Catego

CW00555164

MACK'S

LAND ROVER & 4x4, DIRECTORY '94-95

Independently published by:

McGUIGAN MOTORSPORT

19 PERCY ROAD
PENGE, LONDON
SE20 7QJ
081 778 6498

in conjunction with:

YESTERYEAR BOOKS

60 Woodville Road
London NW11 9TN
Tel. 081 455 6992

Typeset by:

Alexander Associates

London Bureau
PO Box 77, Greenford,
Middlesex, UB6 9TG
Tel. 081 575 8585 - Fax. 081 813 0370

Whilst great attention has been paid to achieve accurate
compilation of the contents herein, the compilers assume
no responsibility for errors or omissions or for any
effect arising therefrom.

It is advisable to contact companies direct when considering
purchase, for although listed costs are to be assumed current
going to press, these prices should be regarded solely
as a guide rather than a fixed quotation.

INTRODUCTION

Welcome to MACK'S LAND ROVER & 4x4 DIRECTORY '94-95, the ultimate quick reference guide to just about "anybody who's anything" within the world of Land Rover in particular, and four wheel drive in general.

MACK'S fully updated categories once again comprise of independent traders, non-franchised dealers and private enthusiasts. Popular with both the trade and public, the only difference to the simple-to-use format is the substantial increase in entries.

Now in its second year, MACK'S pages have swollen from 116 last year to 160 this time around - mind you, so has the price. To those who purchased the inaugural edition it will come as no surprise to learn that printing accounted for 95% of the ridiculously low retail price, let alone those little overheads such as advertising etc! Having now established itself as a credible publication, I am afraid the cover price has had to rise accordingly.

Given the all round increased content (such as the highly-informative 'Travel' category), I believe MACK'S is still excellent value for money ... then again I would, wouldn't I? Seriously though, if you feel a certain area requires improvement, constructive criticism is always welcome. Only with your feedback will MACK'S DIRECTORY grow as you would like to see it - please let me know!

Tom McGuigan (Editor)

FREE ENTRY & ADVERTISING

Every entry in MACK'S is free. No you didn't misread it - FREE!!

Whether a trader, club or private individual, "Free Entry" is open to anyone provided they are connected with four wheel drive i.e. Just because your company happens to manufacture gas fires that Land Rover owners might warm their tootsies on after a hard day's off-roading, this will not automatically qualify you for a "Free Entry"! However, if you market a folding shovel capable of digging themselves out of the mire, that's fine.

SIX SIMPLE STEPS TO QUALIFY FOR "FREE ENTRY" :-

1. Send a large SAE to McGUIGAN MOTORSPORT (address on page 2)
2. Stand by letterbox to receive your '95-96 "Free Entry" form.
3. Complete form (very easy - nothing too taxing).
4. Return form by post.
5. Make cup o'tea, put up feet and rest the brain.
6. Purchase MACK'S LAND ROVER & 4x4 DIRECTORY '95-96 (not compulsory ... unfortunately)

DISPLAY ADVERTISING :-
Low cost advertising rates will be enclosed with your '95-96 "Free Entry" form.
(Advertising is totally optional and will not affect your "Free Entry").

ACCESSORIES

CROSS REFERENCE: See also MECHANICAL PARTS & SPARES - ELECTRICAL PARTS & ACCESSORIES

ENGLAND

AVON
INTEK DISTRIBUTION. 17 Hobbiton Road, Worle, Weston-Super-Mare, Avon BS22 0HP (0934) 518311 MOBILE: (0860) 661730
Thule roofbars, roofboxes and accessories. Approved by the Automobile Association. Roofbox hire. Colour brochure available.
T.G.S. COACHWORKS. Newpit Lane, Bitton, Bristol BS15 6NT   (0272) 329619
Nudge bars - top quality, best prices. Also side steps, light guards and roof racks. Free nationwide delivery.

BERKSHIRE
MOTOR TRAVELLER. 5 Oxford Road East, Windsor, Berks SL4 1DG   (0753) 833442
Car roof box centre. Choose from the U.K.'s top car roof boxes.

BUCKINGHAMSHIRE
BRIAN MORTON. 5 Cottisford Crescent, Great Linford, Milton Keynes, Bucks MK14 5HH (0908) 677866
Aluminium number plates - standard, military and specials. Include sketch with order, £25 for standard pair.
COPLAN LTD. Webb Building, Dawson Road, Milton Keynes, Bucks MK1 1QY (0908) 366055
Keep mud/oil/grease/dirt etc. off cloth with treated nylon one-size seat covers. Front and rear sets available. Trade enquires welcome.
GENESIS INTERNATIONAL. Chancery Court, Lincoln Road, High Wycombe, Bucks HP12 3RE (0494) 461022 FAX: (0494) 464184
Buy direct from the importer and save - High quality USA brushguards & pile car mats. Dealer/rep enquires invited.

CORNWALL
GAINSBOROUGH ACCESSORIES INTERNATIONAL LTD. 35-37 Normandy Way, Walker Lines Ind. Est., Bodmin, Cornwall PL31 1HA (0208) 77527 FAX: (0208) 73626
Accessories manufacturer for most of the 4x4 market, including nudge bars, side steps, light guards and dog guards.

DERBYSHIRE
ASG (ACCESSORIES) LTD. Sandown Road, Derby DE2 8SR (0332) 384260 FAX: (0332) 366316
Suppliers of occasional rear seats for the Range Rover, and additional fuel tanks for Land Rover, Range Rover and Discovery models.
SAMWAYS. 20/22 Ashbourne Road, Derby DE3 3DR (0332) 368849 FAX: (0332) 298593
Cycle rack stockists; Grabers 1060 fits spare wheel 2 bike capacity, Hollywood F4/F5 clips on & off 3/4 bike cap. & Pendle tow ball fitment.
TRANSATLANTIC 4x4 UK LTD. Atlantic House, Venture Crescent, Motorway Link Industrial Estate, Alfreton, Derbys DE55 1BX (0773) 540910
4x4 accessories - Main UK agents for Dick Cepek/Rocket Wheels/Arrigoni De Angelis/Delta 4x4/Rancho suspension. All makes coverage i.e. UK, USA, Jap, European.

DEVON
SOUTHDOWN 4x4 PRODUCTS. "Southdown", Zeal Monachorum, Nr Credition, Devon EX17 6DR (0363) 83819 FAX: (0363) 83472
Manufacturers of under-guard protective systems, winch-mounted bumpers and nudge bars. Specialist vehicle protection.
TRADE SUPPLIES LTD. Unit 6A, Exeter Road Industrial Estate, Okehampton, Devon EX20 1QA (0837) 55330 FAX: (0837) 55332
Nudge bars/rear bars/side steps/light guards/rear window grilles/rigid tow poles/snow chains/dog guards. Fitting service now available.

DORSET
PWS NUDGE BARS. Unit 5, Chalwyn Industrial Estate, St. Clemence Road, Parkdown, Poole, Dorset BH15 3PE (0202) 746851 FAX: (0202) 738135
Our nudge bars will make your 4 wheel drive vehicle (any make and model)more rugged, more stylish, more practical and more protected.

ESSEX
A.J. CYCLE CARRIERS LTD. Civic Square, Tilbury, Essex RM18 8AD
(0375) 841184 FAX: (0375) 855580
Cycle carriers to fit Land Rover Discoveries, Mitsubishi Shoguns and Isuzu Troopers. Colour brochure available on request.

GLOUCESTERSHIRE
COTSWOLD MOTOR SPARES (4WD) LTD. Stonewalls House, Victoria Road, Cirencester,
Glos GL7 1EU (0285) 658015 FAX: (0285) 640335
The most comprehensive range of 4x4 nudge bars in the UK. Roll bars, side bars, light guards/steps and rear bars also available - trade only.
LIFTING & CRANE SERVICES. Unit 5, Merchants Road, Gloucester GL1 5RG
(0452) 504266 FAX: (0452) 504266
The 100 psi max output Magnum air compressor runs drills, inflates tyres etc. Driven by a fan belt & pulley, the unit simply bolts to your engine.

HAMPSHIRE
EBERSPACHER (UK) LTD. Headlands Business Park, Salisbury Road, Ringwood, Hants BH24
3PB (0425) 480151 FAX: (0425) 480152
Independent fuel-burning heating systems for all Land Rover vehicles -heat without the engine running!
TOP TRUNK. P.O. Box 6, Winchester, Hampshire   (0962) 777676 / 777677
Roof-rack mounted storage trunk. Lockable, weatherproof, aerodynamic, stylish. Space to take three family suitcases or seven pairs of skis.
TUBULAR ENGINEERING. 113 Wych Lane, Gosport, Hampshire PO13 0CA
(0329) 289571 MOBILE: (0836) 286773
Hand crafted, highly polished stainless bull bars - Range Rover etc.

HERTFORDSHIRE
EGR PLASTICS. Unit 6, 15-19 Greenhill Crescent, Watford, Herts WD1 8QU
(0923) 211052 FAX: (0923) 254574
Acrylic headlamp protectors & bonnet stoneguards for Land Rover, Discovery, Range Rover. Functional products to save you money & protect your vehicle.

KENT
DAVE COOPER BIKE RACKS. 88 Mountculver Avenue, Sidcup, Kent DA14 5JW
081-302 7246 MOBILE: (0860) 702112
4x4 mountain bike & motorcycle racks, trailers, towbars, wheel clamps. Mail order available - unbeatable prices.
HRG 4 WHEEL DRIVE CENTRE. 87-99 Hawley Road, Dartford, Kent   (0322) 225446
4x4 accessories - Wide tyres, alloy wheels, alloy bull bars, fly screens, side steps, etc. South East agents for Bonx Bars.
CLIMAIR UK. 1 Station Parade, Station Road, Sidcup, Kent DA15 7DB
081-309 7744 FAX: 081-309 5177
Wind deflectors: Manufactured in 3mm TUV approved perspex for vehicle side windows. Full range available.
MERCURY TRAILER CENTRE. 3 Station Parade, Elmers End, Beckenham, Kent BR3 4DR
081-650 3422 FAX: 081-658 9608
Nudgebars - Nudgebars - Nudgebars - Nudgebars. All makes & models supplied and fitted. Access & Visa welcome.
SNOWCHAINS LTD. Wrotham Road, Borough Green, Kent TN15 8TG   (0732) 884408
Top boxes; 25 models & sizes fit all models, stylish and aerodynamic, luggage and ski models, Thule/Jetbag/Hapro/Autoform available ex stock.

LANCASHIRE
ACOUSTIKIT SOUNDPROOFING LTD. Lees Brook Mill, Lees Road, Oldham, Lancs OL4 5JL
061-652 2773 FAX: 061-627 4134
Specialists in Land Rover/Range Rover/Discoverys. Sound deadening kits, full fitting facility available. Open 8.30 am - 5.30 pm.
BLACKBURN ROOF RACKS & TRADE WELDING SERVICES. Unit 4, Walker Street, Lower Audley, Blackburn, Lancs BB1 1BG TEL / FAX: (0254) 263558 / 54776
Manufacturers of heavy duty galvanised commercial roof racks for most
4WD & commercial vehicles/nudge bars/rear side steps etc. European agents required.

LINCOLNSHIRE
CIVIL DEFENCE SUPPLY. Old School, Vicarage Lane, Wellingore, Lincoln LN5 0JF
(0522) 810388 FAX: (0552) 811353
Suppliers of 'Dragon' portable searchlights. Two models - 50/100watts 180/250,000 candle power.
Internal re-chargeable battery (12v/24/240v).

LONDON
CHAMBERLAIN'S SEAT COVERS. 2 Tremaine Road, London SE20 7T2 081-778 7997
More practical than a re-trim, machine washable seat covers. All models tailor-made in authentic
L/Rover-type fabric. 80 designs, samples sent.
WILCO ENGINEERING. 290 Cambridge Heath Road, London E2 9HA
071-729 6619 FAX: (0277) 632991
Manufacturer of high quality, durable roof racks for most 4wds. Design service available. Nudge bars
also supplied and fitted.
WILSTOW LTD. Gardiner House, Broomhill Road, London SW13 4JQ
081-871 5184/5/6 FAX: 081-877 0759
Roof boxes, camping boxes, Maggiolina box beds, cycle racks.

MIDDLESEX
CORDS PISTON RING CO. LTD. 8 Aintree Road, Perivale, Greenford, Middx UB6 7LA
081-998 9923 FAX: 081-998 1214
Piston ring sets for all Land Rover/Range Rover models.

NORFOLK
ROVER PART. Wayside Garage, Holt Road, Horsford, Norwich, Norfolk NR10 3EE
(0603) 891209 FAX: (0603) 890330
Sole importers of Proform engine chrome styling kits for V8 i.e. rocker covers £39.00 pair, also double
chrome breathers to stop oil leaks and crankcase pressure build-up.

NORTHAMPTONSHIRE
COVER SYSTEMS (4WD). 113 High Street South, Rushden, Northants NN10 0RB (0933) 410851
Guard your 4x4 against poor weather, dirt & dust with our protective covers. Indoor & outdoor models
for Land/Range Rover, Frontera, Vitara etc.
MOBILITY ACCESSORIES. 20-22 Dunster Street, Northampton NN1 3JY
(0604) 28223 MOBILE: (0860) 203179 FAX: (0604) 20273
Makers of bull bars, side steps, light guards etc. Trade and retail supplied.
WALTER-BROADLEY MACHINES LTD. Gladstone Road, Northampton NN5 7RX
(0604) 583191 FAX: (0604) 751517
RIC-RAC is a heavy duty commercial roof rack designed to fit Land Rover, Range Rover, most vans etc.
Tested & approved by Rover for LR/RR.

NORTHUMBERLAND
IMPACT COMPOSITES. c/o 30a West Road, Ponteland, Northumberland NE20 9SX (0661) 72827
Roof boxes direct. Made in reinforced marine grade thermoset plastic, ex-works.

OXFORDSHIRE
CROWNFLEET LTD. Island House, Lower High Street, Burford, Oxon OX18 4RR
(0993) 824825 FAX: (0993) 824424
Distributors of the 'Grandstand 4x4', a tubular nudge bar that converts into a stirrup step, viewing
platform or high-level seat.
ALLMAKES. 176 Milton Park, Abingdon, Oxon OX14 4SW (0235) 821122 FAX: (0235) 821133
Land Rover, Range Rover, Discovery and 4x4 accessories including bull bars, side step, roof racks etc.

SUFFOLK
ON THE BALL LTD. Stanchils, Hengrave, Bury St Edmunds, Suffolk IP28 6NB (0284) 704730
Our bike racks are simple, sturdy and easy to use. Carrying 3 bikes, you'll wonder how you ever
managed without one. Phone for colour brochure.
OPTRONICS UK. Debden Way, Melton, Woodbridge, Suffolk IP12 1RB
(0394) 387762 FAX: (0394) 380373
Importers of 4x4 vehicle accessories. Wholesale distributors to the 4x4 industry.

WEST MIDLANDS
ACRON VEHICLE ACCESSORIES. Unit 4, Newfield Close, Walsall, West Midlands WS2 7P
(0922) 30505 FAX: (0922) 35735
World's No. 1 seller of alloy vehicle accessories. Nudge bars/winch bars/side steps + bonnet/headlight
protectors and sheepskin seat covers.

YORKSHIRE, NORTH

ELDWELD. 1 Eldmire Cottages, Eldmire, Dalton, Thirsk YO7 3JQ   (0845) 577352
Small family business producing top quality accessories at low cost. Land Rover/Range Rover/Discovery spare wheel carriers, light guards etc.
R.A.T's REPLACEMENT PARTS AND ACCESSORIES. Brook Farm, Weaverthorpe, Nr Malton, North Yorks YO17 8EY   (09443) 513
Call East Yorkshire's latest outlet - R.A.T's - for a complete range of top quality accessories for Land/ Range Rover, all at competitive prices.

YORKSHIRE, SOUTH

BULLIVANT ENGINEERING. 1 Station Road, Kiveton Park, Nr Sheffield S31 8QP   (0909) 771080
'Pivlock', a practical answer to a 30 year old problem. Rear spare wheel.
WEBASTO THERMOSYSTEMS (UK) LTD. White Rose Way, Doncaster Carr, South Yorks DN4 5JH   (0302) 322232 FAX: (0302) 322231
A Webasto auxiliary heater gives you a pre-warmed car, a pre-heated engine, a clear windscreen and reduced running costs. Send for our brochure.

SCOTLAND

LOTHIAN AND BORDERS

CITY CYCLES. 30 Rodney Street, Edinburgh EH7 4EA   031-556 8229 FAX: 031-557 5273
Roof rack specialists, roof boxes, tow bar cycle carriers, huge range of accessories.

WALES

DYFED

FLEXIBLE IMAGES LTD. Gilfach Farm, Saron, Llandysul, Dyfed SA44 5EJ
(0559) 371191 MOBILE: (0831) 514779 FAX: (0559) 371191
Nudge bars, rear bars, side steps, liners, hard tops, tool boxes plus many more accessories.
TRAVEL TACKLE. Becon Business Park, Warren Road, Brecon, Powys LD3 1XX
(0874) 611953 FAX: (0874) 611954
Distributors of the 'Multi-Rak' & 'Multi-Light' range of accessories.

SOUTH AFRICA

STORM ACCESSORIES CC. 13 Bundo Road, Sebenza, Edenvale, P.O. Box 8522, Edenglen 1613, South Africa DAY: 452-6719 EVENING: 435-2113 FAX: 609-4728
4WD parts & accessories, roof racks, long range tanks, winches, Hi-Lift jacks etc.

BODYWORK
including HOODS, BODY CONVERSIONS GLASS AREA
CROSS REFERENCE: See also TRAVEL category (Sub-section 'Vehicle Conversions')

ENGLAND

CHESHIRE
MMB INTERNATIONAL. Unit A, Calamine Street, Macclesfield, Cheshire SK11 7HU (0625) 615025 FAX: (0625) 511513
Cross country ambulances/specialist vehicles. 110/109 GRP roof extensions. Exports w/wide.
NATIONAL TYRES AND AUTOCARE. 80-82 Wellington Road North, Stockport, Cheshire SK4 1HR 061-480 7461 FREEPHONE: (0800) 626666 FOR NEAREST BRANCH
Windscreens, 4x4 tyres, wheels, other tyres, exhausts, batteries & range of auto services. Check for service before travelling, 400 branches nationwide.

GLOUCESTERSHIRE
COTSWOLD WINDSCREENS. The Cottage, Hooks Lane, Malswick, Newent GL18 1HW (0531) 822424
Family business providing 24 hr mobile replacement service. Specialists in 4x4/cars/van & minibus conversions/trucks/boats/portacabins/caravans.

HERTFORDSHIRE
SUNSEEKERS UNIVERSAL LIMITED. The Rick, Southend, Much Hadham, Herts SG10 6EP (0279) 843345 FAX: (0279) 842171
Sunroofs: Full length fabric electric, glass and steel inbuilts, glass pop roofs. All types fitted, serviced and repaired.

KENT
DAKAR CARS. Rowhill Cottages, Puddledock Lane, Wilmington, Kent DA2 7QF (0322) 614044 FAX: (0322) 668500
Manufacturers of 'Dakar' fibreglass replacement bodies designed for usewith Range Rover chassis & running gear. DIY Kits or complete vehicles.

LANCASHIRE
A & S AUTOCENTRE. Unit 4, Helca Works, Brown Street, Bamber Bridge, Nr Preston, Lancs PR5 6NQ (0772) 34093
Land Rover/Range Rover repairs, welding, bodywork, resprays. Also diesel engine conversions.
CALDWELL & SON. 1 Hartley Avenue, Off Dartlington Street, East Wigan, Lancs WN1 3BW (0942) 826406/207015 FAX: (0942) 826471
Windows for all Land Rover models. Vehicle and marine window conversions direct from the manufacturer.

LEICESTERSHIRE
VENG (UK) LTD. Newton Road, Harrowbrook Industrial Estate, Hinkley, Leics LE10 3DJ (0455) 890303 FAX: (0455) 890178
Body panel distributors to the motor trade.

LINCOLNSHIRE
DAVID HARBY. Little Bytham Garage, Station Road, Little Bytham, Grantham, Lincs NG33 4RA (0780) 410450
R/Rover + L/Rover specialists with 20 years exp. RR inner/outer sills, wheel arches etc. Accident/insurance repair. All major work undertaken

LONDON
McARDLE COACHBUILDERS LIMITED. 25 Park Royal Road, London NW10 7JH 081-961 0616 FAX: 081-9630547
Specialists in Land Rover/Range Rover chassis & body repair. Approved by many leading insurance companies. Free collection & delivery service.
TC BODY MODS. East Acton Lane, London W3 7HD 081-743 2686
Custom bodywork and chassis specialists. Suspension & chassis parts refurbished. Also professional recoating for nudge bars, light guards etc.
VANTAGEFIELD. 4 Shepherd Market, Curzon Street, Mayfair, London W1Y 7HT 071-493 1111 FAX: 071-629 1866
Vantagefield coachbuilders provide luxury 9" or 14" stretch conversions to Range Rover + 4 door power convertible with soft top/hard top option.

MANCHESTER, GREATER
WIGAN ALUMINIUM WINDOW CO. 9 Park Street, Manchester M3 1EU 061-832 6626
FAX: 061-832 6626
Manufacturers of sliding window units for L/Rovers, windscreens for L/Rovers & R/Rovers. Laminated clear/tinted/ambulance shade cut to shape.

NORTHAMPTONSHIRE
MASTER GLASS LTD. 118/122 Wellingborough Road, Northampton NN1 4DR
(0604) 30494 FAX: (0604) 250819
Land Rover glass conversions. Safety glass to fit all models. Bronze, Black, Silver, Grey. Supply only and Exports welcome. Nationwide fitting service.

SUFFOLK
L. STAFFORD DOVEY. 173/4 Acre Road, Carlton, Nr Newmarket, Suffolk CB8 9LF
(0223) 290468
New Series I bulkheads, dash 1954/58. Built to exact replica specification, perfect in every way. Units built to order in small batches - £495 each.

SUSSEX, EAST
MERLIN AUTOMOTIVE. Hendall Gate Farm, Herons Ghyll, Uckfield, E Sussex TN22 4BU
(0825) 733158
Range Rover convertibles - please telephone for details.

SUSSEX, WEST
EAGLE CARS LTD. Gerston Farm, Greyfriars Lane, Storrington, W Sussex RH20 4HE (0903) 743341
Eagle 'Jeep-style' body kits based on Range Rover chassis/running gear - also fibreglass headlinings for Land Rover etc. Phone for details.
PILCHER-GREENE LTD. Consort Way, Burgess Hill, W Sussex RH15 9NA
(0444) 235707 FAX: (0444) 241730 TELEX: 877102
Specialist body builders including ambulances and fire appliances.

WARWICKSHIRE
PWB REPLACEMENT MOTOR PARTS LTD. 11 - 13 Warwick Industrial Estate, Budbrooke
Road, Warwick CV34 5XH (0926) 494782 FAX: (0926) 410185
Manufacturers and suppliers of Land Rover/Range Rover body panels, parts and trim. Prompt and efficient international delivery.

WEST MIDLANDS
P.A. ATKINSON & SONS LTD. 3 Avenue Road, Kings Heath, Birmingham B14 7TH
021-444 1268
Range Rover specialists. Guaranteed quality body and accident repairs to Range Rovers and all makes of vehicle. Servicing, MOT repair & prep.
JUST HOODS. 20 Muswell Close, Solihull, W Midlands B91 2QS 021-705 7354
Quality hoods in khaki, blue or sand for Land Rover models 1948 onwards. Also truck cab hoods & load area tonneau covers. 9am-9pm 6 days per week.

WORCESTERSHIRE
SMITH & DEAKIN. 292 Tolladine Road, Warndon, Worcs WR4 9BA
(0905) 20873 FAX: (0905) 27221
Range Rover heavy duty fibreglass front wings direct from the manufacturer - £33.00 each.

YORKSHIRE, WEST
WADSWORTH PANELS. 1 Steele Lane, Barkisland, Halifax, W Yorks HX4 0ER (0422) 822200
Land Rover Series One panels - all outer wings, all SWB tailgates, all bumpers, early 80" inner wings and door bottoms.

SCOTLAND
STRATHCLYDE
SCOTTISH RANGE ROVER AND DISCOVERY CENTRE. 10 Shaw Road, Larkhall,
Strathclyde ML9 2TR (0698) 886628
Bodywork specialist and producer of 'The Strange Rover', combining Range Rover front half and Discovery rear.

NOW OPEN IN NORTH WEST LONDON ...

... THE
ROVER/LAND ROVER
ENTHUSIAST'S SHOP

... where you will find the most impressive range of Land Rover,
Range Rover, Discovery and Rover saloon car related items
all under one roof:-

* LITERATURE: Technical & historical, new & used, current and out of print, reprints and originals,
lubrication charts, original and reprinted adverts, sales brochures etc.

* VIDEOS, CAR BADGES, BLAZER BADGES, KEY FOBS, MODELS, KITS, RUBBER STAMPS,
ENAMEL SIGNS, FRAMED ORIGINAL ADVERTISING, ETC.

* THE FULL RANGE OF LRO GOODIES: T-shirts, sweats, polos, hats, caps, shorts, mugs,
tea towels, *Land Rover Owner* magazine back issues etc.

* CUT PRICE CAR CARE PRODUCTS

Situated near the M1, North Circular and the Tube
- just phone 081-455 6992

to tell us when you're coming.

(Access & Visa welcome)

YESTERYEAR BOOKS

LAND ROVER, RANGE ROVER, ROVER CAR
LITERATURE SPECIALISTS

LONDON NW11
081-455 6992

Yesteryear Books offer a full range of Land Rover & Range Rover books, including an ever-changing
stock of new & used 'out of print titles'.

The selection includes:

ADVERTISING LAND ROVER, D.Young S/B	96 pp	£ 9.95
LRO, RESTORATION TIPS & TECHNIQUES, R.Green S/B	100pp	£ 8.95
PRACTICAL CLASSICS ON LAND ROVER RESTORATION, S/B	72 pp	£ 8.95
LRO, LAND ROVERS IN MILITARY SERVICE, B.Morrison S/B	100pp	£ 8.95
LRO, BRITISH LAND ROVERS IN THE GULF (Colour), B.Morrison S/B	64 pp	£ 7.99
CLASSICS IN COLOUR, LAND ROVER, J.Taylor S/B	96 pp	£11.95
CHOICE PURCHASE PERFORMANCE, LAND ROVER, J.Taylor S/B	64 pp	£ 8.95
LAND ROVER (Colour), C.Bennett S/B	128pp	£10.99
FOUR WHEEL DRIVING, S.Newitt S/B	128pp	£12.99
LRO, KNOW YOUR LAND ROVER, R.Ivins S/B	114pp	£ 8.95
BROOKLANDS, SERIES I 1948-1958 ROAD TESTS S/B	100pp	£ 8.95
BROOKLANDS, SERIES II, IIA 1958-1971 ROAD TESTS S/B	100pp	£ 8.95
BROOKLANDS, SERIES III 1971-1985 ROAD TESTS S/B	100pp	£ 8.95
BROOKLANDS, 90 & 110 1983-1989 ROAD TESTS S/B	100pp	£ 8.95
NEW: ROVER, THE FIRST 90 YEARS (Colour), E.Dymock H/B	192pp	£19.95
FOUR WHEEL DRIVE & LAND ROVER, N.Baldwin S/B	32 pp	£ 1.50
LAND ROVER, THE UNBEATABLE 4x4, Slavin & Mackie H/B	324pp	£16.99
RANGE ROVER OWNERS & BUYERS GUIDE, J.Taylor S/B	64 pp	£ 8.95
RANGE ROVER SUPER PROFILE, T.Alder H/B	56 pp	£ 5.99
RANGE ROVER GOLD PORTFOLIO 1970-1992 S/B	180pp	£11.95

Also: Numerous handbooks, user manuals, parts books,
workshop manuals and promotional material.

Just ring and fix a time to call and view our stock.

Daniel Young

13

BOOKS

CROSS REFERENCE: See also TRAVEL category (Sub-section 'Books')

ENGLAND

BUCKINGHAMSHIRE

TRANSPORT SOURCE BOOKS LTD. Olney House, Olney High Street, Bucks MK46 4EB
(0234) 240848 FAX: (0234) 240855
Source books on early Range Rovers and Land Rover Discovery. Road tests, Launch articles, advertising etc. £8.95 each.

DORSET

MOTOR BOOKS. 241 Holdenhurst Road, Bournemouth, Dorset BH8 8DA
(0202) 396469 FAX: (0202) 391572
Full range of factory manuals, parts catalogues, etc. General histories, illustrated histories, collectors guides, road tests, etc.

HEREFORDSHIRE

LANDSMAN'S BOOKSHOP LTD. Buckenhill, Bromyard, Hereford HR7 4PG TEL: (0885) 483420
Specialist in books on agriculture, horticulture and allied subjects.

LONDON

CONNOISSEUR CARBOOKS LTD. 11A Devonshire Road, Chiswick, London W4 2EU
081-742 0022 FAX: 081-742 0360 -   Specialist motoring and military book retailer.
MOTOR BOOKS. 36 St Martin's Court, St Martin's Lane, London WC2N 4AL
071-836 5376/6728/3800 FAX: 071-497 2539
Full range of factory manuals, parts catalogues, etc. General histories, illustrated histories, collectors guides, road tests, etc.
YESTERYEAR BOOKS. London NW11 9TN 081-455 6992
New and Used Land Rover/Rover book specialist including many out of print titles. See our advertisements for details. Please phone for full address, appointments easily arranged.

MIDDLESEX

CHATERS MOTORING BOOKSELLERS. 8 South Street, Isleworth, Middx TW7 7BG
081-568 9750 FAX: 081-569 8273
Sellers of motoring books for over thirty years, our main shop in Isleworth is an "Aladdin's Cave" for motoring enthusiasts.

NORFOLK

MARGRET MOTORS. 157 Aylsham Road, Norwich NR3 2AD
DAY: (0603) 407747 EVENING: (026 377) 366
Finding service for manufacturers workshop manuals/handbooks, also purchase of clean manuals/handbooks of all marques.

OXFORDSHIRE

MOTOR BOOKS. 8 The Roundway, Headington, Oxford OX3 8DH (0865) 66215 FAX: (0865) 63555
Full range of factory manuals, parts catalogues, etc. General histories, illustrated histories, collectors guides, road tests, etc.

SOMERSET

HAYNES PUBLISHING GROUP. Sparkford, Nr Yeovil, Somerset BA22 7JJ
(0963) 40635 FAX: (0963) 40001
Land Rover Series I, II & III: Purchase and DIY Restoration Guide by Lindsay Porter - a superb guide, invaluable for any Land Rover owner.

SURREY

BROOKLANDS BOOKS LTD. P.O. Box 146, Cobham, Surrey KT11 1LG (0932) 65051
Distributors of several Land Rover books (Series I - 90/110), Range Rover books and workshop manuals.

WILTSHIRE

MOTOR BOOKS. 10 Theatre Square, Swindon, Wilts SN1 1QN (0793) 523170 FAX: (0793) 432070
Full range of factory manuals, parts catalogues, etc. General histories, illustrated histories, collectors guides, road tests, etc.

ENGLAND

BEDFORDSHIRE

AUTO TECHNIQUE (EMS) LIMITED. Units C & D, Kingsway Industrial Estate, Luton, Beds LU1 1LP (0582) 414000 FAX: (0582) 419690
Land Rover/Range Rover 4WD tuning specialist. New and reconditioned carburettors. Carburettor spares. Also turbos supplied and fitted.

CARBURETTOR EXCHANGE. 28F High Street, Leighton Buzzard, Beds LU7 7EA (0525) 371369
British and continental carburettors, reconditioning and sales.

J.T.S. CARBURETTORS. Stratton Farm, Great North Road, Biggleswade, Beds SG18 9SX (0767) 31291 FAX: (0767) 601150
Suppliers of Zenith, Solex, Stromberg, Weber & SU's at competitive prices. Gasket & diaphragm packs, needle valves, spindles and jets.

CHESHIRE

K & N FILTERS (EUROPE) LTD. Wilderspool Causeway, Warrington, Cheshire WA4 6QP (0925) 36950 FAX: 0925 418948
More off-road races won with K & N than any other filter. Protection high against dust/unaffected by water/cleanable. Extensive 4x4 range.

DEVON

TJ FILTERS LTD. St Modwen Road, Plymouth, Devon PL6 8LH (0752) 667675
Manufacturers & trade suppliers of replacement air, fuel & oil filters for the Land Rover product range.

ESSEX

CARBURETTOR HOSPITAL. 210 Woodgrange Drive, Southend-on-Sea, Essex SS1 2SJ (0702) 615921 (Answerphone after 5pm) FAX: (0702) 601177
All carburettors old & new. Over 1 million carbs & spares on the shelf for: Weber/Solex/Stromberg/ Zenith/S.U./Dellorto/Motocraft/Nikki etc.

HUMBERSIDE

DONALDSON FILTER COMPONENTS LTD. Oslo Road, Sutton Fields Industrial Estate, Hull, Humberside HU8 0XN (0482) 835213
Manufacturers of air filters suited to desert use.

LONDON

CHRIS MONTAGUE CARBURETTER CO. 380-382 Finchley Road, London NW2 2HP
071-794 7766/7 FAX: 071-794 7604
Weber/Solex/Dellorto/SU/Pierburg/Zenith/Stromberg. Also accessories inc Lumenition, Lucas, Cibié, Kenlowe, Facet, Janspeed, K & N and Bilstien.

GOWER & LEE. 24 Brook Mews North, Paddington, London W2 3BW
071-262 0300 MOBILE: (0836) 226241 FAX: 071-706 2250
Carburettor specialists, we are Unipart fuel systems agents stocking SU, Zenith, CD, Solex and Weber carbs/spares. Full engine tuning facilities.

MANCHESTER, GREATER

MARSH & JEFFREY LTD. 18-26 Great Jackson Street, 15 Deansgate, Manchester M15 4NR
061-236 8091
All carburettors and injection systems. Full engine tuning, carburation/ fuel injection problems, 4 wheel drive dynamometer power economy testing

MERSEYSIDE

CARBURETTERS UNLIMITED. 204 Muirhead Avenue, Liverpool L13 0BA
051-256 0366 FAX: 051-270 2044
Carburettors, air filters and associated spares & ancillaries. (Series I, II & III models.)

MIDDLESEX

T.H.A. SOUTH & SON LTD. 17-19 Clayton Road, Hayes, Middx UB3 1AX 081-573 4708/8677
A comprehensive range of Weber/Solex carbs, fuel pumps & filters, manifolds, air filters, carb service kits, linkage systems and Weber Performance Kits.

WEBER CONCESSIONAIRES LTD. Dolphin Road, Sunbury-on-Thames, Middx TW16 7HE
(0932) 788805 FAX: (0932) 782755
Weber replacement carbs including the Rover 3.5 V8 performance kit featuring inlet manifold, air filter &
all necessary gaskets/connections.

NOTTINGHAMSHIRE
CROSLAND FILTERS LTD. Glaisdale Drive, Nottingham NG8 4JX
(0602) 291145 FAX: (0962) 294835
Manufacturers & suppliers to the trade of replacement filters for the Land Rover product range.

OXFORDSHIRE
PROVEN PRODUCTS. 41 Osprey, Langford Village, Bicester, Oxon OX6 0YH
(0869) 322573 FAX: (0869) 322573
Distributors of JR Air Filters, total protection and performance at realistic prices. Also Cooltec heat
protective cloths and exhaust wrap.

SOMERSET
GREENWAYS ENGINEERING. The Green, Ditcheat, Somerset BA4 6QZ (0749) 86267
Specialist carburettor reconditioning; most makes of carburettor restored to "as new" condition. Please
phone for details.

WILTSHIRE
BURLEN FUEL SYSTEMS. Spitfire House, Castle Road, Salisbury, Wilts SP1 3SA
(0722) 412500 FAX: (0722) 334221
Carburettor parts and repair kits for all Land Rovers, Range Rovers and Discovery. We can supply
Weber/SU/Solex/Stromberg and Zenith components.

WALES
MID GLAMORGAN
FRAM EUROPE LTD. Llantrisant, Pontycllin, Mid Glamorgan CF7 8YU
(0443) 223000 FAX: (0443) 225459
Manufacturers of replacement oil/air/fuel filters spanning the entire Land Rover product range. Suppliers
to the motor trade.
FRANCE
TECAFILTERS S.A. BP 32, 93230, Romainville. France.
Pre-cleaning cyclone stage air filters.

CHASSIS

ENGLAND

CHESHIRE
MARSLAND CHASSIS. Salt Pie Works, Whitehough, Chinley, Nr Stockport SK12 6BX
(0663) 750484 FAX: (0663) 751015
Top quality heavy duty chassis finished in galvanised or dipped black. Trade and export enquires welcome.

YORKSHIRE, SOUTH
STEVE WALKER LAND ROVERS. Old Vicarage, Great North Road, Woodlands,
Doncaster DN6 7RA (0302) 727209
New replacement chassis for Series One 80", 86", 88", 2A & 3, 109" truck and station wagon, 109" one ton Series 3 air portable/military one ton.

SCOTLAND

LOTHIAN AND BORDERS
W.R. WOOD. Edenbank Cottage, Ashfield, Duns, Berwickshire, Borders TD11 3TA (0361) 82420
Land Rover chassis 88" & 109". Small volume manufacturer - quality built - no VAT! Finished in black, primer or galvanised. Delivery possible.

CLEANING EQUIPMENT

ENGLAND

CAMBRIDGESHIRE
ELLIOTT ENGINEERING. Unit 44, Viking Way, Bar Hill, Cambridge CB3 8EL
(0954) 781255 FAX: (0954) 782801
Stockists of Kärcher high pressure steam & water cleaners. Discounted prices, special offers throughout the year.

CO. DURHAM
AC ENTERPRISES. 5 Denebridge, Howden le Wear, Bishop Auckland, Co. Durham
(0388) 762001 MOBILE: (0860) 566812
Steam cleaners/pressure washers/car valeting equipment - new, used or contract hire, part exchanges welcome. Service, chemicals, accessories.
AM & CE SUPPLY CO. The Cleaning Equipment Centre, St. Helen Auckland Industrial Estate, Bishop Auckland DL14 9AD (0388) 606701
Do you need the professionals? Then come to us! K.E.W. cleaning equipment.Hot/cold/steam, mobile pressure washers. Sales, service, hire.

CUMBRIA
KEW CLEANING SYSTEMS LTD. KEW House, Gilwilly Industrial Estate, Penrith,
Cumbria CA11 9BN (0768) 65777 FAX: (0768) 64713)
Manufacturers of hot & cold mobile pressure cleaners and accessories, centralised systems, industrial vacuums and floor machines.

HAMPSHIRE
PRESSURE CLEAN LTD. Aldermaston Road, Sherborne St. John, Basingstoke,
Hampshire RG24 9LA (0256) 851272
New and ex-demo Kärcher steam cleaners. At least 25% off, why pay more for cash or lease purchase? We offer lowest prices and 24hr back-up.

NORFOLK
LENNY POWLEY HIGH PRESSURE CLEANING EQUIPMENT. 1 Church Farm Cottage,
Cranworth, Thetford IP25 7SQ (0362) 820682 FAX: (0362) 821146
Main dealer for Kärcher (U.K.) Ltd. Importer for Siro SRL

OXFORDSHIRE

KÄRCHER (UK) LTD. Kärcher House, Beaumont Road, Banbury, Oxon OX16 7TB
(0295) 267511 FAX: (0295) 266436
World leaders in pressure washers and valeting equipment.
WARWICK POWER WASHERS LTD. Oxford Road, Berinsfield, Wallingford, OxonOX10 7LZ
(0865) 340322 FAX: (0865) 341239
High pressure cleaning equipment sales and service - manufacturing for 25 years and still at the forefront
of pressure washer design and technology.

SURREY

PRESSURE CLEAN LTD. Studio Works, Stoats Nest Road, Coulsdon, Surrey CR5 2JD
081-668 3939 FAX: 081-763 1911
New and ex-demo Kärcher steam cleaners. At least 25% off, why pay more for cash or lease purchase?
We offer lowest prices and 24hr back-up.

SUSSEX, EAST

MULTI-CLEAN SYSTEMS. Unit 1, The Square, Diplocks Way, Hailsham, East Sussex BN27 3JF
(0323) 440747 FAX: (0323) 440747
Suppliers and service agents for pressure washers, steam cleaners, industrial vacuum cleaners and
detergents.

WEST MIDLANDS

CAR & COMMERCIAL CLEANING SERVICE. 130 Warwards Lane, Sely Oak, Birmingham B29
7RE 021-4721655 or 021-476 9283
Sales/repair to all makes of steam cleaners, h/p washers, Numatic valeters, vacuums. New & recondi-
tioned equipment/installations/accessories/chemicals.
WEST MERCIA CLEANING EQUIPMENT. The Cott, 195/196 Turls Hill Road, Coseley,
Wolverhampton (0902) 880998 MOBILE: (0836) 635036 FAX: (0691) 828499
Steam cleaners & pressure washers. Sales/service of new & reconditioned equipment including Mistral
power washers. Repairs/service to all makes.

SCOTLAND

GRAMPIAN, HIGHLAND AND ISLANDS

WASHAIR PRODUCTS. 46 Seafield Road, Longman Industrial Estate, Inverness IV1 1SG
(0463) 231235 FAX: (0463) 243559
Highland regions authorised distributor and service centre for Kew pressure washers, accessories and
spare parts. Mail order available by Access/Visa.

CLOTHING

CROSS REFERENCE: See also MILITARY/EX MILITARY

ENGLAND

BERKSHIRE
SEW DESIGNS. Crookhams Willows, Chamberhouse Mill Lane, Thatcham, Berks RG13 4NU (0635) 864188
Specialised embroidery service to order on a range of leisure and riding wear for that personal touch or corporate image incl. horse blankets etc.
SILHOUETTES OF ASCOT. 'The Grange', St. Mary's Road, Ascot, Berks SL5 9AX (0344) 25758
Ladies/gentlemens classic British country clothing incl. Barbour jackets, Mark Regent reversible coats and blousons, caps, hats and genuine Panamas.

BEDFORDSHIRE
SAK ENTERPRISES. 22 The Poplars, Arlesey, Bedfordshire SG15 6UW (0462) 459918
Hats, caps and country clothing including Barbour and Drizabone.

BUCKINGHAMSHIRE
ROHAN DESIGNS. 30 Maryland Road, Tongwell, Milton Keynes, Bucks MK15 8HN (0908) 618888
Designers and suppliers of high quality/high performance outdoor clothing for the enthusiast, worker and traveller.

CAMBRIDGESHIRE
BINDER'S BADGES. 67 Fengate, Peterborough, Cambs PE1 5BA (0733) 340449 FAX: (0733) 340449
Personalised embroidered sew-on badges. No minimum quantity. 4" x 2" rectangular or 3¾" diameter circular. S.A.E. for more details.

CLEVELAND
D.V. TOWNEND & CO. 12 Dundas Street, Saltburn, Cleveland, TS12 1AH (0287) 623754
Country pursuits wear including main Barbour stockists. Also fishing and shooting equipment.

DERBYSHIRE
JOHN BROCKLEHURST. Bridge Street, Bakewell, Derbyshire DE45 1EE (0629) 812089 FAX: (0629) 814777
The countryman's outfitter.

DEVON
DEVON CLOTHING. 6 Temple Street, Aylesbury, Bucks HP20 2RQ (0296) 392263
Ladies and gents country clothing including suede, leather, tweed, loden and hats etc.

DORSET
BLANDFORD SADDLERY. Blandford House, East Street, Blandford Forum, Dorset DT11 7DX (0258) 455377
Good quality country clothing. Also a full range of saddlery, equestrian equipment and riding clothing.
DENEWEAR. Inpark, Cattistock, Dorchester, Dorset DT2 0HJ (0935) 83638 MOBILE: (0836) 271201 FAX: (0935) 83762
Importers of a range of practical country wear from New Zealand and Australia, including "Swanndri", "R.M. Williams" and "Akubra".

HAMPSHIRE
COUNTRY THREADS. The Gate House, Rake, Liss, Hants GU33 7JH (0730) 894012
Quality country clothing by Barbour, John Partridge, Peter Storm etc. Walking boots, hats, sticks, brollies, knitwear. Mail order available.
MALCOLM DUNNING SADDLERY LTD. The Paddock, Catherington Lane, Horndean, Hants PO8 0TD (0705) 592295
We have one of the largest ranges of saddlery, horse clothing and riding wear in the South of England at very competitive prices.

HEREFORDSHIRE
COUNTRYWEAR LTD. Trevadoc, Cusop, Hay-on-Wye, Hereford HR3 5TP (0497) 820896
A large selection of high class outdoor clothing and headwear.

KENT

COTTON ON. Colyers Hill Cottage, Gill Lane, Colliers Hill, Mersham Ashford,Kent TN25 7HZ
(0850) 365954
A wide and varied range of quality country clothing.

LANCASHIRE

COUNTRY STILE CLOTHING. Orcaber Farm, Austwick, Lancaster LA2 8AE (0729) 825446
Country and equestrian clothing for all outdoor pursuits including a wide range of wax jackets, body
warmers and footwear.
CUDWORTH OF NORDEN. Baitings Mill, Norden, Rochdale, Lancs OL12 7TQ (0706) 41771
A genuinely unique range of superior quality and value outdoor & country clothing, in particular our
'Supermole' and 'Supercord' garments.

LINCOLNSHIRE

SPORTING CHOICE. Main Street, Dunsby, Nr. Bourne, Lincs PE10 0UB (0778) 440721
Retailer of country clothing including waterproofs, practical footwear, headwear and accessories.

LONDON

TRANSATLANTIC TRADING CO. 45D Christchurch Street, Chelsea, London SW3 4AS
071-254 1005
A comprehensive range of military clothing, workwear, aviation clothing and country-wear. Also camping
equipment and accessories. Retail - mail order - wholesale.

NORTHAMPTONSHIRE

B & C FARMERS. Unit 1, Robinson Way, Telford Way Industrial Estate, Kettering,
Northants NN16 8PT (0536) 81558
Outdoor country clothiers specialising in waxed jackets, hats, shirts, quilted jackets and bodywarmers.
K & T FOOTWEAR. 7 Clifton Grove, Kettering, Northants NN15 7NB (0536) 512032
Footwear and clothing for farm and country wear including Northamptonshire manufactured Market
Dealer/Stable Boots and Jodhpur Boots. Agents for Trickers, Tecnic, Loake and Grenson.
BOB LILLIE LEISUREWEAR LTD. Unit 1, Robinson Way, Telford Way Industrial Estate,
Kettering, Northants NN16 8PT (0536) 81558 FAX: (0536) 85218
Outdoor country clothiers specialising in waxed jackets, hats, shirts, quilted jackets and bodywarmers.

OXFORDSHIRE

COTSWOLD CLOTHING. The Ridge House, Duns Tew, Oxon OX6 4JL (0869) 40791
Country clothing and footwear for women and children. Please call or write for free mail order catalogue.
SALLTONA LEISURE WEAR. 1 Flemings Road, Woodstock, Oxford OX20 1NA
(0993) 812841
Showerproof jackets and vests, all sizes or can be made to measure. Children's a speciality in cord or
showerproof all colours.

SOMERSET

SOMERSET SHEEPSKIN OF STREET. Griffin Products, Pipers Farm, Ashcott, Nr. Bridgwater,
Somerset TA7 9BN (0458) 210324
Producers of unique country clothing and accessories. Coats/jackets in various materials including tweed,
wool ventile and leather. Also producers of the Nuu-Med range of wool equestrian products.

SURREY

OUTBACK TRADING COMPANY. 51 The Ridgeway, Sanderstead, Surrey CR2 0LJ
081-657 1477
Combining the popular images of Australian and American heritage and successfully merging them with
their own vision of field and workwear fashion.

SUSSEX, EAST

MEECHING COUNTRY WEAR. 39 High Street, Newhaven, Sussex BN9 9PA (0273) 515986
Wholesale & retail suppliers of quality riding, shooting and fishing wear. Wax, cotton, waterproof
country clothing specialists.

WEST MIDLANDS

RENATE. "Cherry Trees", Bellbroughton Road, Flackmans Gate, Clent, Nr Stourbridge,
West Midlands DY9 0EW (0562) 700237
Retailers, wholesalers and manufacturers of country and leisurewear, wax coats, stockman's capes, hats,
fleece jackets, waterproofs, coats, body warmers, shorts, leggings, jogging suits, body suits.

WILTSHIRE
KEVIN'S MENSWEAR (WESTBURY) LTD. 22/24 High Street, Westbury, Wilts BA13 3BW
(0373) 822145/823020
The complete outfitters. Suppliers of agricultural and country clothing. BIG and TALL mens specialists.

YORKSHIRE, EAST
J.C. NICHOLS & CO. 3-5 Market place, Driffield, East Yorks YO25 7AP (0377) 42278
Ladies and gentleman's country clothing.

YORKSHIRE, NORTH
A J COUNTRY WEAR. Long Gill Farm, Wigglesworth, Nr. Settle, N Yorks BD23 4ST(0729) 840208
Country clothing including a range of wax jackets, quilted jackets, bodywarmers, footwear, hats and caps.
FRIMBLE OF RIPON. Pendle House, Ripon, N Yorks HG4 1TT (0765) 603888
Trendy yet classic clothes. Well made, bespoke tailoring for the country lady and gentleman in pure
wools, cottons and silks.

YORKSHIRE, SOUTH
CHRISTINA MARIA - WOODLANDS CLOTHING. 29 Tenter Bank Lane, Adwick-Le-Street, Nr
Doncaster, S Yorks DN6 7EQ (0302) 722622
Pure wool knitwear and quality outdoor clothing including 'Driza-Bone' waxed cotton capes, 'Mountain
Range' gore-tex and polartec fleece jackets.

YORKSHIRE, WEST
PENNINE OUTDOOR SPORTS. 9 Peel Street, Marsden, Huddersfield HD7 6BR
TEL/FAX: (0484) 844201
Producers/distributors of Tyke outdoor clothing. High quality fleece jackets, waterproof clothing &
footwear. Marine specialists.
WOODHEAD & SCOTT. Rockroyd Farm, Keighley Road, Bradley, W Yorks BD20 9HE
(0535) 691025/630625
Retail/wholesale suppliers of farm and country clothing. Specialist in equestrian footwear and clothing -
hats, caps, shirts & outdoor clothing.

SCOTLAND

STRATHCLYDE
FRASERS FARMWEAR. 47 Burns Statue Square, Ayr, Stathclyde KA7 1SZ (0292) 266029
Specialist range of Frasers Farmwear. Harvester overalls and waterproof clothing for all the family.

WALES

GWENT
WAX WORKS COUNTRY CLOTHING. 2 Allt-yr-Yn Road, Newport, Gwent NP9 5EA
TEL & FAX: (0633) 243119
A wide range of quality countrywear.

CLUBS + PUBS

The clubs/groups featured herein have their own officials to thank for being included in MACK'S LAND ROVER & 4x4 DIRECTORY '94-95 - basically they completed and returned their Entry Forms whereas all those clubs missing did not!

Is your club listed below? If not, why not? Inclusion in MACK'S is easy ... just ask your Club Secretary to request a 'Club Booking Form' for MACK'S DIRECTORY '95-96. Entry is free but please include a large stamped addressed envelope, address is on page 2.

Due to constant changes of venue, the PUB MEET category as featured in MACK'S DIRECTORY '93-94 has been discontinued. Should readers require information regarding current meeting venues, contact telephone numbers have been included alongside clubs & groups for this purpose.

ENGLAND

ALL WHEEL DRIVE CLUB. To Join - Send SAE to: AWDC, P.O. Box 6, Fleet, Hants GU13 9YL or c/o Peter Facey (Secretary), 134 Sandyhurst Lane, Ashford, Kent TN25 4NT (0233) 621507
5,000 members nationwide. Trials most weekends for all kinds of vehicles.10-round national Competition Safari championship. Monthly magazine + yearbook, Pub Meets, Rights of Way Officer.

BORDERS OFF-ROAD CLUB. c/o Ray Powell (Founder) 31 St Georges Road, Berwick upon Tweed, Northumberland TD15 1QE (0289) 308790
All marque club - please telephone for further information.

BRECKLAND LAND ROVER CLUB LTD. c/o Mrs Wendy Chandler (Secretary) 8 Acorn Road, North Walsham, Norfolk NR28 0VA (0692) 404453
Breckland Land Rover Club hosts a wide range of activities to suit all Land Rover, Range Rover and Discovery owners.

BUX 4x4. c/o Gary Dawson (Chairman), Willow Cottage, 37 Worton Road, Middle Barton, Chipping Norton, Oxon OX7 7EE (0295) 812080
Friendly Bucks/Oxon based all-makes off-road club. RTV + Beginners Trials, pub meet & newsletter ... all for £5.00

CLUB DISCOVERY. c/o Ray Grater (Secretary) West Farm, Witham on the Hill, Bourne, Lincs PE10 0JN (0778) 33 484 FAX: (0778) 33 466
Specialist club for Discovery owners. Membership is £29.50 inc VAT. Benefits include discounts on spares, service assistance with insurance and a health insurance scheme.

CLUB OFF-ROAD EUROPE. c/o Gill Wood (Treasurer) 28 Field Avenue, Canterbury, Kent (0227) 451222
New independent all-make 4WD club serving the South East. Trials/Green Lanes/Treasure Hunts/show attendances. Links with German/Dutch 4x4 clubs.

THE COUNTRY 4x4 CLUB. c/o Nicholas Moakes (Founder) The Old Forge, London, Wendens Ambo, Saffron Walden, Essex CB11 4JL
Although off-road enthusiasts are most welcome, the club was formed with the 'on-road' 4x4 owner in mind. Services and benefits include a new and used sales/purchase service, discounted parts/insurance, social events.

DORSET LAND ROVER AND RANGE ROVER OWNERS CLUB. c/o Mrs R Cooney (Secretary) 104 Blackmore Road, Shaftesbury, Dorset SP7 8RL (0747) 54377
Club night 1st Friday of month in the skittle alley at the Greyhound Inn, Winterbourne, Kingston. Please telephone for further information.

EAST NORTHANTS LAND ROVER OWNERS CLUB. c/o Dave Vaughan (Secretary) 1 Woodavens Close, Northampton NN4 9TX (0604) 763626
(*This club did reply but forgot to include a description - Ed*)

LAND ROVER 1947-51 REGISTER. c/o Richard Lines (Secretary), 35 Park Road, Yeadon, Leeds S19 7EX (0532) 506546 If no reply ring: (0535) 605310
The earliest 80" Land Rovers. History, restoration, research, originality. The oldest single-model club. Information, technical advice, newsletter.

LAND ROVER SERIES ONE CLUB. c/o David Bowyer, (Secretary), East Foldhay, Zeal Monachorum, Crediton, Devon EX17 6DH (0363) 82666 FAX: (0363) 82782
The world's largest Land Rover club catering for both owners and admirers of vehicles made between 1948-1958.

LAND ROVER SERIES 3 OWNERS CLUB. c/o Frank King (Founder), 16 Holly Street, Cannock, Staffs WS11 2RU (0543) 423326
Although still in its infancy, this recently-formed, friendly club has expanded rapidly to become a must for Series III owners. Local pub meets now stretch across the country - please tel. for details.

LAND ROVER SERIES 3 OWNERS CLUB. c/o Clem Lee (Local Organiser), 43 Tormore Park, Deal, Kent CT14 9UR (0304) 380958 FAX: (0304) 361268
Family club. Greenlaning, 4x4 treasure hunts, off-road events, caravan week-ends etc. Own site. Membership exclusively for Series III's although all Land Rover series are welcome at events.
(Normally restricted to one main entry per club, after phoning and writing to me, how could I possibly refuse this local organiser's enthusiasm? - Ed)

LEA VALLEY LAND ROVER OWNERS CLUB. c/o Harry Stalick (Membership Secretary), 24 Love Lane, Chigwell, Essex IG8 8BB 081-504 3873 MOBILE: (0860) 843400 FAX: (0708) 688391
Lea Valley Land Rover Owners Club is a friendly club for all Land Rover, Range Rover and Discovery enthusiasts.

LEDBURY FOUR-WHEELERS. c/o Steve Monkley (Founder & General Dogsbody), Rye Meadow Cottage, Off Huntleys Farm Lane, Much Marcle, Nr Ledbury, Hereford HR8 2NB HOME: (0531) 6384302 WORK: (0531) 634944
Not a club as such, but an independent group including the All Wheel Drive Club's local area pub meet. Meetings are the 1st Monday of the month (incl. Bank Holidays) at the Beauchamp Arms, Dymock. Good chat, beer, videos, Monkley's waffle - everyone welcome, Land Rover enthusiasts or otherwise.

MIDLAND ROVER OWNERS CLUB LTD. c/o Derek Spooner (Secretary), Bank Cottage, Abbots Morton, Worcester WR7 4NA (0386) 792767
Land Rover & Rover enthusiasts welcome. Events include gymkhanas, 4x4 trials and safaris etc., caravanning and camping, socials & visits.

NEWCASTLE & NANTWICH ROVER OWNERS CLUB. c/o Garry Thompson (Secretary) 70 Cambridge Drive, Clayton, Newcastle-under-Lyme, Staffs ST5 3DQ (0782) 617224.
A club for enthusiasts of all Rover vehicles. Activities range from concours to off-road events.

NORTH LAKES 4x4 CLUB. c/o Andrea Wells (Secretary), 3 East End, Kirkbampton, Carlisle, Cumbria CA5 6HS 1(0228) 576850.
Cumbria's premier all marque off-road association.

101 FORWARD CONTROL CLUB AND REGISTER. c/o Howard Smith (Membership Secretary), 13 Gloucester Gardens, Braintree, Essex CN7 6LG (0376) 552331
For owners and admirers of the 101 Forward Control - to promote and maintain Sohihull's finest vehicles both on & off-road via club events, shows and newsletters.

RANGE ROVER REGISTER LTD. c/o Victor Jones (Membership Secretary), 139 Woodbrook Road, Abbey Wood, London SE2 0PB 081-855 8718
The only club for Range Rover enthusiasts, we offer something for everyone - tech tips, off-roading, concours, show displays, shop, super newsletter. 1200 members, lots of local meets.

RED ROSE LAND ROVER CLUB LTD. c/o B.L. Hart (Secretary), 75 Coniston Road, Fulwood, Preston PR2 4AY (0772) 709391.
A club for all types of Land Rover enthusiasts. Activities from static displays to full trials and winching events.

SOMERSET & WILTSHIRE ROVER OWNERS CLUB. c/o Elizabeth Green (Secretary), 2 The Old School House, Cloford, Frome, Somerset BA11 4PH
Friendly, competitive, local club. Monthly CCV and regular RTV trials.

STAFFS & SHROPS LRC. c/o Mrs V Johnson (Hon. Secretary), 4 Waltham House, Overend Street, West Bromwich, West Midlands B70 6ER 021-553 4070.
Off road motor sports club for Land Rover vehicles (Rover manufacture). We also hold camping weekends and social meets - everyone welcome.

TWICKENHAM OFF-ROADERS. Fullwell Park Residents Assoc. Club House, 1a Fortescue Avenue, Twickenham, Middlesex. Enquires c/o Phil 081-384 7998 or Jerry 081-575 3060

Not a club as such, but a meeting place for an assortment of off-road clubs and individuals under one roof. Twickenham Off-Roaders (TOR) meet every Wednesday, with the largest attendance being the 1st Wednesday of the month.

With an emphasis on informality and friendliness, TOR has its own private room & bar featuring dirty videos (sorry to disappoint - the wet & muddy type), cheap booze/soft drinks, barbeques, daft competitions/ raffles, where to buy cheap spares etc., regular playdays to off-road centres/shows/green laning trips - including excursions and fund-raising for Disabled Off-Road Access (D.O.R.A.). Marshals supplied for competitions and events (over 50 marshalled Bagshot Heath Off Road Show '93), Comp Safari/Rally service support crews supplied to anyone who wants to pay for the beer, African safaris, sponsored charity events, heavy vehicles ... and much, much, more.

The official pub-meet venue for various clubs such as the Range Rover Register, All Wheel Drive Club, 101 Forward Control Club and Military Vehicle Trust, TOR welcomes anyone with an interest in off-road activities. 8.30 pm till late!

WHITE ROSE 4x4 CLUB. c/o Darren Stevens (Chairman), 63 Oak Street, Crofton, Wakefield, W Yorkshire WF4 1JN (0924) 864639
Do you hate formal clubs? Well join us today. We have a monthly pub meet and regular events - all non-formal! Write to address above for application form.

NORTHERN IRELAND

NORTHERN IRELAND 4 WHEEL DRIVE CLUB. c/o Ian Henderson (Secretary), 12 Abbot View, Bowtown Estate, Newtownards, Co. Down BT23 3XT. (0247) 811584 MOBILE: (0860) 443447. Northern Ireland's only "off-road" 4 wheel drive club. Come along and join in the fun. Everyone welcome.

SCOTLAND

AE 4x4 CLUB. c/o Anne Smith (Secretary), Closs Cottage, Closs, Boreland by Lockerbie, Dumfries DG11 2LQ.
All marque club. Barony off-road course + workshop facilities available. Regular newsletters, events, meetings. Club discounts from local dealers etc.

BUCHAN OFF ROAD DRIVERS CLUB. c/o Robert Farquhar (Organiser), 44 Craigpark Place, Ellon, Aberdeenshire AB41 9FG (0358) 22668.
Regular events and meetings for owners and drivers of 4x4 vehicles of all makes. Special events for non-taxed vehicles, rallies/trial/drives etc.

WALES

MID WALES FOUR WHEEL DRIVE CLUB. c/o Jenny Dee (Secretary), Erwyd Garage, Ponterwyd, Aberystwyth, Dyfed SY23 3LA (097085) 664.
All aspects of 4x4 with a lot of fun!

(If any of the following overseas clubs contain outdated or incorrect information, please inform me as soon as possible - Ed.)

AUSTRIA

AUSTRIAN LAND ROVER OWNER CLUB. Autohaus Mathlbacher, Messersschittweg 28, 6175 Kematen Tiroel, Austria

DENMARK

DANSK LAND ROVER KLUB. c/o Claus A. Kjöeller, Gl. Hellebaekvej 61 B, 6 DK 3000 Helsingör, Denmark 49201578 FAX: 48242242. For further information, please contact Club Secretary Claus A. Kjöeller at the above address.

FRANCE

AUTO LOISIRS. 42 c/o Bernard Collas, 2 Le Petit Volvon, 42340 Veauche, France 77.94.83.59 or 77.54.61.12. All types of 4x4 vehicle, club near Lyon.

GERMANY

DEUTSCHER ROVER CLUB. e.v. c/o Roland Koch (Koordinator/Editor), D-6100 Darmstadt, Martinstr. 4, Germany 06151/43304 MOBILE: 06155/4951
Founded 1975, 450 members, 2 national events, bimonthly "Rover Blatt" @ 44p known as the bestL/ Rover club magazine worldwide. Membership DM 150

LROC HESSEN. c/o Günther Schibofski, Ludwigstrasse 5, W6200-Wiesbaden, Germany 0611-372269

HOLLAND

DUTCH LAND ROVER REGISTER. Postbus 46, 2110 AA, Aerdenhout 023-290308

LAND ROVER CLUB HOLLAND. Postbus 1161, 1440 DD, Purmerend 02990 - 32530

ITALY

THE FIRST LAND ROVER CLUB ITALIA. c/o Ferro Roberto (Secretary), Corso, Svizzera 149, 10149 Torino 0039-11-747896

NEW ZEALAND

SOUTHLAND LAND ROVER CLUB INC. c/o Richard Green (Secretary), PO Box 655, Invercargill, New Zealand.
Enjoyment of all makes of four wheel driving. Probably the "southern-most club on the globe!" Driving, sporting & social activities.

NORWAY

NORWEGIAN LAND ROVER CLUB. c/o Eiliv Haakonsen, Gl. Ringeriksvej 206, 1340 Bekkestua, Norway

PORTUGAL

CLUBE LAND ROVER DE PORTUGAL. Lgo. Do Ministro, 3 - Porta 1, 1700 Lisboa, Portugal 351-1-7584239 FAX: 351-1-3523848.
Portuguese Land Rover club which organises several meetings and one annual event open to foreign participants.

SOUTH AFRICA

LAND ROVER OWNERS CLUB OF SOUTHERN AFRICA. c/o Leon Christodoulou (P.R.O.), P.O. Box 23507, Joubert Park 2044, R.S.A (012) 6671 840 FAX: (012) 6671 944
Advice to Land Rover overlanders to sub-Saharan Africa - overseas membership welcome.

SPAIN

LAND ROVER CLUB ESPANIA. c/o Julio Garcia Llama, Centro Com. Entreplazas, 5a pl, 29620 Torremolinos, Malaga, Spain

SWEDEN

LAND ROVER CLUB OF SWEDEN. c/o Ted Persell (Club Secretary), Mossv gen 5 Rydbo, S-184 92 Akersberga, Sweden 08-7329381

SWITZERLAND

AMICALE LAND-ROVER. c/o Rosmarie Berger (Secretary), Rte du Bois 8, CH-1024 Ecublens, Switzerland

LAND ROVER SWITZERLAND. c/o Christian Von Ballmoos (Secretary), Schlyfferenmatt, 3282 Bagen, Switzerland 3

UNITED STATES OF AMERICA

LAND ROVER CLUB OF FLORIDA. c/o Thomas J. La Manna (President), 3324 Pine Hill Trail, Palm Beach Gardens, Florida 33418, U.S.A. 407-627-8752

ATTENTION ALL LAND ROVER & 4x4 CLUBS

Want to help make the countryside accessible to the disabled? Do you have the necessary skills, expertise and vehicles? Then the following voluntary non-profit making organisations might well be for you -

The **GO 4x4 IT** project has had three successful years organising greenlaning excursions in the North of England assisted by RED ROSE LAND ROVER OWNERS CLUB, CUMBRIA ROVER OWNERS CLUB and NORTH LAKES 4x4 CLUB.

By harnessing their professional experience of the land with four wheel drive vehicles, **GO 4x4 IT** enable those with a mobility problem (whether mental, physical or aged), to attain access to the real countryside - the very same countryside normally never seen by most able-bodied people!

Known more readily as **D.O.R.A., Disabled Off-Road Access** is a similar voluntary, non-profit making group who wish to share their passion of four wheel drive with others less able than themselves. Run in conjunction with TWICKENHAM OFF-ROADERS, many 4x4 excursions are scheduled in the South for 1994.

Please note the service provided both by **D.O.R.A.** and **GO 4x4 IT** is absolutely free of charge to recipients, therefore financial support via commercial sponsorship/donations is always welcome.

Whether a 4x4 owner or not, if you or your club would like to participate in either of these worthwhile ventures, please contact the relevant group for further information:

GO 4x4 IT	DISABLED OFF-ROAD ACCESS (D.O.R.A.)
c/o Peter Couch	c/o Wayne Fisher
6 Maple Avenue	97 Jeymer Drive
Haslingden	Greenford
Rossendale	Middlesex
Lancs BB4 5NQ	UB6 8NT
Tel: (0706) 215691	Tel: 081 575 6470

Please mention MACK'S when you phone or fax.

COMMERCIAL/AGRICULTURAL EQUIPMENT

CROSS REFERENCE: See also MECHANICAL SERVICES

ENGLAND

BUCKINGHAMSHIRE

AIRDRIVE LIMITED. London Road, High Wycombe, Bucks HP11 1EU
(0494) 450678 FAX: (0494) 461592
Air compressors, PTO drive, powerful professional units (100 cfm @ 100 psi) for roadbreakers, drills, pumps etc.

CHESHIRE

HYDROLIC MOBILE EQUIPMENT LTD. Unit 5a, Expodite works, Ashton Road, Bredbury, Cheshire SK6 2DS 061-430 8808
A complete design and advice service from the leaders in hydraulic technology. PTO pumps, power packs & systems.

HAMPSHIRE

JASON ENGINEERING (TOTTON) LTD. 27-33 High Street, Totton, Southampton, Hants SO4 4HL
(0703) 663535 FAX: (0703) 663531
PTO's for special vehicles.

HERTFORDSHIRE

HAWKEYE SYSTEMS LTD. 25 Burymead Road, Hitchin, Herts SG5 1RT
(0462) 452712 FAX: (0462) 420065
Surveillance systems manufacturer.

ISLE OF WIGHT

CLARK MASTS TEKSAM LIMITED. Binstead, Isle of Wight PO33 3PA
(0983) 563691 FAX: (0983) 566643
Manufacturer of telescopic and sectional masts up to 30m high. Any application or vehicle. Installation, conversion, power unit, connection

KENT

STALLION HYDROCAR. Stallion House, West Mill, Imperial Business Estate, Gravesend, Kent DA11 0DL (0474) 564707
Your local Nationwide supplier of PTO's, pumps & tipping gear. A complete range of spare parts inc hoses, valves and fitting facilities.

LANCASHIRE

A T VEHICLES. Unit 6, Fallbarn Road, Rawtenstall, Rossendale, Lancs BB4 7NT (0706) 219418.
Live Power Take Off (PTO) and Live Hydraulic Systems.
HYDRAULIC SPARES CENTRE. Unit 5, Lever House, Lever Street, Bolton BL3 6NY (0204) 27594 FAX: (0204) 383037
Pumps and power take-off's. Reconditioned & new. Exchange basis on PTO's. Also hydraulic hose assemblies made while you wait.
R.G.S. DEVELOPMENTS. Unit 6, Fallbarn Road, Rawtenstall, Rossendale, Lancs BB4 7NT
(0706) 219418.
PTO power on demand. Up hill and down dale, for the Power Drive System that leaves the competition standing contact R.G.S.

LEICESTERSHIRE

BEESLEY LTD. Home Barn Farm, Frolesworth Road, Shemford, Leicester LE10 3AD
DAY: (045 527) 3361 EVENING: (045 527) 2406
For all types of agricultural equipment and machinery. Stockists of PTO shafts, hydrualic hoses, seals, pumps, rams + hydraulic repairs.

OXFORDSHIRE

ROGAN FLUID POWER. Bromag Industrial Estate, Burford Road, Minster Lovell, Oxon OX8 5SR
(0993) 776551
Independent live hydraulic PTO's.

SURREY

WINTON ENGINEERING. Unit 4, Monument Way, West Winton Lea, Woking GU21 5EN (0483) 730648
Power Take Off units.

TYNE & WEAR

COMMERCIAL PROPSHAFT SERVICES LTD. Staithes Road, Dunston, Gateshead NE11 9DR
PROPSHAFTS: 091-460 9125 DRIVESHAFTS: 091-460 6003
We manufacture/rebuild/modify/shorten propshafts, PTO's, linkages for car, commercial, plant or machinery. All driveshafts, CV joints supplied/fitted.

WILTSHIRE

WEST FLUID POWER. Unit 1, Deverill Road Industrial Estate, Sutton Veny, Warminster, Wiltshire BA12 7BZ (0985) 40804 FAX: (0985) 40806
For all your hydraulic requirements - system design, valves, fittings, gear, vane & piston pumps, hose assemblies, power packs and PTO units.

NORTHERN IRELAND

CO. ANTRIM

DUNLOP OF CRANKILL STORES. 131-133 Crankill Road, Ballymena, Co. Antrim BT43 5NW (0266) 85507
Hydraulic PTO equipment including rams, valves, fittings and shafts. Repairs and seals distributor.

COMMUNICATIONS

AVON

THE RADIO LICENSING CENTRE. P.O. Box 885, Bristol BS99 (0272) 258333
Official body for the issue of CB licences.

BERKSHIRE

MAIDENHEAD CB RADIO CENTRE. Boyndon Autos, Lower Boyndon Road, Maidenhead, Bucks SL6 4DD (0628) 35312
Full range of CB radios & accessories.

BUCKINGHAMSHIRE

CHILTERN COMMUNICATIONS. Lincoln Road, Cressex Industrial Estate, High Wycombe, Bucks (0494) 459433
Two-way radio systems/Private Mobile Radio/Band 3 service provider. Short term hire, installation & maintenance.
MOONRAKER (UK) LTD. Unit 12, Cranfield Road Units, Cranfield Road, Woburn Sands, Bucks MK17 8QR (0908) 281705 FAX: (0908) 281706
Trade/retail CB radio - complete range of antennas/mikes/power supplies speakers and accessories. Secondhand radios bought/sold.
PREMIERE EUROCOM LTD. Unit 9, Waterside Drive, Langley Business Park, Slough, Bucks (0753) 543713
Sales and service centre for Mobile Radio, Band 3, P.M.R., hand portables, short term hire.

CAMBRIDGESHIRE

COLLINS & PARTNERS. The Communications Tower, Kirkwood Road, Cambridge CB4 2PF (0223) 426155/426384 FAX: (0223) 420218
Mobile communications No.1 in Cambridgeshire for 25 years. Specialist suppliers of two-way radio and National Band 3.

CHESHIRE

CB 37 COMMUNICATIONS. 15 Middlewich Street, Crewe CW1 4BS (0270) 588440
Specialists in CB radio equipment, also radio amateur equipment available. Nationwide mail order.

CORNWALL

RON'S CB & ELECTRICAL SHOP. 46 Lower bore Street, Bodmin, Cornwall PL31 2JY (0208) 74569
CB sales & service.

CUMBRIA
NORTECH RADIO COMMUNICATIONS. Blackdyke Road, Kingstown Industrial Estate, Carlisle, Cumbria (0228) 44678/9 FAX: (0228) 515370
Band III radio * 2-way radio * short and long term hire * repairs to most makes of 2-way radio * rent-buy-lease.
PENRITH COMMUNICATIONS. 14 Castlegate, Penrith, Cumbria CA11 7HZ
(0768) 67146
CB radio equipment - accessories, sales & service.

DERBYSHIRE
ZYCOMM ELECTRONICS LTD. 51 Nottingham Road, Ripley, Derbys DE5 3AN
(0773) 570123 FAX: (0773) 570155
2-way mobile radio, PMR systems, Band III systems, mobile & portable units. Contact Zycomm for all your communication requirements.

DEVON
C.B. SALES (DEVON). Stidston, South Brent, Devon (0364) 73891 FAX: (0364) 72907
Suppliers of CB radio. Full workshop facilities on the premises. Access/Visa accepted.

DORSET
POOLE LOGIC. 49 Kingston Road, Poole, Dorset BH15 2LR (0202) 683093
Your local communication specialists. Private Mobile Radio, CB radio. Repairs carried out on the premises.

ESSEX
LEIGH AUDIO. 1621 London Road, Leigh-on-Sea, Essex (0702) 714330
Sales & service - CB/air band/amateur radio/scanners/aerials and accessories. New & used radio equipment.
R & J ELECTRONIC SERVICES LTD. 2 Birch Avenue, Harwich, Essex CO12 4DB
(0255) 240523 MOBILE:(0860) 485803 FAX:(0255) 240523
Radar, communications, navigation equipment. Mobile & portable radios, marine electronics. Advice/sales/hire/spares/repairs.

HEREFORDSHIRE
TELESERVICE CB. 141 Elgin Street, Hereford (0432) 265378
CB radios and accessories.

KENT
A2 TRUCK STOP. Harbledown Services, C.B. Centre, Upper Harbledown, Canterbury, Kent CT2 9AZ
(0227) 451438
The largest range of CB equipment in East Kent. Accessories, aerials, upgrades and replacement of existing CB's.
HANGARS ELECTRONICS. 3 Victory Street, Sheerness, Kent ME12 1NZ (0795) 663336
C.B.'s - complete range including secondhand models.
ICOM (UK) LTD. Unit 9, Sea Street, Herne Bay, Kent CT6 8LD (0227) 741741 FAX: (0227) 741742
Specialists in all kinds of radio communications equipment.Airband - Marine - Land Mobile - Amateur Radio.
ONE STOP ELECTRONICS. 126A Maidstone Road, Rochester, Kent (0634) 400179
Supply and installation of all communication equipment including CB and marine. Sales, spares and repairs.

HERTFORDSHIRE
RICKMANSWORTH COMMUNICATIONS CENTRE. 37-39 Station Road, Rickmansworth, Herts
(0923) 775577
All your communication needs. Sales, hire, installation, maintenanceof Private Mobile/Band 3/Two-Way Radio systems.

LANCASHIRE
CORRYS TELECOMMUNICATIONS. Rear of 63/67 Handsworth Road, Blackpool FY1 2QZ
(0253) 28218 FAX: (0253) 24455
2 Way Radios/Land, Mobile & Marine Radio - Sales, service, hire, installation & maintenance. Competitive rates.

S.R. ELECTRONICS. 123 Blackburn Road, Accrington BB5 0AA (0254) 397070
CB radio, aerial and accessories.

LONDON

LEE ELECTRONICS. 400 Edgware Road, London W2 1ED 071-723 5521
London's largest communications centre. Marine, amateur radio, land mobile, Band Three etc. Established
for over 20 years.
LONDON COMMUNICATIONS PLC. 134 Gloucester Avenue, Regents Park, London NW1 8JA
071-586 9851 FAX: 071-722 0966
Business two-way systems/Band 3 trunked radio/walkie talkies. Individual systems designed & fitted.
Sales, service & hire.
SOUTH MIDLANDS COMMUNICATIONS LTD. 6 Royal Parade, Hanger Lane, London W5A 1ET
081-997 4476
The complete communications service from one source. All types of radio equipment for governments to
the private individual.

MANCHESTER, GREATER

NETWORK RADIO COMMUNICATIONS LTD. Unit B10, Bolton Enterprise Centre, Washington
Street, Bolton BL3 5EY (0204) 384104
1st choice in the North West for Band 3, Private Mobile Radio, Trunked Radio, Two Way Radio - sales/
service/rental.
STOCKPORT C.B. CENTRE. 14 Buxton Road, Heaviley SK2 061-477 6483
C.B. sales and service.

MERSEYSIDE

C.B. SHACK. 67 Rocky Lane, Tuebrook, Liverpool L6 4BB 051-263 2010
CB radio specialist.

MIDDLESEX

CTL RADIOCOM. CTL House, 200 Windmill Lane, Greenford UB6 9DW 081-575 9929
Base station and mobile two-way radio systems, Band 3 national radio network. Sales, service, radio hire
and installation.

NORFOLK

B.A. YEOMANS & SON. 65 North Walsham Road, Norwich, Norfolk (0603) 426294
C.B. - the low cost 2-way radio system. Quick repairs, often while U wait. Trade & retail.

NORTHAMPTONSHIRE

SUE'S CB CENTRE. 204 Wellingborough Road, Rushden, Northants (0933) 314901
All CB communications equipment and aerials. Please telephone for our competitive prices.

OXFORDSHIRE

C.B. SERVICES (OXFORD). 54 Quarry Road, Headington, Oxford OX3 8NX
(0865) 65126 MOBILE: (0860) 646465
CB/2 way radio - sales, services, installations.

SHROPSHIRE

CAR CARE. 3 Tyrone House, Church Street, Wellington, Telford, Shropshire (0952) 247687
CB radios and accessories. Open 7 days.

SUFFOLK

IPSWICH COMMUNICATIONS & ENG. SERVICES LTD. 297 Bramford Road, Ipswich IP1 4AT
(0473) 462173
We'll keep you in touch! 2-way radio, community base stations, band three - sales/hire/lease/service and
repairs.
RADIOCARE. 48 Eastgate Street, Bury St. Edmunds, Suffolk IP33 1YW (0284) 701823
CB radio - CB radio - CB radio ... Twigs, rigs, repairs. All makes at very competitive prices.

SURREY

MAD BARON ENTERPRISES. 63 Brooklands Road, Weybridge, Surrey KT13 0RU
TEL/FAX: (0932) 336010
CB specialist. Open Tues - Wed - Thurs - Fri 10am-6pm, Sat 10am-4pm.Other times by appointment
only, but I try to accommodate your requirements.
SOCOM GROUP. Head Office: 170 Oval Road, Croydon CR0 6BN 081-680 1585
Sales of complete radio communications inc. Band III trunking. Short term hire/service workshop for
installation/maintenance.

WEST MIDLANDS
C.B. CABIN. 81 Church Street, Brierley Hill, W Midlands DY5 3QP TEL/FAX: (0384) 571905
Citizens Band radio specialists.
CB WORLD. 292 Kitts Green Road, Birmingham B33 021-784 4523
CB radio sales and service.

YORKSHIRE, WEST
EMPRESS TRADING CO. 564 Thornton Road, Bradford BD8 9NF (0274) 499340
Specialists in CB radios. Accessories, aerials etc.
JOHN A. DOBBINS LTD. Bradford Road, East Ardsley, Nr. Wakefield, W Yorks WF3 2DN
(0532) 524586
CB radio specialists. Largest stock in Yorkshire. Trade and retail -the CB centre.
R.F. COMMUNICATIONS. Carphone House, 87 Surrey Street, Parkinson Lane, Halifax HX1
(0422) 344375
CB radio equipment specialist.

SCOTLAND

GRAMPIAN
MAYFIELD MOTORS. South Affleck, Whiterushes, Aberdeen AB2 0RB (0651) 882259
Suppliers of CB radio equipment.

HIGHLAND
TANDY INVERNESS. 4 Eastgate Shopping Centre, Inverness, Highland (0463) 712903
CB radio - scanners - aerials - accessories.

WALES

CLWYD
MOLD CB & RADIO. Indoor Market, Daniel Owen Precinct, Earl Road, Mold CH7 1AP
(0352) 757934
Rigs, antennae, repairs, scanners.

DYFED
ABERYSTWYTH ELECTRONICS. 1 Eastgate Street, Aberryswyth, Dyfed
(0970) 611442 FAX: (0970) 627024
CB specialists, full range of accessories & equipment. Once installed its far cheaper than telephones, all
calls are free!
RIG & RADIO SERVICES. 24 Swansea Road, Llanelli, Dyfed (0554) 754001
CB sales & repair. We probably offer the best prices and range in South and West Wales. Used
equipment bought/sold. Mon-Sat 10-5.30

GLAMORGAN, WEST
TRANSWORLD COMMUNICATIONS (NEATH). 96 Windsor Road, Neath West Glamorgan
(0639) 632374 FAX: (0639) 646003
CB, amateur radio, marine services, radar etc. We are the two way radio people. Advice, fitting & after
sales service.

ELECTRICAL PARTS, ACCESSORIES & SERVICES

ENGLAND

BEDFORDSHIRE
VALEO DISTRIBUTION (UK) LTD. Stewkley Road, Soulbury, Leighton Buzzard, Beds LU7 0EQ (052 527) 511/591 FAX: (052 527) 656
Manufacturer of Halogen headlight conversions for Land/Range Rovers. Marchal and Cibié auxiliary lighting and Valeo alternators & starters.

BERKSHIRE
KENLOWE LTD. Burchetts Green, Maidenhead, Berks SL6 6QU (0628) 823303 FAX: (0628) 823451
Cooling/heating specialists. Kenlowe thermo electric engine cooling fans. Kenlowe hotstart engine/interior pre-heating systems.

BUCKINGHAMSHIRE
DRIFTGATE. Wingbury Farm, Wingrave, Aylesbury, Bucks HP22 4LW
(0296) 682141 FAX: (0296) 681140
The AC Powergen MkIII replacement alternator provides additional 110v or 240v power at 2.5kw. Runs microwave, drills or welding to 170 amps DC.
PACET MANUFACTURING LTD. Wyebridge House, Cores End Road, Bourne End,
Bucks SL8 5HH (0628) 526754 FAX: (0628) 810080
Range of 12v engine cooling fans including a reversible unit. Mounted on either side of the radiator, the CF56 can either draw or blow air according to space availability - ideal for towing/performance mods etc.

ESSEX
CHATAIGNE PRODUCTS. Green Lane, Gt Horkesley, Colchester, Essex CO6 4HD
Crystal frequency controlled inverter converts 12v DC to 240V AC50HZ.Ideal for TV, video, hi-fi, lights etc. Simply connects to 12v battery.
ELECTRICAL CAR SERVICES. 62 Honey Lane, Waltham Abbey, Essex EN9 3BS
(0992) 718439 MOBILE: (0860) 317453 FAX: (0992) 718439
Specialist parts. Complete waterproof switch sets, high output w/screen washer systems/headlight looms & equipment/custom made wiring looms.
REDI-LINE U.K. LTD. Unit 1, Parkside Centre, Potters Way, Temple Farm Ind. Est. Southend,
Essex SS2 5SJ (0702) 617218 FAX: (0702) 469017
Power when you want it. Can be mounted in vehicle. Runs from battery.500w and 1600w 230VAC, 50Hz true Sin Wave output. Send for brochure.

HUMBERSIDE
MALPATECH LTD. Central Buildings, Green Lane, Wincolmlee, Hull HU2 0HG
(0482) 587503 FAX: (0482) 587977
Comprehensive range of wiring looms, braided cable or pvc cable, original specification or converted looms, credit cards accepted.

KENT
BOYER BRANSDEN ELECTRONICS LTD. Frindsbury House, Cox Lane, Detling, Maidstone,
Kent ME14 3HE (0622) 30939
Boyer Bransden Electronic Ignition - guaranteed for life.
RYD DESIGN LTD. Poplar Road, Wittersham, Kent TN30 7NT (0797) 270427 FAX: (0797) 270207
240 volt/250 or 450 watt output inverters. Runs computers, televisions, videos & power tools from a normal 12 volt battery (110v also available)

LONDON
AUTOCAR EQUIPMENT LTD. 77-85 Newington Causeway, London SE1 6BJ
071-403 5959 FAX: 071-378 1270
Lumenition electronic ignition, high specification replacement ignition leads/HT coils, air/fuel ratio gauges, digital fuel management systems.
SPEEDY CABLES LTD. The Mews, St. Paul Street, Islington, London N1 7BU 071-226 9228
Speedometer, clock & rev counter repairs, most types including electronic& recalibration. Most brake/clutch/speedo/throttle cables made to order.

LEICESTERSHIRE
VICTRON (UK) LTD. Jacknell Road, Hinckley, Leics LE10 3BZ (0455) 618666 TEL: (0455) 611446
High quality mobile electric energy systems for car/mobile workshops/marine etc. i.e. a range of ten 12v or 24v inverters rated from 200-4,000 watts!

MERSEYSIDE
JAGRA STARTERS & ALTENATORS. Unit A15, Gardners Row Business Centre, Gardners Row, Liverpool L3 6JT 051-298 2143 FAX: 051-298 2074
Remanufacturer of Land Rover & Range Rover starters and altenators. Please phone for details.

NORFOLK
NORFOLK LAND ROVER CENTRE. Rushall, Diss, Norfolk IP21 4DD (0379) 741607
Manufacturers of 'one off' and special application Land Rover wiring looms.

NORTHAMPTONSHIRE
PULSAR BATTERIES. Unit 15, Silverstone Circuit, Silverstone, Northants NN12 8TL
(0327) 857880 FAX: (0327) 858011
Battery with emergency starting reserve. 1100 cranking amps. Unique design.

NOTTINGHAMSHIRE
AUTO SPARKS. 80-88 Derby Road, Nottingham NG10 5HU (0602) 497211 FAX: (0602) 491955
Wiring looms for Series I, II & IIA, III, early Range Rover - please ring for information. Trade enquires welcome.
MERV PLASTICS. 201 Station Road, Beeston, Notts NA9 2AB (0602) 222783
Wiring materials: Cables, PVC sleeving, 1000's of terminals & connectors, HT & battery cables, lighting, guages, crimp tools, fuse boxes etc.

OXFORDSHIRE
HELLA UK LTD. Wildmere Industrial Estate, Banbury, Oxon OX16 7JU
(0295) 272233 FAX: (0295) 270843
Auxiliary lighting, fire extinguishers, warning triangles, towing accessories.

SURREY
AUTOMOTIVE ELECTRONICS. Oxted Mill, Spring Lane, Oxted, Surrey RH8 9PB
(0883) 715543 FAX: (0883) 716422
Eti 200 electronic ignition suitable for negative earth four, six and eight cylinder engines - not suitable for Series I positive earth.
DATUM FUEL SYSTEMS. 180 Hersham Road, Hersham, Walton on Thames, Surrey KT12 5QE
(0932) 231973 FAX: (0932) 246859
Complete range of 'Facet' electric fuel pumps for road, race or rally.
L.E. PEREI AUTO DEVICES LIMITED. Sunbury House, The Trading Estate, Farnham,
Surrey GU9 9NP (0252) 723434 FAX: (0252) 721788
Manufacturers and trade suppliers of vehicle lighting equipment, incl. Land Rover replacement lamps, lenses, reflectors, flashers etc.

WEST MIDLANDS
VDO INSTRUMENTS LTD. Holford Drive, Holford, Birmingham B6 7UG
021-344 2000 FAX: 021-344 2071
Suppliers of instrumentation and transducers for engine monitoring to the automotive industry.

YORKSHIRE, WEST
D.S. BEAL (UK) SUPPLIES. Church Street, Morley, W Yorkshire LS27 9JS
(0532) 533033 FAX: (0532) 530223
Workshop consumables - cable ties, electrical terminals, fuses,
PVC tape, etc.

ENGINE CONVERSIONS

CROSS REFERENCE: See also ENGINES,INDEPENDENT 4WD SPECIALISTS

ENGLAND

BERKSHIRE
TURBO ROVER. 260 Kidmore Road, Caversham, Reading RG4 7NE
(0734) 482853 EVENING: (0734) 477147 FAX: (0734) 461932
We enjoy the reputation of being one of the country's leading specialists in diesel conversions - complete with 12 months warranty.

CAMBRIDGESHIRE
MOTOR & DIESEL ENGINEERING. Station Works, Old North Road, Bourn, Cambridge CB3 7TZ
(0954) 719549/719633 FAX: (0954) 718915
Land Rover/Range Rover diesel conversions include Perkins 4.182T, Mazada SL35Ti and VM units.
Options for 3 & 4 speed Automatic Range Rovers.

CHESHIRE
FROGGATT'S RANGE ROVER SALES. Unit 2 Whirley Quarry, Sandy Lane, Whirley,
Macclesfield SK10 4RJ (0625) 425524 MOBILE (0860) 479462 FAX (0625) 619494
Diesel conversion specialists - Mazada, Perkins, Nissan etc. Please telephone (0625) 425524 for all your Range Rover requirements.

DERBYSHIRE
MILNER CONVERSIONS. The Old Bus Garage, Hackney Lane, Darley Dale, Derbys DE4 2QJ
(0629) 734411 FAX: (0629) 733906
Diesel Conversion Kits for Range Rover: Perkins, Toyota, Daihatsu, Peugeot, Isuzu, Ford + Turbo Kits for Land Rover Series I to 110.

DEVON
COUNTRY VEHICLE SERVICES. Livingshayes, Silverton, Exeter EX5 4JT
(0392) 860604 MOBILE: (0860) 893838 FAX: (0392) 860604
All 4x4 repairs. Specialist in diesel conversions for Range Rover and Land Rover.

GLOUCESTERSHIRE
GRETTON MOTORS LTD. Unit 11, Whimsey Industrial Estate, Cinderford, Glos GL14 3JA
(0594) 826040
Diesel power for your Range Rover, Discovery, Land Rover 90/110. Our 3.9 litre Tdi conversion gives performance, fuel economy and value for money.

HAMPSHIRE
B & H SERVICES. Unit 3, Beavers Yard, Pack Lane, Basingstoke, Hants RG22 5HR
(0256) 810144 MOBILE: (0860) 509248 FAX: (0256) 810144
Range Rover/Land Rover 5.0 litre engine conversions and kits. Servicing and repairs, new/used spares, Rover V8 Weber carburettor conversions.

HUMBERSIDE
BRENT ENGINEERING SERVICES. Plantation Farm, Breck Lane, North Cave, Brough,
N Humberside HU15 2PF (0430) 422153
Range Rover diesel conversions including 4-speed autos. Perkins Phaser Turbo engines supplied and fitted. Conversion kits at competitive prices.

LANCASHIRE
A & S AUTOCENTRE. Unit 4, Helca Works, Brown Street, Bamber Bridge, Nr Preston,
Lancs PR5 6NQ (0772) 34093
Land Rover conversions, V8, V6, Perkins. All repair work, welding, bodywork, resprays.
STEVE PARKER LAND ROVERS. Unit 72, Healey Hall Mills, Healey Dell, Rochdale,
Lancs OL12 6BG (0706) 350140 FAX: (0706) 43878
Ford 2.3/2.5/2.8/3.0 litre V6 petrol engines, Isuzu & peugeot diesel conversions for Land/Range Rover.
Lead free heads for LR 2.25 petrol.

MERSEYSIDE
WIRRAL DIESEL CONVERSIONS. Unit 8, Corporation Road Industrial Estate, Birkenhead, Wirral,
Merseyside 051-653 3322
Range Rover & Land Rover diesel conversions, choice of new or used engines.Engine reconditioning, sales, service, fuel injection, refurbishment.

SHROPSHIRE
W.E. PHILLIPS ENGINEERING. Preens Eddy, Coalport, Telford TF8 7JG
(0952) 882199 MOBILE: (0831) 125286
Suitable for LR/RR/101 conversion: Isuzu, Nissan, Toyota, Perkins, Ford,Peugeot, York, Daihatsu.
Please telephone for conversion kit details.

SOMERSET
COASTAL ENGINEERING. Higher Buckland Farm, Buckland St Mary, Chard,
Somerset TA20 3QZ (0460) 234724 MOBILE: (0831) 862855 FAX: (0460) 234722
LR/RR/Discovery diesel conversions by us or DIY kits. New/secondhand engines - Daihatsu/Mazda/
Nissan/Perkins/Toyota. Send large SAE or phone.

SUSSEX, EAST
ROBERTS RANGE ROVERS. Ninfield Garage, Bexhill Road, Ninfield, Battle,E Sussex TN33 9EE
(0424) 893280 FAX: (0424) 892178
Range Rover specialist - diesel conversions, parts, servicing, repairs, breaking all vehicles, vehicle sales,
export welcome.

SUSSEX, WEST
D. LOCK & ASSOCIATES. Woodcote, Chalk Road, Ifold, Billingshurst, W Sussex RH14 0UE
(0403) 753396 FAX: (0403) 752879
Easy low-cost conversion to unleaded with Broquet Fuel Catalyst;cleaner engine, more mpg, better
performance, fully guaranteed.

WEST MIDLANDS

J.E. ENGINEERING LTD. Siskin Drive, Coventry CV3 4FJ
(0203) 305018 FAX: (0203) 305913
Rover V8 specialists. New or exchange, short or full 3.5, 3.9, 4.2, 4.5 litre engines/parts. Fast road/race/rally or standard spec. Anything V8.
MERCIA 4x4. Unit 27A, Yates Brothers Industrial Estate, Lime Lane, Pelsall, Walsall WS3 5AS
(0543) 375641
Conversion manufacturers. Kits include Rover V8, Mazda, Isuzu or Perkins into L/Rover, R/Rover, Discovery. Also full servicing, chassis refits etc.

WILTSHIRE

AMERICAN ENGINE SERVICES LTD. Unit 1, Avon Terrace, Salisbury, Wilts SP2 7BT
(0722) 414111 FAX: (0722) 411906
BMW 6 cylinder diesel engines for Range Rovers. Ford/Chevy engines & parts.

NORTHERN IRELAND

CO.DOWN

JAPANESE ENGINE CENTRE. 16 Old Road, Mayorbridge, Newry, Co. Down, Northern Ireland
(069385) 724
Diesel engine conversion of Land Rover & Range Rover. Same day fitting service, fully guaranteed. All makes of Japanese engines available.

WALES

POWYS

M. BURGINS & SON. Fronwen Garage, Dolau, Llandrindod Wells, Powys LD1 5TL
(0597851) 236 FAX: (0597851) 862
Isuzu Turbo Diesel for Range Rover, Discovery V8, Land Rover. Amazing power & economy from the makers of the finest diesels - auto or manual.

CROSS REFERENCE: See also ENGINE CONVERSIONS

ENGLAND

BEDFORDSHIRE

AUTO TECHNIQUE (EMS) LIMITED. Units C & D, Kingsway Industrial Estate, Luton, Beds LU1 1LP (0582) 414000 FAX: (0582) 419690
Land Rover/Range Rover 4WD tuning specialist. Sun 4WD rolling road 720 bhp. Turbos supplied and fitted. New and reconditioned carburettors.

BUCKINGHAMSHIRE

BELGRADE SERVICES LTD. London Road, Woburn, Milton Keynes MK17 9PY (0525) 290635 FAX: (0525) 290249
New Land Rover and Range Rover engines. 3.5 or 3.9 EFi from £2,200 + VAT fitted.

CHESHIRE

C M A. Unit 1, Dale Street, Broughton, Chester, Cheshire (0244) 311578
Full engine machine service and V8 re-conditioning. Also sales of timing chains/pistons/cam shafts/hydraulic followers/rocker arms & shafts etc.
FROGGATT'S RANGE ROVER SALES. Unit 2 Whirley Quarry, Sandy Lane, Whirley, Macclesfield SK10 4RJ (0625) 425524 MOBILE (0860) 479462 FAX (0625) 619494
New and second-hand petrol & diesel engines always in stock. Please telephone (0625) 425524 for all your Range Rover requirements.

DERBYSHIRE

"THE VM SPECIALIST". G Force Diesel Power & Engineering, 3 Darwin Road, Newbold, Chesterfield, Derbys S40 4RX (0246) 221399 MOBILE: (0836) 362152
New, used, exchange or own recon VM 2.4/2.5 turbo diesel engines. Large stocks of new & used spares off the shelf, conversion & soundproofing kits.

DEVON

SAMURAI MOTOR COMPONENTS LTD. Stenwood House, Station Road, Colyton, Devon EX13 6HD TEL/FAX: (0297) 552234 MOBILE: (0836) 331168
Suppliers of new Nissan diesel engines & fitting kits for Land Rover, Range Rover etc.
ZEUS DESIGN PATENTS EXETER & LONDON LTD. 8 Devon Units, Budlake Road, Marsh Barton, Exeter, Devon EX2 8PY (0392) 438833 FAX: (0392) 422099
Land Rover 2.25/2.5 and Discovery timing conversions. Re-conditioned full engines. Phone for full details.

DORSET

V8 ENGINEERING LTD. Manor Farm, Berwick St. John, Dorset SP7 0EX (0747) 828070
230 bhp Ford V8 302 cu.in. or 270 bhp Chevrolet 350 units supplied ready to fit. Also budget American V8 engine and transmission parts.
SMC INDUSTRIAL LIMITED. Airfield Way Estate, Airfield way, Christchurch, Dorset BH23 3TA (0202) 480414 FAX: (0202) 480404
UK agents for Isuzu engines. 2.8 litre turbo/intercooled diesel engine conversions for Range Rover/Discovery/Land Rover. Phone for specifications.

ESSEX

DIAMOND ENGINE CENTRE. 573-585 High Road, Ilford, Essex IG3 081-983 8855
Range Rover Efi - full engine £995.00 + VAT (exchange). Supply & free fitting. Open 7 days a week. Phone for details.

HEREFORDSHIRE

F.G.R. PO Box 6, Bromyard, Herefordshire (0885) 400639
Performance V8 specialists, engines, engine parts, suspension, fibreglass supplied home & abroad. Export enquires welcome.

HERTFORDSHIRE

ROVER POWER, OBLIC ENGINEERS LTD. Church Street, Litlington, Royston, Herts SG8 0QB (0763) 852217 FAX: (0763) 852985
V8 specialists; 3.9 & 4.2 litre engines for Discovery and Range Rover. Suspension systems and ancillary modifications.

KENT

DUBLAR DIESELS. Fair Folly Garage, Gravesend Road, Higham, Kent ME3 7NX
(0634) 295285
Diesel Problems? We supply/fit low mileage engines/heads/pumps cranks etc. Range Rover conversions.
Try us for anything diesel.

KENT COMBUSTION. Unit 8, Castle Road, Sittingbourne, Kent (0795) 430546
V8i/carb petrol £475, 2.5 Turbo Diesel £950 - remanufactured service ex units, free fitting & guarantee
OR D.I.Y. exchange/no exchange OR used.

ROVERCRAFT. Unit One Progress Estate, Parkwood, Maidstone, Kent ME15 9YH
(0622) 687070 FAX: (0622) 692273
Complete 250+ bhp V8 race engines or 3.5/3.9 performance kits ready to assemble. Also machining
services by mail order - cylinder head work a speciality, plus boring/balancing/grinding/tuftriding/welding
etc.

LEICESTERSHIRE

HEATHROW ENGINE CENTRE (LEIC) LTD. 312/314 Green Lane Road, Leicester
(0533) 460746 MOBILE: (0860) 508404 FAX: (0533) 461192
British or Japanese replacement engines and gearboxes. All work fully guaranteed. Nationwide delivery
(POA) 8.30am-8pm Mon-Fri, 8.30am-4pm

NORFOLK

ROVER PART. Wayside Garage, Holt Road, Horsford, Norwich, Norfolk NR10 3EE
(0603) 891209 FAX: (0603) 890330
V8 engines are our speciality. We can build full or part engines, high performance or standard - or supply
all parts from stock for DIY.

R.P.i. INTERNATIONAL. Wayside Garage, Holt Road, Horsford, Norwich, Norfolk NR10 3EE
(0603) 891209 FAX: (0603) 890330
Rover 3.5 & 3.9 performance engine specialists. Engines built to customer's spec. Massive on-the-shelf
stocks of used, recon'd & new SD1 & 800 spares.

SURREY

TURNER ENGINEERING. Churchill House, West Park Road, Lingfield, Surrey RH7 6HT
(0342) 834713 FAX: (0342) 834042
The only UK engine re-manufacturer specialising in Land Rover. BS5750
part 2. All 4 cyl 2.25/2.5 petrol/diesel 90/110 Turbo Diesel & Tdi. Cylinder heads, short, stripped
engines etc. & parts from stock.

SUSSEX, WEST

SOUTHERN ENGINE CENTRE. A23 London Road, Bolney, West Sussex (0444) 881305
Full R/Rover engines incl fitting - £895 + VAT Subject to availability, exchange units being serviceable,
fitted units do not incl service parts

TYNE & WEAR

ENGINE & GEARBOX EXCHANGE. Wellington Road, Dunston, Gateshead NE11 9JJ
091-460 6024/6049
The North East's leading engine re-manufacturer. Guaranteed 12 months or 12,000 miles, most units
supplied from stock. Removal/fitting service.

WEST MIDLANDS

BREAKWELL THE ENGINE MAN. Unit 2, Wallows Road Industrial Estate, Brierley Hill, Dudley,
West Midlands (0384) 483989
Any & every engine (many diesels). Run & tested salvage engines, stripped & rebuilt engines, cylinder
heads, blocks, pistons, cranks etc.

WALSH DIESEL'S. Unit 11, Edgwick Park Industrial Estate, Foleshill, Coventry CV6 5RB
(0203) 687092 FAX: (0203) 662751
Land Rover/Range Rover/Freight Rover specialists. Remanufactured engines and gearboxes. Wide range
of parts and accessories.

WILTSHIRE

WEST COUNTRY DIESELS. Unit 46, Okus Trading Estate, Swindon, Wiltshire (0793) 420749
Top quality, reliable remanufactured diesel/petrol engines - or phone us for a quote to repair your existing
engine effectively and economically.

WORCESTERSHIRE
GRINALL CARS. Westridge House, Heightington, Bewdley, Worcs DY12 2YJ
(02993) 2862 FAX: (02993) 2889
4043cc Rover V8 engines producing 225-275 bhp - depending on Cam Spec. and Carburation. 3500cc
engines & 5-speed gearboxes fully reconditioned.

YORKSHIRE, WEST
A.E. AUTOPARTS LTD. PO Box 10, Legrams Lane, Bradford, W Yorks BD7 INQ (0274) 723481
FAX: (0274) 308746
Manufacturers of short and full engines. Trade only.

SCOTLAND
LOTHIAN
EAST OF SCOTLAND ENGINEERING LTD. 11 Bankhead Drive, Sighthill Industrial Estate,
Edinburgh EH11 4EJ 031-664 5054
Replacement AE Autoparts short or full engines. Also full machine shop facilities incl. cylinder head
grinding, pistons, bearings, gaskets etc.

EXHAUSTS
ENGLAND

CHESHIRE
NATIONAL TYRES AND AUTOCARE. 80-82 Wellington Road North, Stockport,
Cheshire SK4 1HR 061-480 7461 FREEPHONE: (0800) 626666 FOR NEAREST BRANCH
Exhausts, 4x4 tyres, wheels, other tyres, exhausts, batteries & range of auto services. Check for service
before travelling, 400 branches nationwide.
TUBE TORQUE COMPETITION MANIFOLDS & SYSTEMS. Unit 10, Brook St. Mill,
Brook Street, Macclesfield, Cheshire SK11 7AA (0625) 511153
One off's for off-roaders, rally, race and performance road-going vehicles i.e. Patterns for RR/110 Paris-
Dakar spec. V8 manifolds.
WELCROFT PRODUCTS. Bramhall Auto Centre, Ack Lane East, Bramhall, Cheshire SK7 1AW
061-439 5578 FAX: (06637) 46944
Mild steel & stainless steel exhaust systems for 88"/90"/101"/109"/110"and Range Rover. Phone now for
an immediate quote. Open 7 days.

DEVON
DOUBLE 'S' EXHAUSTS LTD. Station House, Station Road, Cullompton, Devon EX15 1BN
(0884) 33454 FAX: (0884) 32829 - Manufacturers of stainless steel exhaust systems. Stocks for most
Land Rover/Range Rover models and other 4x4's held for immediate delivery.

HEREFORDSHIRE
F.G.R. PO Box 6, Bromyard, Herefordshire (0885) 400639 FAX: (0885) 400639
FGR Range Rover Dakar/Tubular manifolds and exhaust systems.

LINCOLNSHIRE
RIMMER BROTHERS LIMITED. Triumph House, Sleaford Road, Bracebridge Heath,
Lincoln LN4 2NA (0522) 568000 FAX: (0522) 567600
Stainless Steel Exhausts with life-time guarantee. Land Rover/Discovery/Range Rover (inc V8 Sports
exhaust systems), Europ'n/Japanese models. Fast mail order. Prices inc VAT & free next day delivery.

LONDON
JAYSTOCK LTD. Hampden Centre, Hampden Road, London N10 2PA
081-444 1003 FAX: 081-883 3411
Exhaust specialist distributor, massive stocks, all models old and new, nationwide delivery.
LONDON STAINLESS STEEL EXHAUST CENTRE. 249-253 Queenstown Road, Battersea,
London SW8 3NP 071-622 2120 FAX: 071-627 0991
Stainless exhausts for all Land Rover & Range Rover vehicles from earliest to latest.
RALLY & RACE TECHNOLOGY. Unit 14 H/K, Stonehill Bus. Pk, Angel Rd, Edmonton, London
N18 3LD 081-345 5656 MOBILE: (0836) 252416 FAX: 081-345 5185
Performance road & race exhausts made to order in stainless steel using information gained on our
Bosch Rolling Road Dyno - V8 specialists.

MIDDLESEX

THE EXHAUST FACTORY. Unit 2, Staines Central Trading Estate, Staines, Middx TW18 4UP
081-754 7900 FAX: (0784) 464489 - Europe's largest stock of stainless steel exhausts - fitted while-u-wait or worldwide dispatch - also built to order.

NORTHAMPTONSHIRE

BTB EXHAUSTS LTD. Unit 3, Great Central Way, Woodford Halse, Daventry NN11 6PZ (0327)
61797 24 HOUR FAX: (0295) 750233
Specialist manufacturers of high performance exhaust manifolds and systems. Rover V8 and diesel conversion exhaust systems fabricated and fitted.

WEST MIDLANDS

BAINBRIDGE SILENCERS LTD. Unit 26, Aston Church Trad. Est., Aston Church Road, Nechells, Birmingham B7 5RU 021-3284700 FAX: 021-328 8338
Exhaust manufacturers & suppliers to the motor trade.

YORKSHIRE, WEST

TONY LAW EXHAUSTS. Unit 3, Queen Street, Stourton, Leeds LS10 1SL
(0532) 715422
All hand made one-offs - rally cars or off-road racers.

GEARBOXES & DIFFERENTIALS

ENGLAND

CAMBRIDGESHIRE

CAMBS 4x4 TRANSMISSIONS. 36 London Road, Wansford, PE8 6JE (0780) 783513
4 speed Range Rover transmission specialists. Guaranteed reconditioned gearboxes with transfer box and brake from £375. Fitting service avail.

ESSEX

DIAMOND GEARBOX CENTRE. Chadwell Heath Lane, Romford, Essex IG3 081-598 9440
Range Rover Efi - 5 speed manual gearbox £695.00, auto gearbox £795.00 Supply & free fitting. Phone for details.
LAND SPARES LTD. 3 Woodside Parade, 261 Woodside, Leigh on Sea,
Essex SS9 4SS (0702) 512110
Gearboxes reconditioned to original equipment. Standard parts guaranteed 12 months/12,000 miles or up to two years road use only.
MARQUEZ MOTORS. Mount Hill, Halstead, Essex CO9 1AA (0787) 477556
Range Rover automatic transmission specialists. Also repairs, servicing and tuning.

HERTFORDSHIRE

BASAND LTD. Terrace Gardens, St Albans Road, Watford, Herts WD1 1RB
(0923) 244044 FAX: (0923) 818020
Crownwheels & pinions, heavy duty sets 3.56 & 4.7 ratios to suit Land Rover and Range Rover.
IAN ASHCROFT. 24 Wells Close, Harpenden, Herts AL5 3LQ (0582) 761081
4x4 automatic conversions i.e. Customised transmissions with optional transfer ratios. Also improved half shafts and differentials.

KENT

RT QUAIFE ENGINEERING LTD. Botany Industrial Estate, Sovereign Way, Tonbridge,
Kent TN9 1RS (0732) 353747 FAX: (0732) 770137
Specialists in the design and manufacture of gearboxes & differentials.

LONDON

FWD GARAGE. Units 15-18 Lombard Business Park, 8 Lombard Road, London SW19 3TZ
081-545 7227 MOBILE: (0860) 817324 FAX: 081-544 1311
Automatic gearbox specialists i.e. Land Rover ZF, although all makes catered for.

NOTTINGHAMSHIRE

Z.F. GEARS LTD. Abbeyfield Road, Lenton, Notts NG7 2SZ (0602) 869211
Manufacturers of the Series DL limited-slip differential. Ideal for snow, icy inclines, slippery roads after heavy rain, towing etc.

SHROPSHIRE
L.E.G.S. LTD. Whittington Road, Gobowen, Oswestry, Shropshire
DAY: (0691) 653737 EVENING: (0691) 653524
Land Rover gearbox specialists. All units warranted, collection & delivery service, old units wanted for reconditioning.

SURREY
KAM DIFFERENTIALS LTD. Clock Barn House, Hambledon Road, Godalming, Surrey GU8 4AY
(0483) 417558 MOBILE: (0860) 508280 FAX: (0483) 417558
High ratio crown wheel & pinions for Land/Range Rovers. Cheaper than an overdrive, these diffs are ideal for Comp. Safari or vehicle conversion. Benefits include increased overall speed & strength, high bhp handling, lower fuel consumption. R/Rover ratio 2.83 & L/Rover ratio 3.8 & 4.1

YORKSHIRE, WEST
DAVE BEAUMONT. Lumb Cottage, Wainstalls, Halifax HX2 7UJ (0422) 244587
4x4 gearbox specialist. Land/Range Rover 5-speed & transfer boxes. Land Rover Series IIA and III.
Range Rover 4-speed.

SCOTLAND
TAYSIDE, CENTRAL & FIFE
ROVER TRANSMISSION SERVICES. Falkirk & District Business Park, Newhouse Road,
Grangemouth FK3 8LL (0324) 814453 FAX: (0324) 665908
4x4 Rover gearboxes - quality products offering excellent value
for money.

AUSTRALIA
JACK McNAMARA. 25 Levanswell Road, Moorabbin, Vic 3189, Australia
TEL: 61.3.555 2213 FAX: 61.3.555 0251
Front/rear heavy duty replacement differentials to fit Land Rover & Range Rover. Ratios 3.54, 3.73, 3.9, 4.1, 4.3, 4.7 supplied with Salisbury axles.

ENGLAND

BUCKINGHAMSHIRE
MARK SMITH & CO. Tower Farm, Boarstall, Nr Brill, Aylesbury, Bucks HP18 9UX
(0844) 238066 FAX: (0844) 238017
Range Rover hire from Buckinghamshire's Range Rover specialists.
RANGE FINDER. 27 Green Lane, Chesham Bois, Bucks HP6 5LQ
(0494) 725451 MOBILE: (0831) 294228 FAX: (0494) 432400
Exclusive 4x4 self-drive hire. Land Rover, Discovery, Range Rover and Japanese - countrywide.
RANGE LAND. Fagnall Farmhouse, Fagnall Lane, Winchmore Hill, Bucks (0494) 433028 (4 lines)
4x4 hire & sales. Best U.K. prices - Range Rover, Discovery, Defender 110/90. U.K. delivery.

CHESHIRE
COUNTY 4x4 HIRE. St Mary's Way, Stockport, Cheshire SK1 4AP
DAY: 061-474 1515 EVENING (MOBILE) : (0860) 736682 FAX: 061-476 0776
Defender 90/110 County models, Discovery Tdi's, Range Rover Vogue SE & LSE models available.
Servicing work also undertaken in our own workshops.

CLEVELAND
HALL & HALL VEHICLE HIRE. Graythorp Industrial Estate, Hartlepool TS25 2DF
(0429) 234141 AFTER HOURS: (0429) 860345/279511
Land Rovers for short or long term hire. Also Land Rover parts stockist, LR/commercial repairs, towing
and light haulage work.

DERBYSHIRE
THORNTON ARMSTRONG HIRE. 163 Ashbourne Road, Derby DE3 3AJ (0332) 550682
Off-road, 4 wheel drive vehicle hire specialists.

DEVON
FAR MOOR 4x4. Little Woodlands, Old Newton Road, Bovey Tracey, Devon TQ13 9TH
TEL/FAX: (0626) 833992 MOBILE: (0831) 415727
Hire a Land Rover, Discovery, diesel 7 Seater (other self drive 4x4's available). All 4x4's urgently
required for cash.
ENG >> LAND >> ROVER LTD. Unit 2, Barratt Industrial Estate, St. Oswalds Road, Gloucester GL1
DAY: (0452) 303190 EVENING: (0531) 820631
Short term Land Rover hire. Travel in safety and comfort with our new vehicles. Ideal for towing, 12-
seaters, fully insured.

ESSEX
FRANKLIN SELF DRIVE. Unit 1, Rawreth Industrial Estate, Rawreth Lane, Rayleigh,
Essex SS6 9RL (0268) 784544
Land Rovers available (contract hire only).

HAMPSHIRE
INTERCITY CAR RENTALS LTD. The Pump House, 32 Oakley Lane, Oakley, Basingstoke,
Hants RG23 7JY (0256) 782105
Self-Drive car rental - "From a Fiesta to a Range Rover Vogue".
TRACTION ACTION. Hadley Dene, Reading Road, Rotherwick, Hants RG27 9BD (0256) 764240
Full range of Range Rovers/Land Rovers/Discoveries - petrol and diesel. Self Drive hire in vehicles under
1 year-old, very competitive rates.

HUMBERSIDE
K.W. SADLER. The Tower, 65-71 Kent Street, Grimsby, Humberside
(0472) 345706(4 lines) FAX: (0472) 241238
Land Rover self drive hire. Long or short term rental. Continental hire our speciality.
READY RENT-A-CAR. Abbey Road, Grimsby, Humberside
(0472) 355801/346702/340366 AFTER HOURS: (0472) 812447
Big on choice - low on price. Land Rovers/Discovery. Automatics available, unlimited mileage, free
insurance, daily/weekly/contract hire
T.J.S. SELF DRIVE. 7 Hebden Road, Scunthorpe, Humberside (0724) 863684
Full range of Land Rover hardtops & 4x4 pick-ups available for hire from any of our four depots:
Scunthorpe, Lincoln, Bolton, Rugby.

KENT

LANCASTER SEVENOAKS LIMITED. 92 London Road, Sevenoaks, Kent TN13 1BA
(0732) 456300 FAX: (0732) 740470
Specialist vehicles including four wheel drive, Jaguar saloon and Jaguar coupé.

LEICESTERSHIRE

PROFESSIONAL 4x4 HIRE. Eye Kettleby Hall, Melton Mowbray, Leics LE14 2TS
(0664) 480195 MOBILE: (0860) 653748 FAX: (0664) 69029
Exclusive vehicle hire. Self-Drive or Chauffeur Driven Range Rovers, Discoverys, Land Rovers. Please
contact Robert Barber for information.
RICHARD'S SELF DRIVE. Plot B, Prince William Road, Loughborough, Leics LE11 0GU
(0509) 218138
Land Rover Discovery for hire. Also car, vans, minibuses, 7 seat Renault Espace, 8 seat Toyota Previa,
4x4 and 7½ trucks. Also vehicles for sale.

LONDON

DELTA CAR RENTAL. Poplar Place, Bayswater, London W2 071-586 5001 FAX: 071-722 8572
Range Rover hire. Delivery & collection service. Open 7 days per week. Monday-Saturday 8am-6.30pm
Sunday 10am-2pm.
EXPRESS RENT-A-CAR. 104b Finchley Road, Swiss Cottage, London NW3
071-722 3763 FAX: 071-722 8572
Range Rover hire. Unlimited mileage on rental of 3 days or more. Delivery & collection service. Open 7
days a week. Mon-Sat 8am-6.30pm Sun 10am-2pm.
LANDROVER SUPPORT. 50 Iverson Road, West Hampstead, London NW6 2HE
071-624 3246 Contact: Nick Hayden
Land Rover 10 seat Stationwagon available for hire with friendly helpful driver. Ideal vehicle to assist
climbers/cyclists/ramblers/paragliding/watersports/expeditions. Available by the hour, day or week.

MIDDLESEX
WHEELS CAR RENTAL LTD. Garrick House, 161 High Street, Hampton Hill, MiddxTW12 1NL
081-941 5331/9363 MOBILE: (0831) 653887 FAX: 081-941 8804
Range Rover specialist hire outlet, convenient to London Heathrow and all major road networks in the
south of England.

SHROPSHIRE
BURNT TREE VEHICLE HIRE. March Way, Battlefield Enterprise Park, Harlescott Lane,
Harlescott, Shrewsbury, Shropshire (0743) 236929
Four Wheel Drive self-drive hire including Range Rovers.

WEST MIDLANDS
4x4 MOTORS. Saxon Park Industrial Estate, Hanbury Road, Bromsgrove B60 4AD (0527) 576777
Land Rover & Range Rover self drive hire. Other 4x4's also available.
READ PERFORMANCE CARS. Unit 5/6, Selly Oak Industrial Estate, Dawlish Road,
Birmingham B29 7AR 021-414 1747
Executive car hire specialists from a Ford to a Ferrari - from a Range Rover to a Rolls Royce. "Try one
before you buy one".

WILTSHIRE
WESSEX 4x4 HIRE. 9 Meadow Lane, Westbury, Wilts BA13 3AD (0373) 822986
Land Rover County Station Wagons - Self Drive or Chauffeur Driven. Also service, repair and towing.
HARFORDS 4x4. St Edith, Stanton St Quinton, Chippenham, Wilts SN14 6AB
(0666) 837522 MOBILE: (0860) 451725 FAX: (0666) 837300
Wide range of 4x4's. Range Rover, Discovery, Land Rover, Isuzu, Daihatsu etc. Long or short term
hire. Insurance available. UK delivery.

SCOTLAND

GRAMPIAN, HIGHLAND AND ISLANDS
4x4 HIRE. Highland Rail House, Station Square, Academy Street, InvernessIV1 1LE (0463) 710048
Specialists in 4 wheel drive. Latest long & short wheelbase 3-12 seaters, Land Rovers/Discovery/Nissan.
Delivery/collect service throughout Scotland.
TREK-OVER LAND ROVER HIRE. 127 Culduthel Road, Inverness, Scotland (0463) 235054
Modern fleet of diesel 90 & 110 models. Also Shogun 7-seaters.

LOTHIAN AND BORDERS
PENNYWISE SELF-DRIVE. 27 Poplar Road, Glenrothes, Edinburgh, Lothian (0592) 610222
Self drive Land Rovers for hire.

TAYSIDE, CENTRAL AND FIFE
COUNTRY CAR HIRE. 66-68 High Street, Auchterarder PH3 1BN
DAY: (0764) 64052 EVENING: (0764) 62896 FAX: (0764) 64362
Specialists in four wheel drive, Land Rover/Range Rover/Discovery and all terrain vehicles. 7 day service.
Delivery/collection throughout Scotland.

IMPORT/EXPORT

ENGLAND

HAMPSHIRE

KEITH GOTT LANDROVERS. Greenwood Farm, Old Odiham Road, Alton, Hants GU34 4BW (0420) 544330 MOBILE: (0860) 737925 FAX: (0420) 544331
Land Rover & Range Rover exports to over 45 countries. F.C.O., British Council and O.D.A. being customers for over 15 years.

KENT

HOLMES-BLACKBURN IMPORT/EXPORT. Unit 1, Thayers Farm Road, Beckenham, Kent BR3 4RH 081-650 0678 FAX: 081-663 3551
Importers of Ford, Chevy, Dodge, Jeep, trucks, vans, ATV's and custom built race trailers.

LANCASHIRE

BLACKBURN ROOF RACKS & TRADE WELDING SERVICES. Unit 4, Walker Street, Lower Audley, Blackburn, Lancs BB1 1BG TEL/FAX: (0254) 263558/54776
Manufacturers of heavy duty galvanised commercial roof racks for most 4WD and commercial vehicles/ nudge bars/rear side steps etc. European agents required.

LONDON

TRANSAUTEX. 65 Grosvenor Street, London W1X 9DB
071-495 2848 FAX: 071-408 4401 TELEX: 267782 Trans G
Exports of 4x4 vehicles, spare parts and workshop equipment. Sea and airfreight service worldwide.

MERSEYSIDE

CARBURETTERS UNLIMITED. 204 Muirhead Avenue, Liverpool L13 0BA
051-256 0366 FAX: 051-270 2044
Import and export of Nikki Carburetters - adapted by us to suit almost every 4, 5 & 6 cylinder car in the world.

WARWICKSHIRE

PWB REPLACEMENT MOTOR PARTS LTD. 11 - 13 Warwick Industrial Estate, Budbrooke Road, Warwick CV34 5XH (0926) 494782 FAX: (0926) 410185
Manufacturers and suppliers of Land Rover/Range Rover parts and trim. Prompt and efficient international delivery.

INDEPENDENT 4WD SPECIALISTS

CROSS REFERENCE: See also ENGINE CONVERSIONS PARTS & SPARES

ENGLAND

AVON

BRISTOL LAND ROVER CENTRE. Old Gaol Workshops, Cumberland Road, Bristol BS1 6XW (0272) 294896 FAX: (0272) 294495
Land Rover/Range Rover/Discovery sales & service, engines/gearboxes, full rebuilds, parts/accessories - see our advert in MACK'S '94 Parts category.
NAILSEA LAND ROVER CENTRE. Unit 17, Southfield Trading Estate, Nailsea, Bristol BS19 1JE (0272) 85655/852142
Full repairs and service facilities, spares and accessories for LandRovers, Range Rovers & Discoverys. Vehicles bought and sold.
STEVE GAY LANDROVERS. Dramway Cottage, Nibley, Bristol, Avon (0454) 322729
Discovery, Land Rover and Range Rover - Service & repairs.

BERKSHIRE

FOX AUTO ENGINEERS. Fox Farm Workshop, Baydon Road, Lambourn Woodlands, Berks RG16 7TR (0488) 73392 or (0793) 814960
Rover and off-road vehicle specialists. Servicing/repairs/welding/gearboxrebuilds/V8 & diesel turbos/tuning/used sales/engine conversions/MOT prep.
NEWBURY 4WD CENTRE. 1 Bone Lane, Newbury, Berks RG14 5SH (0635) 38511/32028
Land Rover & Range Rover specialists. Full repair service. Free local collection and delivery service.
NICK KERNER ENGINEERING. Bracknell, Berks (0344) 487869 MOBILE: (0831) 453578
Servicing, repairs, welding etc. Sales of standard/refurbished ex-MOD and civilian vehicles from Land Rovers to Bedford MK 4x4's. Exports welcome.
OAKES BROS. Station Works, Station Road, Hungerford RG17 0DY (0488) 684431
West Berkshire's leading Land/Range Rover service centre. Only genuine L/Rover parts, sales, fixed servicing charges, full workshop facilities.

BUCKINGHAMSHIRE

TRING 4 WHEEL DRIVE. A.J. Flanders Services, Woodview Farm, Hog Lane, Ashley Green, Bucks HP5 (0442) 872523
Land Rover, Range Rover, Discovery servicing specialist. Full workshop facilities. Mon-Fri 8.30am-5.50pm Sat 9.00am-12.30pm Bucks/Herts border.
LEE PERRY MOTOR ENGINEERS. Horsley Green, Stokenchurch, Bucks HP14 (0494) 883451
Full workshop facilities at competitive prices. MOT preparation inc. full gas analysing/welding/Land Rover engine conversions. New & used LR parts.
MARK SMITH & CO. Tower Farm, Boarstall, Nr Brill, Aylesbury, Bucks HP18 9UX (0844) 238066
Range Rover specialists. We offer full workshop facilities, parts and accessories, Range Rovers for sale, servicing and engine conversions.

CAMBRIDGESHIRE

A.P. DENNIS. Long View, Millfield, Cottenham, Cambridgeshire CB4 4RE (0954) 51973 MOBILE: (0831) 128567 FAX: (0954) 52348
Andrew Dennis Land & Range Rover specialists. Spares, repairs and servicing. Engine and gearbox conversions.
WICKEN 4 WHEEL DRIVE (FIELD SERVICES CO.) 7 Lower Road, Wicken, Ely, Cambs CB7 5YB (0353) 722434
Specialists in servicing, repairs, conversions to Land Rover/Range Rover/Discovery and all 4 wheel drive. New and secondhand parts & accessories.

CHESHIRE

BROOKSIDE MOTORS. Grange Road, Brook Lane, Chester, Cheshire CH2 2AN (0244) 390119
Land Rover & Range Rover specialists. Mechanical/body repairs, insurance work, crypton tuning, MOT preparation, car valeting - Mon to Midday Sat.
FROGGATT'S RANGE ROVER SALES. Unit 2 Whirley Quarry, Sandy Lane, Whirley, Macclesfield SK10 4RJ (0625) 425524 MOBILE: (0860) 479462 FAX (0625) 619494
Sales, service, repair and diesel conversions. Please telephone (0625) 425524 for all your Range Rover requirements.
LAND ROVER CONVERSIONS 4x4 LTD. King Street, Buglawton, Congleton, Cheshire CW12 2DP (0260) 273672
Land Rover sales, service, spares, repairs, MOT preparation, recovery, trailer hire - all at competitive prices. Land Rovers bought for cash.

☰ MARK SMITH ☰

Range Rover Specialists

BUCKS / OXFORDSHIRE

Established 10 years

We offer:
FULL WORKSHOP FACILITIES
NEW AND USED SPARES
AND ACCESSORIES
VEHICLE SERVICE
DIESEL ENGINE CONVERSIONS
VEHICLES FOR SALE
Ring:
Mark Smith Range Rovers

0844
238066

Tower Farm,
Boarstall,
Nr. Brill, Aylesbury,
Buckinghamshire

Please mention MACK'S when you phone or fax.

LEES AUTOS. 1 Davies Avenue, Heald Green, Cheshire SK8 3PF
061-437 8258 MOBILE: (0860) 516828
Land Rover specialists - mobile repairs, servicing, welding, electrical fault finding, pre MOT's, diesel conversions. Over 19 years experience.

CO. DURHAM
DICK GRAHAM LAND ROVERS. Sinkers Row Garage, Wingate Industrial Estate, Wingate, Co Durham TS28 5AJ (0429) 837222 FAX: (0429) 83266
Land Rover servicing, welding, respraying, new/used parts. Sales: Ex-army, civilian 12 & 7-seaters etc. Always 40 diesel/petrol vehicles in stock.

CORNWALL
CORNISH LAND ROVER SERVICES. The Old Brewery, Treluswell, Four Cross, Penryn, Cornwall TR10 9AN (0326) 372511
Full workshop facilities. Used Land Rover & Range Rover sales. Large comprehensive stock of spares and accessories.
G & J LANDROVERS. Chy-An-Bre, Pit Lane, Higher Fraddon, St Coloumb, Cornwall TR9 6LG (0726) 860388
Gerald Pascoe - Land Rover and Range Rover specialists.
HICKS & SON LTD. Lemon Quay, Truro, Cornwall TR1 2JG (0872) 74321
Service, repairs, modifications, collection and delivery service available. M.O.D. contractor. Low West Country rates - 22 years experience.
LAND ROVER DISCOUNT CENTRE. Unit 7, Victoria Mill, Threemilestone, Truro, Cornwall TR3 6BX (0872) 79772
Service, repair, MOT, bodywork. Sales of used, re-built/reconditionedLand Rovers & Range Rovers.
LAND ROVER CENTRE. Rosevear Road Industrial Estate, Bugle, St Austell, Cornwall PL26 8HP (0726) 851958
Sales, service, parts, repair and hire.

CUMBRIA
NEATKENT LTD. Mintsfeet Industrial Estate, Mintsfeet Road South, Kendal LA9 6ND (0539) 732637
Land Rover/Range Rover spares, servicing, repairs, insurance estimates,MOT preparation. All parts at competitive prices. Scrap vehicles required.
PENNINE 4x4. Penrith Industrial Estate, Penrith, Cumbria CA11 9EH (0768) 890309/65628/899102
Land Rover, Range Rover & all 4x4 spares. Service, repairs, vehicle sales. All 4x4's wanted - good, bad & ugly. New spares & reconditioned units.

DERBYSHIRE
D L S. Water Lane, Wirksworth, Matlock, Derbys DE4 4AA (0629) 822185 FAX: (0629) 825683
Land Rover/Range Rover accident repairs/recovery service/MOT station and servicing to makers spec. Specialists in parts mail order including export.
LANDROVER AGRICULTURAL. Nunsfield Farm, Fairfield, Buxton, Derbys SK17 7HN (0298) 77827/72132
Land Rover services, spares & repairs.
WORTHINGTON 4x4. Church Fields, Edlaston, Ashbourne, Derbys DE6 2DQ (0335) 300720
Land Rover/Discovery/Range Rover servicing, M.O.T., chassis repair, diesel conversions, mechanical and electrical repair, modifications, rebuilds.

DEVON
HAYDEN MOTORS. Unit 3B, Mullacott Cross Industrial Estate, Nr Ilfracombe, North Devon EX34 8PL (0271) 864101
Exmoor's Land Rover/Range Rover centre. Repairs, renovations, servicing and an extensive range of parts at competitive prices.
U.L.R. 17 Chantry Court, Plympton, Plymouth, Devon PL7 3YB (0752) 343443
Land Rover/Range Rover parts & vehicle specialists.

DORSET
BAILIE CROSS GARAGE. Poole Road, Sturminster Marshall, Bournemouth, Dorset BH21 4AE (0258) 857309
Range Rover, Land Rover & all 4WD. Servicing, crypton tuning, breakdown service, welding, steam cleaning, MOT, tyres, batteries and exhausts.
SEMLEY LAN-TRAC SERVICES. Newbridge House, Station Road, Semley, Nr Shaftesbury, Dorset SP7 9AH (0747) 52527/51588
4 wheel drive dealers. Specialists in Land Rover, Range Rover & 4x4. Parts/accessories distributors, repairs, servicing and vehicle sales.

ESSEX

CANDOL. Bansons Yard, High Street, Ongar, Essex CM5 9AA (0277) 364205 FAX: (0277) 364055
Land Rover/Range Rover/Discovery sales, servicing, parts (mail order orcollect). Also general purpose, trailers and horse trailers.

CLARKE'S 4x4. Park Farm, Blackheath, Colchester, Essex CO2 0DB
(0206) 44954 FAX: (0206) 549544
Range Rover & Discovery specialist * Parts - new/used/recon * Service *Sales * Insurance/bodywork * Conversions * Salvage parts bought & sold.

C.Y. REPAIR SERVICES. 6 Curzon Drive, Manor Way Industrial Estate, Grays, Essex RM17 6BG
(0375) 371655
Land Rover spares and repair. MOT testing, chassis welding and trailer repairs.

D. GARRARD LAND ROVERS. Unit 3, Alresford Business Centre, Colchester Main Road, Arlesford, Essex CO7 (0206) 823499
All models of Land Rover/Range Rover rebuilt, refinished, serviced, bought and sold. Genuine/pattern parts, used engines/gearboxes/body panels.

FERRARI TRANSMISSIONS. r/o 714 Cranbrook Road, Barkingside, Ilford, Essex IG6 1HU
081-551 3015 MOBILE: (0836) 645229
Range Rover specialist est.15 years; servicing, repairs, auto transmissions on late models, fuel injections, air conditioning, recovery service.

FOLEY SPECIALIST VEHICLES LTD. Cut Maple Garage, Hedingham Road, Gosfield, Halstead, Essex CO9 1UP (0787) 60496 MOBILE: (0836) 625443 FAX:(0787) 60099
Vehicle sales new/used R/LHD, export, vehicle converters & body builders engine, steering & chassis conversions. Ex-military, reconditioners.

GRAWALL AUTO'S. Patch Park Farm, Ongar Road, Abridge, Essex RM4 1AA
(0708) 688391 MOBILE: (0860) 843400 FAX: (0708) 688391
Mechanical & body repairs/services, plus conversions to allLand Rovers, Range Rovers and Discoverys.

LAND ROVER SERVICE CENTRE. Grafton Farm, Curtis Mill Green, Stapleford Abbotts, Nr Romford, Essex RM4 1RT (0708) 688502 FAX: (0708) 688678
Near Chigwell in Essex, we specialise solely in service & repairs to all Land Rover models. Fixed price servicing at very competitive rates.

Q B MOTOR SERVICES. Unit 13, Aviation Way, Southend, Essex SS2 6UN (0702) 549188
Land Rover/Range Rover/Discovery full servicing and repairs. Also Sun diagnostic engine tuning and MOT repairs. We are interested in your vehicle!

R.J. HARVEY. Unit 5, Quest End, Rawreth Lane, Rayleigh, Essex SS6 9PZ (0268) 784928
Land Rovers/Range Rovers/all 4x4's. Welding specialist. Chassis rebuilds, winch fitting, parts, servicing, petrol/diesel repairs to MOT standard.

THURROCK LAND ROVER CENTRE. Oliver Road, West Thurrock, Essex RM16 1ED
(0708) 866327
Everything for the Land Rover enthusiast. Used vehicle sales, new & used parts, servicing.

GLOUCESTERSHIRE

COTSWOLD LAND ROVERS. Pike Lane, Frampton Mansell, Stroud, Glos GL6 8JA
(0285) 760463 PARTS DEPT: (0285) 760660
Land Rover/Range Rover specialists. Repairs, servicing, MOT, sales, spares, accessories (new & secondhand), hire, trailer servicing and repair.

GEOFF BILLETT FOUR WHEEL DRIVE CENTRE. Broadfield Farm, Moreton Valance, Glos GL2 7NH (0452) 722544
Servicing & repairs, new & secondhand parts, gearbox reconditioning, performance tuning, full facilities and free friendly advice.

TIM FRY LANDROVERS. 24-28 Sherborne Street, Cheltenham, Glos GL52 2JU
PARTS/ACCESSORIES: (0242) 516028 SALES/SERVICE: (0242) 23543
Vehicle sales/servicing, all models. New and secondhand spares for all models. Mail order/credit card sales/export sales welcomed.

HAMPSHIRE

FAREHAM 4x4 CENTRE. 99b Mays Lane, Stubbington, Hampshire PO14 2ED (0329) 661800
Land Rover/Range Rover specialists. Full workshop facilities including chassis welding, engine conversions, MOT preparation. Mail order parts.

KEITH GOTT LANDROVERS. Greenwood Farm, Old Odiham Road, Alton, Hants GU34 4BW
(0420) 544330 MOBILE: (0860) 737925 FAX: (0420) 544331
Specialists in ex-MOD and civilian Land Rovers, cheapies to full reconditioned. Full workshop facilities. 25 years experience.

LEWIS LANDROVER SPECIALISTS. Wychwood, Portsmouth Road, Fishers Pond, Eastleigh, Hants SO5 7HF (0703) 600190 MOBILE: (0836) 240878
Land Rover/Range Rover servicing and repairs. New & used secondhand spares. Vehicles bought and sold, all at competitive rates.

R.A LLOYD ENGINEERS. Balstone Farm, Ibworth, Basingstoke, Hants RG26 5TJ
(0256) 85077 MOBILE: (0836) 522162
L/Rover, R/Rover & Toyota Hi-Lux specialists. Service, repairs, new & used spares, competitive rates, free del/collection. Friendly personal service.
RAPID ROVERS. Dean Farm, Kingsley, Bordon, Hampshire GU35 9NG (0420) 475303
Full workshop facilities for all models, diagnostic equipment for fuel injection, major components re-built, specialist preparation for both on & off-road, general servicing, repairs and refurbishment.
VSM ENGINEERING. Budds Lane, Romsey, Hants SO51 0HA (0794) 511727
4x4 servicing/repairs. Land Rover & Range Rover specialists. Competitive rates, 20 years experience. Also horse trailers repaired and serviced.

HEREFORDSHIRE
CLYRO SPARES. Ashbrook Garage, Clyro, Hereford HR3 5SD (0497) 821046 FAX: (0497) 821182
Land Rover/Range Rover/Pampas sales & service. New and secondhand spares, accessories, MOT testing. Always breaking Land Rover, Range Rover, Pampas.
P.M. WHISTANCE. The Workshop, The Garage, Much Birch, Hereford HR4 0DG (0981) 540850
Service & mechanics, body repairs, MOT testing station. Land Rover & Range Rover specialists. 24 hour breakdown service.

HERTFORDSHIRE
HARRIS MAYES. Watford Field Road, Watford, Hertford WD1 (0923) 224026
Range Rover & Land Rover. Personal service by factory trained experts. Maintenance, repairs, parts, accessories. Nissan Turbo D conversions.
J.M.T. COMMERCIALS. The Sawmills, Fullers End, Elsenham, Nr Bishops Stortford, Herts CM22 (0279) 647006
Land Rover/Range Rover/4x4 specialists. Sales/servicing/re-sprays/recon engines/restorations/welding/gearboxes. Phone us with your requirements.
KEVIN N. MARTIN MOTOR ENGINEER. 20 Bell lane, Widford, Nr Ware, Herts SG12 8SH
(0279) 843561 MOBILE: (0860) 860701
Land Rover specialist. All servicing work undertaken, repairs including bodywork, recovery service. Business users and fleet enquires welcome.
LUMSDON LAND ROVERS. Green End Farm, High Road, Shillington, Herts SG5 3LT
WORKSHOP: (0850) 785322 MOBILE: (0462) 711830 AFTER 6pm: (0525) 861965
Land Rover specialists - sales, new & secondhand spares, repairs.
THE OAK TREE GARAGE. Kimpton Road, Peters Green, Kimpton, Herts LU2 9PR
DAY: (0438) 832580 EVENING: (0582) 840260
We specialise in all aspects of Land & Range Rover. New spares all at discount prices, over 50,000 used spares, buying/selling, repair/service
SAFARI SERVICES. Holly Hedges Lane, Bovingdon, Hertfordshire HP3 0NW
(0442) 833413 FAX: (0442) 832946
Land Rover and Range Rover specialists. Spares, servicing, sales, safari preparation, Isuzu diesel engine conversions.

HUMBERSIDE
LAND ROVER SERVICES. 100/102 West Dock Avenue, Hull HU3 4JR (0482) 20900
Land Rover servicing, repair, sales, new & used spares stc. - basically anything Land Rover. Manual gearbox overhaul specialist, 20 yrs experience.

ISLE OF WIGHT
JOHN DIXON (I.W.) LTD. Forest Road, Newport, Isle of Wight PO30 5QJ (0983) 526517
Land Rover servicing and parts.

JERSEY
FOUR WHEEL DRIVE CENTRE. Fareways, Five Oaks, St Saviour, Jersey (0534) 66144
The Channel Island's 4x4 specialist.

KENT
ASHFORD LANDROVER CENTRE. Ashford Market, Ashford, Kent TN23 1PG
TEL/FAX: (0233) 613237
Land Rover/Range Rover/Discovery full servicing/repair facilities. Parts department for competitive prices on all parts/accessories. Secondhand parts available.
DAKAR CARS. Rowhill Cottages, Puddledock Lane, Wilmington, Kent DA2 7QF
(0322) 614044 FAX: (0322) 668500
Range Rover repairs/servicing. Large stock of new parts. Breaking 2 doorand early 4 door models. Mail order service. 10 mins from Dartford Tunnel.

RAY ROSS AUTOS. The Workshop, Ivy Works, Jail Lane, Biggin Hill, Kent TA16 3AU
(0959) 571931
Land Rover/Range Rover specialists. Mechanical, bodywork, overhauls, chassis welding, high-tech diagnostics and V8 tuning. 30 yrs experience.
FOUR x FOURNEAU. Unit 6, Westwood Cottage, Rockhill, Chelsfield, Kent (0959) 533130
Restoration specialists. Welding, autoelectrics, chassis & bodywork, prototypes/specials to your specification. No job too big or too small.
FOUR BY FOUR SPECIALISTS. Knight Road, Stood, Rochester, Kent ME2 2AH
(0634) 713164/713313 MOBILE: (0850) 335387
Range Rover and Land Rover s/hand parts, repairs, rebuilds & servicing. Mobile service available for speedy and cost conscious repairs.

GOOODMAN 4x4 MOBILE VEHICLE SERVICES.
(0689) 859186 day & evening

*   **Land Rover/Range Rover mobile servicing**
*   **Tuning**
*   **M.O.T. preparation**
*   **Welding to M.O.T. satndard**
*   **Non-starters**
*   **Virtually all other makes of vehicle serviced**
*   **All work carried out at your home**
*   **No VAT! Very competitive rates**

ALL SURROUNDING AREAS OF BROMLEY, KENT

HIGHWAY MOTORS. Sandwich Road, Hacklinge, Deal, Kent CT14 0AS (0304) 615318
Land Rover, Range Rover and Discovery sales/service/accessories inc. all mechanical & body repairs/insurance work/MOT testing/vehicles purchase.
KENT ROVER SERVICE. Unit 5, New Road Business Estate, New Road, Ditton, Maidstone ME20 6AF (0732) 840617
Central Kent's major independent Land Rover & Range Rover specialist repair service. Servicing/bodywork/alloy welding/rebuilds/specials built
SITE SERVICES. r/o 3-5 West Street, Sittingbourne, Kent ME10 1QB
DAY: (0795) 426360 MOBILE: (0836) 542070 EVENING: (0795) 471526
Land Rover/Range Rover specialists. Repairs, servicing, MOT, breakdown service, spare parts stockist, new and secondhand conversions undertaken.

LANCASHIRE
AJAX MOTORS. Willow Lane, Lancaster LA1 5NA (0524) 381313
Land Rover specialist. Crypton tuning, servicing, repairs, welding. Parts inc exhausts/clutches/brakes. Free delivery/collection. Competitive rates.
C & A LANDROVERS. Skipton Road, Colne, Lancs BB8 (0282) 868874/861503
The North West's largest independent stockists of Land & Range Roverparts/servicing/accessories/accident repairs/Rover V8 building & tuning.
I & A BARTRAM. Oxford Street Mill, Victoria Street, Clayton-le-Moors, Lancs BB5 5PD
DAY: (0254) 386935 or EVE: (0254) 883603
Full workshop facilities from a service to a full rebuild. Engines and gearboxes reconditioned. Used spares, new parts, tyres and accessories.
'K' MOTORS. 164 Chapel Lane, Longton, Preston, Lancs PR4 5FB (0772) 613329
Land Rover/Range Rover sales, repairs, spares & accessories. Specialists in Land Rovers prepared to your specification.
HARRISON MOTORS. 39-41 Bispham Road, Layton, Blackpool, Lancs FY3 7HQ
(0253) 396654 MOBILE: (0850) 941312
Land Rover/Range Rover/Discovery. Service, breakdown, spares and breaking.
NORTH WEST FOUR WHEEL DRIVE. 71 Gorsey Lane, Southport, Lancs PR9 8ED
(0704) 29014/64916 FAX: (0704) 232911
A complete service for the 4x4 owner. Mechanical/electrical/chassis repairs/MOT's/servicing/rebuilds/vehicle sales/full range of accessories

LEICESTERSHIRE
SHERWOODS. Lion Garage, Main Road, Nether Broughton, Leics LE14 3HB (0664) 823151
Land Rover spares, sales & servicing.
SWINFIELD COOPER. 50 Commercial Square, Freemans Common, Leics LE2 (0533) 545657
Specialist welding, gearbox rebuilds, chassis repairs/rebuilds, bodywork conversions, MOT Testing, discount parts/accessories, winch stockists.

LINCOLNSHIRE

4 WHEEL DRIVE TRUCK CENTRE. Country Workshops, Risegate, Nr. Spalding, Lincs PE11 4EZ
TEL/FAX: (0775) 750223
Specialist engineers. Land Rover new and used parts service 1948 to date. Retail/trade exports.
UK 24 hour delivery. Access & Visa.
FAMOUS FOUR PRODUCTS. Fairfield Industrial Estate, Tattershall Way, Louth, Lincs LN11 0YA
(0507) 609444 FAX: (0507) 609555 Open 9-6 weekdays 9-12 Sat.
All specialist and service work undertaken in a fully equipped workshop. Sales of new/secondhand Land
Rover/Range Rover parts + all 4WD accessories.
LOVELL LANDROVERS. Westminster Industrial Estate, Station Road, North Hykeham,
Lincoln LN6 3QY TEL/FAX: (0522) 500361
Spares, repairs, accessories, conversions, bodywork, breakdown service. Visa welcome.
PARKSIDE. 101 London Road, Kirton, Boston, Lincs PE20 1JH (0205) 722110
Land Rover & Range Rover sales, service, parts.

LONDON

BROWNES ENGINEERING. 9a Shandon Road, Clapham, London SW2 4XN 081-673 3699
Land Rover/Range Rover service, bodywork, rebuilds - full workshop facilities. New parts & accessories.
Breaking Land Rovers.
FWD GARAGE. Units 15-18 Lombard Business Park, 8 Lombard Road, London SW19 3TZ
081-545 7227 MOBILE: (0860) 817324 FAX: 081-544 1311
Repairs, servicing welding etc. to all Land Rover models. All other makes of 4x4 catered for. Automatic
gearbox specialists.
GOODMAN ENGINEERING. r/o 59 Jasmine Grove, Penge, London SE20 8JY 081-778 0948
Land Rover/Range Rover servicing, welding, bodywork including crash repair, steam cleaning, all
mechanical repairs. Small friendly family business.
GO-T-EL LANDROVERS. Office: 14 Cliffsend House, Normandy Rd, London SW9 6HE
071-820 0959 Workshop: 55 Woolwich Church St, Woolwich SE18 081-855 3201
Land Rover sales, service, repair, new parts, mountains of secondhand spares. Also a comprehensive
range of new tools. See our advertisement in the 'USED SPARES' category for details.
M.H. LEADER. 126-132 Leyton Road, Stratford, London E15 081-534 1060
Selection of Land Rovers for sale. New & used spares, repairs carried out. Also Land Rovers wanted.
REARRANGED ROVERS. Unit 14F, Stonehill Business Park, Angel Road, London N18 1RT
081-807 9806 (24 hour answerphone) MOBILE: (0831) 474654
Sales & service of all Land Rovers, Range Rovers and Discovery. Used spares for all models. Series I
specialist repair and restoration.
ROVERCARE. 34 Aylmer Parade, Aylmer Road (A1), London N2 0PE 081-340 0733
4x4 service centre established 1976. Range Rover, Land Rover and Discovery repairs, servicing,
bodywork & parts.

MANCHESTER, GREATER

FIELD MOTOR SERVICES LTD. Pilot Mill, Chapel Street, Whitworth, Rochdale OL12 8PP
(0706) 49947
Repairs, spares & service including chassis repairs, exchange gearboxes etc. Land Rover, Range Rover
and all 4x4 vehicles.
MANCHESTER LAND ROVER & GYPSY BREAKERS. Hopes Carr Garage,
36 Upper Brook Street, Stockport SK1 3BP 061-480 3165
Full range of garage services for Land Rover & Range Rover.
SERVICETUNE. 8 Parkside Avenue, Worsley, Manchester M28 5FT
061-799 8543 MOBILE: (0850) 799889
Land Rover servicing, repair and tuning specialist. New parts and accessories including aluminium wing-
tops. Large stock of used spares.
WATSON & TURNER. Hayfield Road, Chapel en le Frith, Stockport SK12 6JF
(0298) 816177 FAX: (0298) 816206
L/Rover, R/Rover, Discovery specialists and all 4x4 servicing/engineering. Diesel conversions/M.O.T.'s/
chassis renewals/gear & transfer box rebuilds.

MERSEYSIDE

WIRRAL RANGE ROVER. 1D Carterton Road, Carr Lane, Hoylake, Wirral, Merseyside L47
051-632 6665
Land Rover & Range Rover specialists.

MIDDLESEX
GREEN LANE MOTOR ENGINEERING. Wayemeadows, Chertsey Road, Shepperton,
Middx TW17 9NF (0932) 564869
LR/RR servicing/repairs/used sales/chassis welding/MOT prep. Breakdown,towing, collection and
delivery service. Ring for courteous, personal attention.

NORFOLK
D & C ROBERTS ENGINEERS. Bradfield Road, Swafield, North Walsham, Norfolk NR28 0QX
(0692) 403109
Land Rover/Range Rover/Discovery specialists. Servicing/repairs, MOT prep.roll bars & cages, unit
rebuilds, new & s/h spares, vehicles bought & sold.
DEREHAM 4x4 VEHICLE CENTRE. The Old Coach House, Yaxham Industrial Estate, Station Road,
Yaxham, Dereham NR19 (0362) 693336
Specialists for Land Rover and Range Rover. Repairs, servicing, spares, competitive rates, M.O.T.
preparation.
IVES MAINTENANCE & RECOVERY. Unit A, Station Yard, Cawston, Norfolk NR10 4BB
(0603) 870921/666704
Land Rover mechanical overhauls. Repairs to MOT standard. Crash repairs. Breaking for spares.
24 hour recovery service.
JSF LANDROVERS. 1 Spar Road, Vulcan Road Industrial Estate, Norwich, Norfolk NR6 6BY
(0603) 787064 FAX: (0603) 482845
Land Rover/Range Rover/Discovery parts, accessories, servicing to all models. Over 7,000 stock lines for
Land Rover & Range Rover parts.
KINGS LYNN FOUR WHEEL DRIVE. Saddlebow Industrial Estate, Saddlebow Road,
Kings Lynn PE30 5BN (0553) 775416
Land Rover and Range Rover specialists.
NORFOLK LAND ROVER CENTRE. Rushall, Diss, Norfolk IP21 4DD (0379) 741607
Land Rover specialists serving S Norfolk. Land Rover/Range Rover breakdown service, repairs/servicing,
engine conversions, new spares and accessories.
OVERLAND VEHICLE SERVICES. The Glebe Workshop, Brandon Road, Methwold, Thetford,
Norfolk IP26 4RH (0366) 728119 MOBILE: (0860) 877265
Land Rover/Range Rover repairs & servicing. 24 hour breakdown recovery.

NORTHAMPTONSHIRE
GLENFIELD 4x4. Unit 16, Francis Court, Wellingborough Road, Rushden, Northants NN10 9AY
(0933) 413846 FAX: (0933) 316382
Land Rover/Range Rover/Discovery service, bodywork, full workshop facilities.
NENE VALLEY OFF ROAD. Old Brickyard, Mill Road, Wellingborough, Northants NN8 1QP
(0933) 276579 MOBILE: (0860) 860490
Land Rover, Range Rover and all types of 4x4 serviced & repaired. Spares, parts and accessories for
most vehicles.
STALLION MOTORS LTD. Unit 4, Midas Workshops, St Lukes Road, St James Industrial Estate,
Corby, Northants NN18 8AJ (0536) 403671
General repairs and servicing of all types of 4x4 vehicles.
THREE COUNTIES LANDROVERS. Boddington Road, Byfield, Northants NN11 6XU
(0327) 61752
The Land & Range Rover specialists. Vehicles for sale/wanted and fully reconditioned. Chassis welding/
servicing/diesel engine conversions/parts

NORTHUMBERLAND
M.M.S. LAND ROVERS. 60/62 Maddison Street, Blyth, Northd NE24 1EY
(0670) 366679 MOBILE: (0860) 486724
Repair and service specialist for Land Rover, Range Rover, Discovery and Defender. Also chassis
welding and MOT work. See our advert for more info.
MOBILE MAINTENANCE SERVICES. 60 Maddison Street, Blyth, Northd NE24 1EY
(0670) 366679 MOBILE: (0860) 486724
Land Rover & Range Rover specialists. Full workshop facilities. Service, repairs and tuning.
R.S. JOHNSON (MORPETH) LTD. Coopies Lane Industrial Estate, Morpeth, Northd NE61
(0670) 519905/519970 MOBILE: (0860) 428884
4WD specialists. New/used parts & accessories. Engine tuning/conversions full workshop facilities/
repair/servicing/rebuilds/24 hr breakdown service.

NOTTINGHAMSHIRE
LAND ROVER SPECIALISTS. Cottage Farm, Chapel Lane, Epperstone, Notts NG14 6AQ
(0602) 663266 FAX: (0602) 664482
Land Rover, Range Rover, Discovery sales/spares/repairs/insurance repairs bodywork/exports/M.O.T.'s/
hire/parts/accessories/renovations, Isuzu conversions.

NEWARK LAND ROVER REPAIRS. Unit 1, Northern Road, Newark, Notts NG24 2EH
(0636) 708793 FAX: (0636) 701308
For a specialised service to none - speak to the experts. New & used spares, all kinds of repairs, MIG welding, MOT preparation.

OXFORDSHIRE

CROSS COUNTRY VEHICLES LTD. Hailey, Witney, Oxon OX8 5UF
(0993) 776622 FAX: (0993) 773218
Land Rover parts, sales and service.
E.H. DOUGLAS. 'Gilpins', Edgecote Lane, Wardington, Nr Banbury, Oxon OX17 1SH
PARTS: (029575) 8380 SERVICE: (029586) 673
Extensive range of new Land Rover parts. Gearbox specialist. Hydraulic hoses. Full workshop facilities, Land Rover servicing.
HYRANGE. 94 Bell Street, Henley-on-Thames, Oxon RG9 2BN (0491) 410877
Range/Land Rover servicing, repairs, modifications, spares and accessories. Chassis welding, engine tuning, brakes, clutches etc.
SHIRE FOUR BY FOUR LTD. Unit 9, Station Yard Ind. Est., Adderbury, Oxon OX17 3HJ
(0295) 812080 MOBILE: (0860) 841988 FAX: (0295) 812132
L/Rover, Discovery, R/Rover servicing & repairs. Large stocks of new parts, genuine & replacement. Diesel engine conversions.
SYLVAN GARAGE. South Green, Kirtlington, Oxford OX5 3HJ (0869) 50385 FAX: (0869) 50921
Servicing, parts and accessories - our workshops can carry out any Range & Land Rover work incl. diesel conversions/gearbox changes/bodywork etc.

SOMERSET

ANDREW CAMERON. Pikes Garage, St Georges Street, Dunster, Somerset (0643) 821777
Land Rover specialists - service - spares.
COUNTRY MOTORS. Shaftesbury Road, Henstridge, Somerset BA8 (0963) 63110
Can we quote for your Land Rover and Range Rover overhaul? Competitive prices. All work fully guaranteed.
COUNTRY ROVERS (CHARD). Unit 6, Bartlett Park, Millfield Industrial Estate, Chard, Somerset (0460) 67584
Your local independent Land Rover/Range Rover suppliers. Original equipment at competitive prices. Spares, repairs, servicing and accessories.
GREENSHIELDS ENGINEERING. Park Farm, Wellington, Somerset TA21 9NP
(0823) 663490 MOBILE: (0836) 563246
Range Rover & Land Rover specialists. Nissan/Perkins diesel conversions,new & s/hand spares, Rover 4x4 hire, vehicle sales, horse box repairs.
NICOLAS PAXTON. The Workshop, Cloford, Nr Frome, Somerset BA11 4PM
Please Ring Before 10am: (0373 836) 661 (24 hr) FAX: (0373 836) 663
Land Rover/Range Rover parts, expedition/export preparation, ex Ministry L/Rovers available, Perkins/ Mazda diesel engine conversions, 10 yrs exp.

STAFFORDSHIRE

BURTON AUTO SERVICE. Lancaster Park, Newborough Road, Needwood, Burton-on-Trent, Staffs DE13 9PP (0283) 75600
Land Rover specialists. Spares, service & vehicles for sale including thoroughly rebuilt Land Rovers from £3,600 to various specifications.
K & S LANDROVER SERVICES. 69 Lightwood Road, Longton, Stoke on Trent, Staffs ST3 4HU (0782) 342379
All forms of Land Rover work undertaken: body/mechanical/rebuilds/diesel conversions/rollbars/ competition vehicles. Also new & secondhand parts.
VALLEY MOTORS. Stoney Rock Farm, Waterhouses, Stoke-on-Trent, Staffs ST10 3LH (0538) 308352
Land Rover, Range Rover and Discovery spares, repairs & sales.

SUFFOLK

C.A.R.S. SALES & HIRE LTD. The Friston Business Centre, Aldeburgh Road, Friston, Suffolk IP17 1NP (0728) 688770/688307 FAX:(0728) 688326
Land Rover and Range Rover specialists. Vehicle sales, hire, service, repairs, modifications, rebuilds, new and secondhand parts/accessories.
DERWOODS 4x4. Rustic Cottage, Half Moon Lane, Grundisburgh, Woodbridge, Suffolk IP13 6UE
(0473) 735388 MOBILE: (0860) 540659 FAX: (0473) 735410
Land Rover, Range Rover & Discovery sales, servicing, refurbishing. New and s/hand spares. Exchange gearboxes for all models, engines, bodies etc.

MARK PEACOCK LANDROVERS. Southview, Laxfield Road, Stradbroke, Eye, Suffolk IP21 5JT
(0379) 384280 24 hours
All types of Land/Range Rover repair. Constantly breaking vehicles, vast stock of new/used spares.
Customers encourged to remove parts themselves
PARK GARAGE SERVICES. Unit 1, Wetherden Business Park, Stowmarket, Suffolk
(0359) 42479 MOBILE: (0850) 742372/3
Land Rover/Range Rover/Discovery specialists. Servicing & repairs for all makes of car and commercial
vehicles. 24 hour recovery service.
SAS LANDROVERS. Unit 1, Wetherden Business Park, Wetherden IP14 3JU (0359) 42479 (24 hours)
Full workshop facilities, engine conversions, servicing & welding, new and used parts (LR/RR's wanted
for breaking). Phone for friendly advice.
TREVOR MURRAY. Church Road, Kessingland, Suffolk NR33
(0502) 741635 MOBILE: (0836) 371765
Over 10 years experience as Land Rover & Range Rover specialists. Sales, service, repairs, diesel engine
conversions, new/used spares in stock.

SURREY

ALVIN SMITH RANGE ROVERS. Wallis Wood, Dorking, Surrey RH5 5RD (0306) 627396
Sales * service * modifications * coachwork * race preparation.
For excellent servicing, diagnosis, suspension mods and major overhauls.
THE COUNTRY CAR. Unit 4, Charlwood Place, Norwood Hill Road, Charlwood, Surrey RH6 0EB
(0293) 863444 FAX: (0293) 862863
Land Rover trained factory personnel using manufacturer's procedures. Service, repairs, welding,
fabrication, engines - performance/unleaded/economy.
DORKING VEHICLE SERVICES. 82 Oakdean Road, Dorking, Surrey (0737) 843586
Land Rover sales, repairs, overhaul, recovery, servicing.
L.J. HALL MOTORS. Grove Mill Industrial Estate, 475 London Road, Mitcham, Surrey CR4 4YP
081-648 0621
Land Rover servicing and repairs. New & used spares. Pre-M.O.T. and chassis repairs. No job too
small ...
SURREY OFF-ROAD SPECIALISTS LTD. Alford Road, Dunsfold, Surrey GU8 4NP
(0483) 200046 FAX: (0483) 200047
E.F.I./diesel/4 speed ZF auto box/Weber V8 conversions to all L/Rover models. ARB airlockers/nudge
and winch Bars, tyres, wheels, full workshop.
WOKING LANDROVER SERVICES. 17 North Street, Woking, Surrey GU21 5DT (0483) 768965
Servicing, repairs, MOT preparation, welding, fabrication, custom roll cages & bull bars, used spares,
vehicles prepared to customer's spec.

SUSSEX, EAST

GUMTREE ENTERPRISES. Fallbrook, Plumpton, Lewes, East Sussex BN7 3AH
(0273) 890259 FAX: (0273) 891010
L/Rover, R/Rover & Discovery service, repairs, renovation, welding, spares, diesel conversions, breaking
all models. Mail order & export welcome.
"THE LAND ROVER MAN". The Thatched Garage, Park Corner, East Hoathly, E Sussex BN8 6RD
(0825) 841148 MOBILE: (0860) 204850
Sales, service, spares, repairs - for Land Rovers ancient and modern.
ROBERTS RANGE ROVERS. Ninfield Garage, Bexhill Road, Ninfield, Battle, East Sussex TN33 9EE
(0424) 893280 FAX: (0424) 892178
Range Rover specialist - parts, servicing, repairs, breaking all vehicles, diesel conversions, vehicle sales,
export welcome.
SUSSEX 4 WHEEL DRIVE. Unit 11, Millbrook Business Park, Jarvis Brook, Crowborough,
E Sussex TN6 (0892) 663320
Specialists in Land Rover/Range Rover servicing, spares and repairs. Sun computer engine tuning. All
makes of 4x4 serviced and repaired.

SUSSEX, WEST

PAUL RUTTER. Haybourne Engineering Works, Blackgate Lane, Pulborough, W Sussex RH20 1DE
(0403) 700941 MOBILE: (0831) 460475
Low cost Land & Range Rover servicing/repairs/bodywork/accessories/new & used parts. Secondhand
vehicle sales - AVG, choice of 30. Power Plus agents.

TYNE & WEAR

NORTH EASTERN MOTORS LTD. Leamington, Newcastle NE15 8SJ 091-267 6271
Land Rover Defender, Discovery, Range Rover - new & used vehicles sales, parts, accessories and
service. Fast friendly staff.

WARWICKSHIRE

LAND ROVER CENTRAL. 283 Watling Street, Nuneaton, Warwicks CV11 6BQ (0203) 347023
Parts, accessories, vehicle sales, servicing.

LEAMINGTON LAND ROVER SERVICES. 32 Rugby Road, Cubbington, Leamington Spa,
Warwicks CV32 6DG (0926) 335630 or (0926) 428606
Large selection of L/Rover and R/Rover new & used parts, service, sales (usually a minimum of 15
vehicles). Run by enthusiasts for enthusiasts.

WARWICK 4x4 LTD. Budbrook Industrial Estate, Warwick CV34 5XH
(0926) 410090 SPARES HOTLINE: (0926) 411246 FAX: (0926) 411250
A friendly, professional service specialising in Land Rover/Range Rover.Sales, refurbishment/resprays/
custom builds, servicing, new/used spares.

WEST MIDLANDS

ANDY'S LANDY'S. Unit 4, Stoney Court, Binley Industrial Estate, Hotchkiss Way, Coventry CV3 2SF
(0203) 444041/450719 MOBILE: (0831) 33671
Specialists in Land Rover, Range Rover, 4x4 and private vehicle repairs.

EARLSWOOD GARAGE. 133 The Common, Earlswood, Solihull B94 5SH (056 46) 2254
Land Rover & Range Rover specialists. Repair, servicing, MOT work, accident repair, bodywork,
insurance repairs.

WALSALL LAND ROVER CENTRE. Superservice Motoring Centre, 60-66 Sandwell Street,
Walsall, West Midlands WS1 3EB (0922) 614057
Servicing, repairs, parts, M.O.T's, welding. Land Rover and Range Rover specialists.

WILTSHIRE

CHURCH FARM MOTORS. Church Farm, 6 Bath Road, Shaw, Melksham, Wiltshire (0225) 704269
Land Rover & Range Rover specialists. Service, parts, diesel/V6/V8 conv. Vehicles fully rebuilt + new/
used vehicles prepared and exported.

LUDGERSHALL VEHICLE SERVICES LTD. 39- 41 Andover Road, Ludgershall, Nr Andover,
Wilts SP11 9LY (0264) 791555
Land Rover and all 4x4 servicing & repair. 'One off' engine conversions a speciality i.e. V12 or diesel
conversions such as BMW.

W.J. JOYCE (ENGINEERS) LTD. Polebarn Road Garage, Polebarn Road, Trowbridge, Wilts BA14
DAY: (0225) 752358/754460 EVENING: (0225) 755258
Land Rover & Range Rover specialists. Repairs, M.O.T. testing, new and secondhand spares supplied.

WORCESTERSHIRE

APB TRADING LTD. 38 Hartlebury Trading Estate, Kidderminster, Worcs DY10 4JB (0299) 250174
FAX: (0299) 251752
Land Rover/Range Rover spares, repairs and accessories. Full workshop facilities. Insurance work
undertaken.

EVESHAM FOUR WHEEL DRIVE CENTRE. r/o 119 High Street, Evesham, Worcs WR11 4EQ
(0386) 45500
For all your sales, servicing & repairs. Contact us to keep your offroad vehicle on the road (Land Rover/
Range Rover/Discovery specialists)

TOWER 4x4. Unit 17, Weston Industrial Estate, Honeybourne, Weston-sub-Edge, Evesham,
Worcs WR11 5QB (0386) 841395
Land Rover sales & service.

YORKSHIRE, NORTH

BISHOPDALE MOTORS. Edgley Garth, West Burton, Leyburn, N Yorks DL8 4UW (0969) 663650
Land Rover sales, service, spares. Specialists in pre-1984 refurbishment/re-chassis. New/second hand
spares. Est 1981, helpful advice given freely.

C MACDONALD-SMITH LAND ROVER SPECIALIST. Laburnum Cottage, Fadmoor,
York YO6 6HY (0751) 31202
New & used vehicles supplied, serviced and repaired. Also new and used spares available.

M.C. MOTORS. Sheepcote Lane, Darley, Harrogate, N Yorks HG3
(0423) 780189 EVENING: (0943) 461610
4x4 specialists - Land Rover, Range Rover etc.

NORTH RIDING AUTOMOTIVE. Lake Farm, Eavestone, Ripon HG4 (0765) 620684
Land Rover & Range Rover sales, service and spares.

YORKSHIRE, SOUTH

MIDDLEWOOD LANDROVERS. Middlewood Quarry, off Mowson Lane, Sheffield S30 3AJ
(0742) 864438
Servicing, repairs, welding, chassis replacement - petrol & diesel.

YORKSHIRE, WEST

JAKE WRIGHT (4x4). Hilltop, Burley-in-Wharfedale, Ilkley, W Yorks LS29 7JW
(0943) 863530 FAX: (0943) 864840
Land Rover/Range Rover rebuilds, service, repair, diesel conversions. Rover V8 to Land Rover. Used vehicle sales. Parts, tyres & accessories
LANDROVER REPLACEMENTS. Clarks Mill, Storrs Hill Road, Ossett, Nr Wakefield, West Yorkshire (0924) 274587
Everything for your Land Rover/Range Rover/Discovery from Series Ionwards. Service/repair (24hr breakdown), new/used spares, vehicle sales
RECYCLED LAND ROVERS. Unit 7, Healey New Mills, Healey Road, Ossett, West Yorkshire (0924) 401010
All repair work undertaken, chassis welding, vehicle rebuilds, pre-MOT work, servicing, all at competitive rates + sales, new & used spares.
ROVER PLUS. Beecroft Street, Leeds LS5 3BD
(0532) 304023 MOBILE: (0831) 372023 FAX: (0532) 745437
Range Rover/Land Rover/Discovery specialists. Servicing, repairs, parts, accessories, tuning & modifications. Full workshop facilities/parts dept.

SCOTLAND

STRATHCLYDE

CROSS COUNTRY VEHICLES. 133 Main Street, Newmains, Wishaw, Strathclyde ML2 9BG
(0698) 381645/382414
Four wheel drive specialists. L/Rover parts, sales, servicing, diesel conversions, refurb. Spares: breaking Land Rover/Toyota/Suzuki/Daihatsu
GLASGOW 4x4 CENTRE. 52 Springboig Road, Glasgow G32 041-774 5011 FAX: 041-774 5656
Land/Range Rover specialists. Vehicle sales, new/replacement parts & accessories, used spares, new & s/hand diesel conversions + mail order.
MONARCH GARAGE. 49 Colvend Street, Glasgow G40 4DU 041-554 3844 FAX: 041-554 2833
Land & Range Rover specialist. Accident/insurance work, mechanical and body repairs. MOT preparation, fast efficient service. 24 hr recovery.

GRAMPIAN, HIGHLAND AND ISLANDS

KIRKSTYLE GARAGE. Victoria Terrace, Kemnay, Inverurie, Aberdeenshire (0467) 42248
Used Land Rover sales, specialist in refurbished vehicles, full servicing and repairs.
NEWTON HILL GARAGE. By Stone Haven, Aberdeen AB3 2NN (0569) 30204
Land Rover/Range Rover service & sales. For private and commercial use.

TAYSIDE, CENTRAL AND FIFE

DREADNOUGHT GARAGE. G Luti & Sons, Leny Road, Callander, Perthshire FK17 8EL
DAY: (0877) 31099 EVENING: (0877) 30655
Land Rover, Discovery & Range Rover service. Warwick Banks agent in Scotland for suspension & engine modifications. Supercharger specialists
LIX TOLL GARAGE. Lix Toll, Killin, Perthshire FK21 8RB (0567) 820280
Land Rover sales specialists in refurbishment including engine replacement& conversion/chassis/paintwork/bodywork. Also mail order parts/accessories.

WALES

CLWYD

D.K. MOTOR SERVICES. Unit 9, Oak Road, Isycoed, Wrexham Industrial Estate, Wrexham, Clwyd (0978) 660472 AFTER HOURS: (0978) 356157 or 757560
Specialising in Land Rover spares, repairs and sales. Also car collection and delivery service.
D LAWRENCE LANDROVERS. Padeswood Service Station, Padeswood, Mold, Clwyd (0244) 550312
Land Rover sales - repairs - service.
M & M LAND ROVER SERVICES LTD. The Filline Station, Bychau, Denbigh, Clwyd LL16 5LS
(074570) 237 FAX: (074570) 237
The most comprehensive range of services for Land Rover owners in North Wales. Militay & civilian used sales/repairs/servicing/new & used spares
MICHAEL FLETCHER LTD. 50 Welsh Road, Queensferry, Deeside, Clwyd CH5 2HT (0244) 830168
Land Rover specialists - sales & service. Land Rover and Range Rover hire.

DYFED

PAUL JENKINS MOTORS. New Unit 5, Thornton Business Park, Milford Haven, Dyfed SA73 (0646) 697724
Land/Range Rover service & repairs. MOT preparation including welding.Engine & gearbox repair/rebuilds. Diesel specialist.

GLAMORGAN, SOUTH

VALE 4x4 CENTRE. Vale Forge, North Road, Cowbridge, South Glam LF7 7DF
DAY: (0446) 773768 EVENING: (0446) 772772
Land Rover/Range Rover sales & service. Large parts dept./full workshop facilities/welding/resprays/insurance work. Long & short term LR hire.

GLAMORGAN, WEST

A.J. MOTOR SERVICES & 4x4 SPECIALISTS. Neath Road, Tonna Neath, West Glam SA11 3BZ
(0639) 639917/750516 MOBILE: (0831) 294848 FAX: (0639) 638209
4x4 sales & hire, recovery, full workshop facilities, welding specialists, accessories, personal imports & exports.
H.G. REES & SONS (VALE OF NEATH LAND ROVER CENTRE). Riverside Engineering Works, Abergawed, Resolven, Nr Neath, West Glamorgan SA11 4AA
DAY: (0639) 711553 EVENING: (0639) 710965
Land Rover/Range Rover sales, servicing, repairs, spraying and welding. Long term contract hire, MOT bay, new & used spares, plenty of breakers.

GWENT

4x4 UNLIMITED. Pill Farm, Severn Bridge Industrial Estate, Caldicot, Gwent NP6 4JH (0291) 421262
Land Rover/Range Rover/Discovery specialists. Servicing & repairs to 4x4's, cars, light commercials and plant. V6 and V8 conversions.

CANADA

PAUL SAFARI COMPONENTS. Box 39, 61 Queenston Street, Queenston, Ontario, Canada LOS ILO TEL: 416.262.448/6 FAX: 416.262.5967
New & used Land Rover spares, accessories, vehicles. Galvanised chassis and good used Land Rovers - all models - plus pre-1967 for USA market.

FRANCE

JEAN-LUC GUYOT 4x4. 46 Boulevard de l'Egalitß, 62100 Calais, France
TEL: 21.97.00.47 Contact: Jean-Luc Guyot
Specialist in every class of all terrain vehicle, especially Land Rover and Range Rover. Repairs, sales, accessories, spares and tourism.
LAND SERVICE IN FRANCE. BP9 95710, Ambleville, France
TEL: (1) 34.67.76.85 FAX: (1) 34.67.71.85
The French Mail Order specialists. New/used parts/accessories for Land Rover and Range Rover at competitive prices. We also have details of specialist workshops throughout France + ex-French colony specialists.

GERMANY

DM LAND ROVER SERVICE. Am Triften 7, 2806 Oyten 1, Germany
TEL: (04207) 5700 Contact: C Wiegenhagen
4WD Gmbh. Marwinkel 3, D-3401 Waake, Germany
TEL: 49 05507 847 FAX: 49 5507 1565 Contact: Emanuel Ebner
H. SQUERESSIG. Hans-Sachs-Strasse 14, 4010 Hilden, Germany TEL: (02103) 47701
JEVER-WILLI. Poppenbuettelerstrasse 31, 2000 Norderstedt, Germany
TEL: 040-529 1070 Contact: Willi Ditters
LAND ROVER CENTRE RHEIN-MAIN. Ludwigstrasse 5, 6200 Wiesbaden, Germany
TEL: (0611) 372269 FAX: (0611) 304136 Contact: Guenter Schiebofski
RINKERT LAND & RANGE ROVER. Glasbronnenstrasse 26, 7131 Neubaerental, Germany
TEL: (07044) 43156 FAX: (07044) 43150
ROVER ALLRAD SERVICE. Moellner Landstrasse 76, 2000 Oststeinbeck, Germany
TEL: 040-712 8459 FAX: 040-712 8448 Contact: Paul Nitschke

REPUBLIC OF IRELAND

J & C MOTORS. Rere 264, Rathdown Road, Dublin NCR 7, Eire TEL: 38 85 33
4x4 specialists. Bosch engine tuning, all servicing & auto electrics.

SOUTH AFRICA

STEINFELD GARAGE. Steinfeld 117, P.O. Box 35, Keetmanshoop, Namibia 9000
South Africa TEL: 0638 ask for 11831 FAX: 0631 2725 c/o Johann Strauss
Land Rover, Range Rover, Discovery - full workshop facilities, new spares, breaking Land Rovers,
breakdown service. 3,000 Km touring 4x4 routes.

UNITED STATES OF AMERICA

WEST COAST BRITISH. 6398 Dougherty Road, 34 Dublin, CA 94568 USA
TEL: (415) 829 6091 FAX: (415) 829 0494 Contact: Michael Green
Range Rover/Land Rover specialists. Service, parts and accessories. Factory trained staff. Bearmach
agent/DLR.

INSURANCE

CROSS REFERENCE: See also TRAVEL (Sub Heading 'Insurance')

ENGLAND

BERKSHIRE

ALAC INSURANCE SERVICES. 2 Bulldog House, Reading Road, Wokingham, Berks RG11 5AB
(0734) 793953/4/5 FAX: (0734) 772702
4 wheel drive specialists. Any area, any vehicle, any driver. Scheme discounts incl. legal protection/
claims & accident emergency recovery.

DEVON

GRAHAM SYKES INSURANCE. 16 Rolle Street, Exmouth, Devon EX8 1NJ (0395) 266621
Special 4x4 scheme rates. Up to 60% introductory bonus, immediate cover, limited mileage, modified
cars, young drivers, convicted drivers.

DORSET

QUAY 4x4 INSURANCE. 446 Ashley Road, Parkstone, Poole, Dorset BH14 0AD
(0202) 732976 (3 lines)
We specialise in standard 4x4 insurance (i.e. not specials). Scheme rates FREE road rescue, FREE legal
protection, FREE 24 hour car hire.

HAMPSHIRE

DEBRACEY INSURANCE SERVICES. 29 Silverdale Road, Tadley, Hants RG26 6JL (0734) 813395
Horses, dogs, cats. We are specialists in this type of animal insurance re. transportation etc. Please phone
for cover details/free quotation.

STAFFORDSHIRE

MARLOW INSURANCE BROKERS. Suite 3, Georgian Mews, 24a Bird Street, Lichfield,
Staffs WS13 6PR (0543) 414224
4x4 specialist insurance. We track down the best deal for you!
SNOWBALL INSURANCE BROKERS LTD. 58/60 Wetmore Road, Burton-on-Trent,
Staffs DE14 1SN (0283) 31391
True specialists in 4 wheel drive insurance i.e. Items such as bull bars/additional lighting/roof-racks/
winches etc. are regarded as standard accessories. Insurance also arranged for off-road business use such
as farming, competition, trailers/horseboxes & low milage classics.

BELGIUM

I.S.I. NV INTERNATIONAL SERVICES & INSURANCES. Heuvelstraat 9, 3850 Nieuwerkerken,
Belgium TEL: 00 32 11 671 671 FAX: 00 32 11 673 906
Rally insurance including desert Rally Raids. First risk cover, engine, gearbox, mechanical parts, labour
all included.

ENGLAND

BEDFORDSHIRE
G W BARTLETT CO. Unit 8, Union Park, Triumph Way, Woburn Road Industrial Estate, Kempston, Bedford MK42 7QB (0234) 843331 FAX: (0234) 843340
Colour-coordinated leather seating for Discovery models.

ESSEX
PREMIER AUTOMOTIF. 67 Beedell-on-Sea, Essex SS0 9JR (0702) 335343
Tailored car mats for off-road vehicles. Luxury front and rear carpet, embroidered heal pad logo.
4 colours, 2 year guarantee.
R.D.S. PROJECTS LTD. 5 Suffolk Drive, Chelmsford, Essex CM2 6UN
(0245) 450730 FAX: (0245) 450735
Range Rover retrim specialists - leather seats, door inserts, gearstick gaiter, steering wheel, headrests, passenger grab handle + wood veneer.

HERTFORDSHIRE
HRS TRIMMING. Units 13-14 Nazeing Glassworks, Nazeing New Road, Broxbourne, Herts EN10 6SU (0992) 451622
All interior trim including Range Rover leather * Full sunroof supply, fitting & repair * Seat covers by post * Recaro seats * Trade welcome.
SUNSEEKERS UNIVERSAL LIMITED. The Rick, Southend, Much Hadham, Herts SG10 6EP
(0279) 843345 FAX: (0279) 842171
Range Rover/Land Rover/Discovery trim including headlining, carpets, cloth & hide seats, wood trim and sound-proofing.

KENT
CASS BROTHERS. 153 Hastings Road, Bromley, Kent BR2 8NQ 081-462 2387
Specialists in retrimming/repairing all upholstery old or modern. We can also supply hoods, materials etc. for DIY.

LANCASHIRE
COVERDALE CARPETS. The Saw Mills, Frith Street, Wigan, Lancs WN5 0XQ
(0942) 44001 FAX: (0942) 820458
Manufacturers of luxury quality car carpet and tailor made sets for 100's of classic cars, all with handbound edges. Most colours available.

LONDON
CHAMBERLAINS SEAT COVERS. 2 Tremaine Road, London SE20 7T2 081-778 7997
More practical than a re-trim - machine washable seat covers tailor-made in original Land Rover material.
80 designs for Land Rover / Range Rover / Discovery, samples sent.

MANCHESTER, GREATER
SHERLOCK FOAMS LTD. Unit 1, Sheffield Street, Heaton Norris, Stockport SK4 1RU 061-429 9769
Anti-condensation kit for Land Rover, any model. Replacement headlining for Range Rover, grey or original. Under bonnet sound proofing kit, LR/RR.

MERSEYSIDE
AUTO INTERIORS & HOODS. 56 Norfolk Street, Liverpool L1 0BE
051-708 8881 FAX: 051-708 6002
Interior soundproofing and fitted carpets for Discovery, Range Rover, Land Rover and all 4x4 vehicles.
Full fitting service if required.
PRESTIGE AUTO TRIM PRODUCTS LTD. 3 Prenton Way, North Cheshire Trading Est.
Birkenhead, Merseyside L43 3DU 051-608 8683 FAX: 051-608 0439
Range Rover 14-piece superior quality carpets. Tailored to fit precisely based on manuf. original patterns
- Velour: £90.47 - Deep Pile: £122.77

NORFOLK
AIS AUTO INTERIOR SPECIALISTS. Unit 5, 36 Lothian Street, Norwich, Norfolk NR2 4PH
(0603) 632641
Conversions, original and custom seat covers, carpets, headlinings, door panels, hoods, vinyl tops and sunroofs. Call us for a quote.

Range Rover • Discovery • Defender

TAILOR MADE SEAT COVERS

In Original Land Rover Material

PROTECT YOUR NEW SEATS
OR REVIVE YOUR OLD ONES

- Manufactured in authentic Car Upholstery Fabric
- Easy to Fit
- Machine Washable
- Robust Quality
- Flame Retardent
- Ultra violet Ray Resistant

These uniquely designed seat covers slide easily over the existing seats and attach underneath.

As they are made from high grade car upholstery material, and are machine washable, they enable you to maintain the immaculate interior of your car.

They will equally transform your old seats with the minimum of effort.

LESS EXPENSIVE AND MORE CONVENIENT
THAN THE ALTERNATIVES

Wendy Chamberlain
2 Tremaine Road
London SE20 7TZ

081-778 7997

Est. 1975

NORTHAMPTONSHIRE
MOTOR UPHOLSTERY SUPPLIES. 14 Anne Road, Wellingborough, Northants NN8 2HH (0933) 223602 or (0933) 227166
Rot proof carpets for Land Rover & Range Rover. All parts included, not just floor. 100% polypropylene with pad for drivers heel. 9 colours.

OXFORDSHIRE
KIM JOHNSON. Unit F, Swain Court, Avenue 2, Station Lane, Whitney, Oxford OX8 6YA (0993) 776800 MOBILE: (0860) 245386 FAX: (0993) 705352
Land Rover and Range Rover trim, specialising in hood making and seat covers, including one-off hoods and covers in vinyl and leather.

SURREY
TEK SEATING. 1 Manorgate Road, Kingston on Thames, Surrey KT2 7AP 081-546 2508
Main distributors for KAB seating, part of Bostrom Plc. Suppliers of static & suspension seats.

SUSSEX, EAST
AUTOMOTIVE INTERIORS. 16A Beamsley Road, Eastbourne, E Sussex BN22 7EH (0323) 416606/765953
Full carpet sets (100% wool/wool rayon), standard/de luxe door panels, standard/de luxe seat covers and conversions, dashboard speaker mounts.
CORBEAU GT SEATS (PROTECH SEATING LTD.) Haywood Way, Ivyhouse Ind. Est. The Ridge, Hastings TN35 4NN (0424) 435480 FAX: (0424) 431480
High quality replacement car seats for road, race & rally. For free catalogue send S.A.E. to the above address.

WARWICKSHIRE
PWB REPLACEMENT MOTOR PARTS LTD. 11-13 Warwick Industrial Estate, Budbrooke Road, Warwick CV34 5XH (0926) 494782 FAX: (0926) 410185
Manufacturers and suppliers of Land Rover/Range Rover parts and trim.Prompt and efficient international delivery.
TRAKKERS LIMITED. Unit 3A, Budbrooke Industrial Estate, Warwick CV34 5XH (0926) 411922
L/Rover interiors. Designer seats Series II upwards, 109/110 second row seats. Hoods for every LR made. Luxury door trims, headlining, carpets.

WEST MIDLANDS
IMPACT SPORTS. Unit 9, Watery Lane Industrial Estate, Wednesfield, Wolverhampton WV13 3RU (0902) 637555 FAX: (0902) 609860
The famous original Tee Pee seat saver. Water/dirt/grease/oil proof nyloncover. All 4x4's catered for in various colours.
NATIONWIDE TRIM. Unit 6, Sloane Hse, Sloane St, Hockley, Birmingham B1 3BX
021-233 9410 FAX: 021-233 9429
Cloth/leather retrims, Range Rover and Discovery. Carpets, casings, fibreglass headlinings, accessories. Full fitting service. Free brochure on request. See our display advertisement FRONT INSIDE COVER.

WORCESTERSHIRE
BARRY HAYLINGS COACHTRIMMINGS. Sunnyside, Droitwich Road, Hartlebury, Kidderminster, Worcestershire DY10 4EH (0299) 251474
Range Rover/Suzuki Jeep seats trimmed, for exchange. Carpet sets, hoods, door casings and accessories. Price list and samples on request.

SCOTLAND
LOTHIAN
RAMSAY COACHTRIMMING. Unit 11, Pentland Industrial Estate, Loanhead, Midlothian EH20 9HL TEL/FAX: 031-440 0555
All interior work carried out to a high standard. Seat repairs welcome or retrims in leather. Private cars and vintage vehicles also catered for.

WALES
DYFED
LA SALLE. Golygfa, Pontrhydfewdigaid, Ystrad Meurig, Dyfed SY25 6BB (09745) 659
High quality moulded interior trim panels including headlinings anddoortrims for Land Rovers and Range Rovers.

TRAKKERS

Quality Comfort Style

ATTENTION ALL 12 SEATER OWNERS

(Reg. design)

Mums & Dads.
Have you ever travelled any distance in the incredibly uncomfortable second row seats (the Weenies)? They are (in our opinion) dangerous without headrests - give no lateral support - in other words are only suitable for very small children, if then.

ASK THE CHILDREN WHAT THEY THINK.
Now you have the opportunity to put it right. The HI-BACK WEENIES exclusive Trakkers design is comfortable, safer and affordable at the modest price of £75.00 each. Available in all Land Rover cloths and PVC, beautifully made by craftsmen who are proud of their products. GIVE THE CHILDREN A BREAK and ease your earache!

THINK OF THEIR SAFETY

SII & SIII & LIGHTWEIGHTS

Increase the comfort and pleasure of your Land Rover by fitting our High Quality Hi-BACK FRONT SEATS. Fit to standard fittings.

COUNTY CLOTH or PVC
£88.00 each.

DISCOVERY OWNERS discover TRAKKERS range of products for your vehicle.
THE DISCOBOX (Reg. design)

The one major omission most owners complain about is a central storage compartment and somewhere to rest ones's elbow. This beautifully made Discobox is a must for every owner. You will wonder how you managed without it.

IN MATCHING VELOUR & TWEED CLOTH.
£75.00 each.
Ask for details of our range of waterproof seat covers for all L.R. models.

0926 - 411922

Prices include VAT - CARRIAGE IS EXTRA - ASK FOR OUR CATALOGUE

ENGLAND

BUCKINGHAMSHIRE

OAKWOOD ENTERPRISES. 31 Worminghall Road, Oakley, Aylesbury, Bucks HP18 9QU
(0844) 237867 FAX: (0844) 238083
Save up to 20% on fuel costs and reduce exhaust pollutants by 50% Ecoflow is suitable for all petrol &
diesel engines - £44.65 inc. VAT

DEVON

FUELSAVER U.K. Clyst Road, Exeter, Devon EX3 0DB (0392) 874972 FAX: (0392) 873798
Save fuel, save money, save the environment. Petrol/diesel, easy to fit.As featured on TV. For full
details, please telephone the above number.

HAMPSHIRE

FUEL DYNAMICS LTD. 9 Woodlands Way, Northlands Rd, Southampton, Hants SO1 2TJ
(0703) 632716 MOBILE: (0850) 355638 FAX: (0703) 632716
Fuelsaver fuel conditioning system. Proven reductions in toxic emissions with a fuel saving and added
power.
OAKFORD RESOURCES LTD. Millbridge House, Middlebridge Street, Romsey, Hants SO51 8HJ
(0794) 511103 FAX: (0794) 511167
Fuelset fuel additive. Independently tested and found to improve fuel economy by over 10% , increased
power output, reduced exhaust emissions.
TRAFALGER AUTOMOTIVE LTD. Unit 4, Limberline Spur, Hilsea, Portsmouth, Hampshire
(0705) 651188 FAX: (0705) 651199
Distributors of Wynns and STP oils and engine treatments. Quantity discounts and export prices available
to the trade.

HERTFORDSHIRE

QUAYHEAD INDUSTRIES LTD. P.O. Box 285, Harpenden, Herts AL5 2HP
(0582) 461123 FAX: (0582) 461117
Distributors of Nulon PTFE-based friction reducer. Fully compatible with all normal engine oils inc.
synthetics. Suitable for petrol/diesel engines.

LEICESTERSHIRE

NEO SYNTHETIC OIL CO. U.K. Unit 4B, Soarbank Way, Bishop Meadow Road, Loughborough,
Leics LE11 0RE (0509) 234792
Neo synthetic oil gives increases of 10-20% mpg and 6% horsepower, reduced oil consumtion, reduced
engine wear.

LONDON

GASOX-FUEL CAT LTD. Merlin Hse, 122/126 Kilburn High Rd, London NW6 4HY
071-624 0613 MOBILE: (0831) 509291 FAX : 071-372 2775
Fuel Cat catalytic fuel treatment. Lower fuel costs (8-15%), better performance, quieter engines, cleaner
environment.
SPORTSCRAFT. 36 Shrewsbury Lane, Shooters Hill, Woolwich, London SE18 3JF
081-856 0692 FAX: 081-856 0657
Total seal gapless piston rings reduce piston 'blow by' thus increasing power/torque, oil remains cleaner/
lasts longer - and less fuel is used!

MERSEYSIDE

KRAUSE LABORATORIES. 53 Kentmere Drive, Pensby, Wirral L61 5XW MOBILE: (0860) 874460
Smoking exhaust? MOT emission failure? New Krause Moryb-based treatment for poor compression/
uneven idling/wasted fuel & oil.

MIDDLESEX

PERFORMANCE OILS LTD. 31 York Street, Twickenham, Middx TW1 3JZ
081-892 0061 MOBILE: (0860) 807847 FAX: 081-892 5500
Importer of Amsoil fully synthetic engine and gear oils, A.T.F., diesel and petrol fuel additives. By-pass
and replacement oil filters.

OXFORDSHIRE
REED AUTOMOTIVE LTD. 7B Avenue Two, Station Lane Industrial Estate, Witney,
Oxon OX8 6YD (0993) 778711 FAX: (0993) 778951
RESTORE engine additive fills internal metal scratches & grooves in high mileage motors restoring
compression, horsepower & life to tired engines

SUFFOLK
BORDER ASSOCIATES. 24 Roman Way, Haverhill, Suffolk CB9 0NG (0440) 714755
Fuel Cat catalytic fuel treatment. Suitable for all diesel, leaded& unleaded petrol engines. Improve
exhaust emissions, mpg & power.

SURREY
SHURFLO LTD. Euro Division, Liberty House, 105 Bell Street, Reigate, Surrey RH2 7JB
(0737) 242290 FAX: (0737) 242282
'Aquasolve' diesel fuel additive absorbs/bonds water enhancing fuel performance, improving combustion,
reducing exhaust emissions.

SUSSEX, WEST
D. LOCK & ASSOCIATES. Woodcote, Chalk Road, Ifold, Billingshurst, West Sussex RH14 0UE
(0403) 753396 FAX: (0403) 752879
Broquet Fuel Catalyst; low-cost conversion to unleaded, more mpg, better performance, cleaner engine,
full guarantee.

WEST MIDLANDS
FORTÉ LUBRICANTS LIMITED. 1 Portway Close, Torrington Avenue, Coventry CV4 9UY
(0203) 474069
Forté Oil Seal Conditioner additive assists in preventing engine oil leaks, especially older, high mileage
motors.

WORCESTERSHIRE
SPIRRIT ENVIRONMENTAL TECHNOLOGY LTD. Unit 6, Thornhill Road, North Moors Moat,
Redditch, Worcs B98 9ND (0527) 62808 MOBILE: (0831) 525085
The S.E.T. Advanced Fuel System for Diesel Engines. Substantial increase in power/exhaust emissions
reduced/fuel savings/smoother quieter engine.

SCOTLAND
LOTHIAN
HOME AND AWAY. Axwell House, Westerton Road, Broxbourn, West Lothian EA52 5AU
(0506) 858865
Distributors of the IMT magnetic induction device - up to 18% increase in bhp, 25% improvement in mpg.
Call for information.

MECHANICAL SERVICES

CROSS REFERENCE: See also COMMERCIAL/AGRICULTURAL EQUIPMENT

ENGLAND

AVON

THE AXLE CENTRE. 79 Fishponds Road, Eastville, Bristol BS5 6SF (0272) 513656
Your axle problems solved by the specialists. Reconditioning and parts sold separately. Export & mail order. Regional branches.

BUCKINGHAMSHIRE

BRYANT & RILEY. Holmer Green Vehicle Service Centre, Unit 20, Earl Howe Road, Holmer Green, Bucks HP15 6QT (0494) 715058/713907
Specialist supply/fitment of genuine Borg & Beck clutches for all models of Land Rover, Range Rover & Discovery + mechanical and bodywork repairs.

CHESHIRE

G.B. ENGINEERING. Westfield, Wybunbury Road, Walgherton, Nantwich, Cheshire CW5 7NG (0270) 841081
Most makes/models, remote gearchanges, driveshafts manufactured to anyCV joint/length. Engine-gearbox adapters to suit unusual combinations.

ESSEX

TRS. Transeurope Refrigeration Services, 50 Bentfield Road, Stansted, Essex CM24 8HP(0279) 812232
Vehicle air conditioning. All makes repaired & serviced.
MOBILE MECHANICAL REMEDIES. Boreham, Chelmsford Essex CM3 3JW (0245) 461037
General engineering, servicing, repairs, alterations, conversions.Evenings, nights and weekends. Reliable, friendly service.

GLOUCESTERSHIRE

AIRSTREAM LTD. Unit 13, Stonehouse Commercial Centre, Stonehouse, GlosGL10 3RH (045382) 8781
Auto air conditioning installation, service and spares.
MOBILE AIR PRODUCTS LTD. Unit 6, Springhill Estate, Avening Road, Nailsworth, Glos GL6 0BS (0453) 834894 FAX: (0453) 835442
Vehicle air conditioning, components & replacement parts.

HERTFORDSHIRE

M P P. 8A High Street, Old Town, Stevenage, Herts SG1 3EJ (0438) 740901 FAX: (0438) 740896
Blast cleaning service, chassis etc.

KENT

DARTFORD VEHICLE RADIATORS. Unit 5, Parker Knight Industrial Estate, Watling Street, Dartford, Kent DA2 6BP (0322) 291177
Radiator, fuel tank and spring specialists. Repairs, box radiators, re-cores fuel tanks repaired. Tow bars/alarms/sunroofs/upholstery.
ROVERCRAFT. Unit One Progress Estate, Parkwood, Maidstone, Kent ME15 9YH (0622) 687070 FAX: (0622) 692273
Machining services by mail order - cylinder head work a speciality, plusboring/balancing/grinding/tuftriding/welding etc.

LONDON

AXLE-WISE. 34D Fairview Road, Norbury, London SW16 5PT 081-679 7090
The axle, differential, propshaft & driveshaft shop. Reconditioned and repaired with guarantee. Free fitting.
McCARTNEYS. 168 Parkview Road, Tottenham, London N17 8DP 081-808 0582
Axles, gearboxes and steering boxes reconditioned & exchanged secondhand. Established over 45 years.

MANCHESTER, GREATER

MIKE AGER MOBILE. 39 Brinkshaw Avenue, Wythenshawe, Manchester M22 5FE
061-436 3149 MOBILE: (0860) 384951
Servicing, MOT preparation, repairs, welding, chassis repairs.24 hour breakdown recovery service.

Please mention MACK'S when you phone or fax.

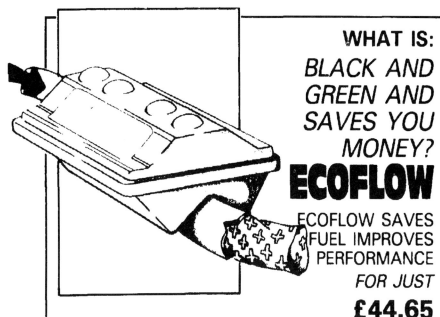

WHAT IS:

BLACK AND GREEN AND SAVES YOU MONEY?

ECOFLOW

ECOFLOW SAVES FUEL IMPROVES PERFORMANCE

FOR JUST

£44.65
inc VAT

The **Ecoflow** clamps onto the fuel line to give:

★ 5%-20% more miles to every gallon

★ Improved Power and Torque

★ Reduces Carbon Monoxide up to 60%

★ Reduces Hydro-Carbons by up to 25%

★ Prevents Carbon build-up in Cylinder Head

★ Fitted in second (D.I.Y.)

★ Maintenance free for life

★ Smoother engine and easier starting

★ Transfers to your new car

SUITABLE FOR DIESEL/PETROL

D.T.I. TESTED

60 day money back guarantee if, for any reason, you are not satisfied with your Ecofow.

Send cheques or postal orders payable to 'Oakwood Enterprises', 31 Worminghall Road, Oakley, Aylesbury, Bucks HP18 9QU.

Tel: (0844) 237867
7.30 am to 10 pm
Fax: (0844) 238083

MIDDLESEX

VEHICLE REFRIGERATION SERVICES. Unit 24, Ashford Industrial Estate, Shield Road, Ashford, Middx TW15 1AU (0784) 248905 FAX: (0784) 242540
Vehicle air conditioning service, repair, installations, parts.
PROPSHAFT SERVICE. Central Way, Feltham, Middx TW14 0RD 081-844 2265/7
Specialists in the maintenance, reconditioning, repair and balancing of all propshafts - young or old. Same day service.

NORTHHAMPTONSHIRE

SUTRAK UK. 24/25 Saddleback Road, Westgate Industrial Estate, Northampton NN5 5HL (0604) 581468 FAX: (0604) 758132
Call the experts for vehicle air conditioning. 4x4's, cars, trucks, agricultural machinery, coaches.

SHROPSHIRE

HEADMASTERS INTERNATIONAL LTD. Shrewsbury Road, Prees, Nr Whitchurch, Salop SY13 2DJ (0948) 841184 FAX: (0948) 841122
Land Rover reconditioned cylinder heads rebuilt to the highest spec. using manufacturer OE new parts. Nationwide del. Export/trade enquires welcome.

WEST MIDLANDS

CYLINDER HEADS (UK). Bobbington Airport, Nr Stourbridge, West Midlands (0384) 221550 FAX: (0384) 221549
Exchange new & reconditioned, petrol/diesel. All units pressure tested. Gaskets available.
24 hr nationwide delivery. Free advice & estimates.
MOTOR CLIMATE SERVICES. 66-68 Cherrywood Road, Bordesley Green, Birmingham B9 4UD 021-766 5006 FAX: 021-771 3004
4x4 air conditioning specialists. Contact us for all your air conditioning needs including Range Rover, Discovery and Defender.

SCOTLAND

LOTHIAN AND BORDERS

INCH DIESEL LTD. 9-11 Old Dalkeith Road, Edinburgh, Lothian EH16 4TE   031-664 5054
Specialists in removal, reconditioning & re-timing of diesel fuel injection systems. Diesel diagnostics for private & commercial vehicles.

ENGLAND

BEDFORDSHIRE
THATCHREED. Hayes West End, Bedford MK45 3QU (0234) 740327 FAX: (0234) 741708
Army surplus - trade only. 20,000 sq ft cash & carry warehouse. Surplus plus camping goods etc.
Phone for information and catalogue.

CHESHIRE
SOLDIER OF FORTUNE. Unit 3A, Brymau 3 Estate, River Lane, Saltney, Cheshire CH4 8RQ
(0244) 681090 FAX: (0244) 674651
American, German and British clothing & equipment from World War II to present day. Large selection
of books and T-shirts. Catalogue £1.
MILITARY & CIVILIAN. Unit C, Ringstones Ind. Est., Bridgemont, Whaley Bridge, Stockport,
Cheshire SK12 7PD TEL/FAX: (0663) 734042
Ex-MOD & civilian used vehicle sales: Land Rover/Range Rover/Abbot DDRG-Wagen/Ferret/Saracen/
trailers/plant etc + winches, parts & accessories

DEVON
MILITARY SCENE. 6 Hillcrest, Ottery St Mary, Devon EX11 1XY
(0404) 814164 FAX: (0404) 814164
Bob Morrison: Specialist defence and off-road vehicle author & photographer. 30,000 image library.
Assignments undertaken.

DORSET
G.I.'s. 305 Holdenhurst Road, Bournemouth, Dorset (0202) 393245 FAX: (0202) 398504
Trade only army surplus: Large selection of German, Dutch, French, U.S. and British army surplus.
Phone for information.

HAMPSHIRE
BROOKLYN ENGINEERING. Hursley Road, Chandlers Ford, Nr Southampton, Hants SO5 1JH
(0703) 252281 FAX: (0703) 269990
Ex Ministry of Defence Land Rover's, Bedford's, trailers. 88"/101"/109"/fire/ambulance, civilian County/
Range Rover/Discovery. Spares/servicing
KEITH GOTT LANDROVERS. Greenwood Farm, Old Odiham Road, Alton, Hants GU34 4BW
(0420) 544330 MOBILE: (0860) 737925 FAX: (0420) 544331
Specialists in all types of MOD Land Rovers - LT/WT, SWB, LWB, 90. 110, 101 and ambulances.
RHD & LHD. Soft top or hard top.
SAFARI ENGINEERING. West Winner, Eversley Centre, Eversley, Hants RG27 0LY
(0734) 732732 MOBILE: (0836) 384505
Ex-Ministry Land Rovers refurbished and ready for work, including LWB, Lightweights, Ambulances,
SWB & 24 volt. Spares/welding/servicing/repair

HUMBERSIDE
P.A. BLANCHARD & CO. Clay Lane, Shiptonthorpe, York YO4 3RU
(0430) 872765 FAX: (0430) 872777
Ex MOD vehicle sales/spares/surplus stores/equipment. Military/civilian FC's IIA & IIB, Lightweights,
Series I 1948-57, II, IIA, III, 90 & 110.

LANCASHIRE
CROOK BROTHERS. Blackburn Old Road, Hoghton, Preston, Lancs PR5 0RX
TEL: (0254) 852660 HOME TEL: (0254) 852021 FAX: (0254) 853334
Specialist in ex Ministry of Defence Land Rovers/Range Rovers for over 30 years, including lightweights,
101's and ambulances.

SOMERSET
THE LIGHTWEIGHT CENTRE. (0823) 666505 (Telephone for address)
The only company in the UK specialising in ex-MOD lightweights. All vehicles carefully selected for
quality. Over 30 in stock.

STAFFORDSHIRE
LEAVESLEY INTERNATIONAL. Rykneld Street, Alrewas, Burton on Trent, Staffs DE13 7AB
(0283) 791071 FAX: (0283) 791392
International dealers in Ex-Ministry specialist vehicles, plant & equip.Refurbished L/Rovers & Bedford
trucks supplied. New/recon/used spares.

WARWICKSHIRE
J.H. MERRIS. Fennis Fields Farm, Little Lawford, Nr Rugby, Warwicks CV23 0JL
(0788) 833185 MOBILE: (0831) 805930
Specialist and ex-military vehicles including FC101. Spares, repair, engine/gearbox/axle rebuilds. New
genuine Land Rover parts.

YORKSHIRE, SOUTH
L. JACKSON & CO. Rocket Site, Mission, Nr. Bawtry, Doncaster DN10 6ET
(0302) 770485/770491 FAX: (0302) 770050
M.O.D. vehicles, plant, equipment and parts.

YORKSHIRE, WEST
GRIBBINS. Victor Mills, 227 Bradford Road, Batley, W Yorks WF17 6JL
(0924) 463550 FAX: (0924) 464199
Wholesale only - Huge quantities of German para boots/camouflage clothing/ Dutch waterproofs/camping
equipment, etc. Traders, ring for price list.
P.R.B. SERVICES. Wortley Moor Garage, Tong Road, Leeds 12 (0532) 796039 FAX: (0532 310708)
Ex-Military L/Rover specialists, all models in stock. Choice of 35 sold fully prepared or "as is". Repairs/
servicing/conversions/dismantling.

WALES

CLWD
M & M. LAND ROVER SERVICES LTD. Bylchau, Denbigh, Clwyd. TEL/FAX (074) 570237
Quality recycled parts for all Land Rovers specialising in 101's and Light Weights. MOT's Sales of new
parts large workshop facility.

MODELS/COLLECTING

ENGLAND

AVON

J.R. PARKER OFF-ROAD MODELS. 6 Cherry Road, Chipping Sodbury, Bristol BS17 6HJ (0454) 321502
For all types of off-road models including Land Rover, Range Rover andujerj Discovery. Kit building, promotional models and restorations.

KENT

ANY CAR. Unit 1, Thayers Farm Road, Beckenham, Kent BR3 4RH 081-650 0678 081-663 3551
Importers of American Revell, Monogram, AMT plastic kits. Collectors die-cast - Bang & Best, Vitesse, Trax, Ertel, Brum, Onyx and Solido.

DANNY PIKE. 127 View Road, Cliff Woods, Rochester, Kent ME3 8UQ (0634) 221106
Range Rover sales brochures required by private collector; also price lists, colour charts, conversions, promotional literature ... basically anything in print!

LONDON

TOM McGUIGAN. 19 Percy Road, Penge, London SE20 7QJ 081-778 6498
Land Rover, Range Rover and Discovery models required by Editor of *Mack's Directory*. Cash waiting for interesting items such as promotional models, unusual foreign, plastic kits, mint boxed, limited editions etc. Tin/plastic/pottery/glass/wood etc. Especially interested in 'one off' home-made models or interesting creations.

SUSSEX, WEST

TRANSPORT OF DELIGHT. PO Box 130, East Grinstead, W Sussex RH19 3FS (0342) 410502
1.48 scale mainly metal hand-built models of modern & historic Land Rovers. Military & civilian liveries, factory produced by enthusiasts, some as kits.

WEST MIDLANDS

DIAL AUTO MODELS. 29 Cathedral Lanes, Broadgate, Coventry CV1 1LL
(0203) 551633 FAX: (0203) 551921
Stockists of well-known brands such as Brumm, Best, Vitesse, Bang, Onyx, Minichamps & Burago. Mail order service available.

WILTSHIRE

TURLEIGH MODELS. 'Trees', Turleigh Hill, Bradford-on-Avon, Wilts BA15 2HE (0225) 862386
Comprehensive stock of Britains current farming models including Land Rovers plus a selection of obsolete items, also restoration of cattle/farm animals.

YORKSHIRE, SOUTH

CAR CRAZY PROMOTIONS. 63 Doncaster Road, Goldthorpe, Rotherham S63 9HJ (0709) 880888
Suppliers of die-cast models, mail order available. Phone us with your requirements.

YORKSHIRE, WEST

PETER GALILEE. 96 Glen lee Lane, Keighley, W Yorkshire BD21 5QY (0535) 605310
Wanted for Land Rovers 1948-53 : Catalogues, manuals, original photos, service bulletins, etc. Also unusual P.T.O. equipment, engine governors, etc. (Private collector).

WALES

GWYNEDD

LANDCRAFT OFF ROAD TUITION & DRIVING CENTRES. Plas-yn-dre, Top Floor, 23 High Street, Bala, Gwynedd LL23 7LU (0678) 520820 FAX: (0678) 520152
Landcraft & LRO Model Shop: Full range of Land Rover/4WD models, die-cast and kits. Please send S.A.E. for list.

NEW ZEALAND

KEN SIBLY. 97 Palmers Road, Christchurch 9, New Zealand
Willing to swop Land Rover, Range Rover and Discovery sales brochures from the 60's & 70's with similar enthusiasts.

OFF-ROAD DRIVING CENTRES
(including rally tuition)
CROSS REFERENCE: See also SCHOOLS (4x4 TUITION)

ENGLAND

CHESHIRE
4x4 DRIVE OFF-ROAD DRIVING CENTRE. The Castle House, Rock Park, Wirral L42 1PJ
051-6458124
Tuition in centre's Land Rovers or non-damaging self-drive in own vehicle.
PARAMOUNT CIRCUIT. Unit 22, King Street Trading Estate, Middlewitch,Cheshire CW10 9LF
(0606) 737030
'Drive Factor' - the ultimate driving experience. Your chance to try your hand at Honda Pilots, Quads,
Hovercrafts and Outdoor Karting.

CO. DURHAM
WEARDALE OFF ROAD CENTRE. Coves House Farm, Wolsingham, Co. Durham DL13 3BG
(0388) 527375 FAX: (0388) 526157
Quad bikes, Honda Pilots, Range Rovers for hire. Extensive off road course.Qualified ATV/4 wheel drive
instruction available. Corporate entertainment.

CUMBRIA
LAKELAND FOUR WHEEL DRIVE SAFARI. "Duddon View", Kirkby-in-Furness,
Cumbria LA17 7UW (0229) 89333 MOBILE: (0831) 874646 (24 hour answerphone)
Experience genuine off-roading whilst exploring the natural beauty of the English Lake District.
Individual tuition, group & corporate events.

ESSEX
GRAVELMANIA. CY Repair Services, 6 Curzon Drive, Manor Way Industrial Estate, Grays,
Essex RM17 6BG (0375) 377164 or (0375) 371655 (daytime)
The perfect venue for 4x4's with mud and water in abundance. Individuals or groups welcome.
TUF GOING. Freightmaster's Estate, Coldharbour Lane, off Ferry Lane, Rainham, Essex
(0268) 764830
Mainly for the individual, corporate groups can be accommodated. Tuition available. Vehicles supplied
or bring your own.

HAMPSHIRE
OFF ROAD MOTIVATIONS. Andover Garden Machinery, Salisbury Road, Andover,
Hants SP11 7DN
Vehicles supplied or bring your own. Individuals to corporate groups.

HEREFORDSHIRE
BASKERVILLE CHALLENGE. The Garrison Cottage, Brilley, Whitney-on-Wye,Hereford
(04973) 357 or (0497) 820085
4x4 Supertrack in The Baskerville Challenge. Bring your four wheel drive to the heart of Herefordshire.

HERTFORDSHIRE
DEAVINSONS LEISURE. Kart Raceway, Rye House Stadium, Rye Road, Hoddesdon,
Herts EN11 0EH (0992) 451170
The venue for kart racing and all terrain rallying: Corporate days, individuals welcome, day and evening
sessions. Open 7 days for your fun!
FRESH TRACKS. Head Office: Haultwick Farm, Ware, Herts SG11 1JQ
(0920) 438758 MOBILE: (0831) 247775
Off-road driving centres throughout the UK ranging in size from 500 to 4,500 acres. Tuition, day passes
and group bookings available.

HUMBERSIDE
RALLYDRIVE. 153 High Street, Hull HU1 1PA (0482) 588891
Your chance to drive a Sierra Cosworth/VW Golf Gti 16v rally car against the clock! Full day's tuition,
send SAE or phone.

KENT
FAST LANE LEISURE LTD. Knight Road, Strood, Kent ME2 2EZ (0634) 713383
The ultimate fast moving corporate event. Outdoors: Full suspension 400cc all terrain Dune Buggies.
Indoors: 160cc Zip Karts. Please phone.

OFF ROAD EXPERIENCE. 115a St Johns Hill, Sevenoaks, Kent TN13 3PE
(0732) 742426 FAX: (0732) 461794
100 acre off-road site in Kent for open days, club days, 4x4 tuition and leisure events with driving.
Vehicles supplied or bring your own.

LINCOLNSHIRE
MANBY SHOWGROUND PERFORMANCE DRIVING CENTRE. Sunny Oak, Little Cawthorpe,
Louth, Lincs LN11 8ND (0507) 604375
Vehicles supplied - Quads, Pilots, Land Rovers, Stalwarts - or bring your own. From individuals to
corporate groups.

MANCHESTER, GREATER
WILD ROVERS. 38 Chatsworth Road, Hazel Grove, Stockport SK7 6BT 061-449 0725
Corporate days to individuals. Vehicles supplied or bring your own.

MERSEYSIDE
4x4 FUNDAY LTD. The Castle House, Rock Park, Wirral L42 1PJ
051-645 8124 MOBILE: (0831) 296454
Non-competitive off-road events, drives and exploration for your 4x4 from only £10 a day. Over 10
centres in U.K. Phone Richard Walsh for details.

NORFOLK
MID NORFOLK OFF ROAD CENTRE. Wood Farm, Runhall, Nr Dereham, Norfolk NR9 4DW
(0362) 850233
Off road driving - hills, humps, water, bumps and more! Specifically designed 1 mile course. Use your
4WD or the Centre's. Tuition available

NORTHAMPTONSHIRE
TRITON LEISURE LTD. Arkwright Road, Willowbrook North Industrial Estate, Corby,
Northants NN17 1FG (0536) 403500
25 acre purpose built off-road centre. Bring your 4x4/Quad and play, or Pilots & Land Rovers for hire.
Corporate/group entertainment specialists.
TUF-TRAX OFF ROAD CENTER. Office Address: Westerings, Station Road, West Haddon,
Northants NN6 7AU (0788) 510575 MOBILE: (0831) 526165
Training in Land Rover/Range Rover/Bedford trucks near Kettering. Fun days, corporate entertainment,
individual and groups. Send for brochure.

SUSSEX, EAST
OFF ROAD ADVENTURE. Gotwick Wood Farm, Holtye Road, Hammerwood, East Grinstead,
E Sussex RH19 3PP (0342) 315504
8 acres of easy to hard off-road obstacles to test the beginner to experienced driver. Vehicles supplied or
bring your own. Tuition available.

SUSSEX, WEST
COPTHORNE OFF-ROAD CENTER. 2 Longacre Cottage, Ardingly Road, Cuckfield,
W Sussex RH17 6HF GUY: (0444) 458929 MARTIN: (0403) 711648
Here is your chance to drive your Landy off-road. We offer easy or hard tracks - £15 per vehicle per day.
Tuition available.
LEISURE PURSUITS. Chartin, Hammerwood Road, Ashurst Wood, East Grinstead,
W Sussex RH19 3RX (0342) 825522 FAX: (0342) 824722
Off-road driving/fun days/tuition/drive your own vehicle events. Could you? Would you? Dare you?
Drive our amphibious tanks/quads/Argocat/4x4's

WEST MIDLANDS
4x4 AT PLAY. Tazin House, 695 Washwood Heath Road, Birmingham B8 2LH
021-327 5223 or 021-328 4846 MOBILE: (0850) 376226 FAX: 021-328 4846
Non-competitive off-road playdays for all 4x4's at all skill levels. Catering/toilets/St.John's. £12 per
vehicle pre-booked, £15 on day.

WILTSHIRE
FRONTIER TRAILS. Home Farm, Cholderton, Nr Salisbury, Wilts SP4 0DW (0980) 54162
Corporate days or for the individual - bring your own vehicle.

YORKSHIRE, NORTH
MOORLAND OFF-ROAD ADVENTURE SPORT. Park House, Church End, Sheriff Hutton, York YO6 1PY
'Moors Safari', 'Forest Trail' or 'Weekend Break' - 3 packages featuring adventure days on the Yorkshire Moors, vehicles supplied or bring your own.
NORTH YORKSHIRE OFF ROAD CENTRE. Bay Ness Farm, Robin Hoods Bay, Whitby, N Yorks YO22 4PJ TEL/FAX: (0947) 880371 MOBILE: (0831) 694294
Open every day. Expert tuition in your own 4x4 or a school four wheel drive vehicle. Drive your own 4x4 @ £15.00 per day - quads etc.

YORKSHIRE, SOUTH
SPECTRUM CORPORATE SERVICES. Unit 3, Swinton Meadows Business Park, Meadow Way, Swinton, Mexborough, S Yorks S64 8AQ (0226) 748822
4x4 off-road driving tuition, 30 min. taster sessions, courses half & full day. Corporate days/staff incentives. Quads/remote buggies/our vehicles.

SCOTLAND
HIGHLAND
LANDWISE. Rothiemurchus Estate, By Aviemore, Inverness-shire PH22 1QH(0479) 810858
Corporate days and for the individual. Vehicles supplied, tuition available.

TAYSIDE, CENTRAL AND FIFE
COLZIE HILL RECREATION. Easter Colzie Autchermuchty, Fife, KY14 7EQ Scotland (0337) 27075 FAX: (0337) 27077
Corporate hospitality: Off-roading, JCB diggers, quads, Honda Pilots, tractor & trailer manouvering, Argocats, helicopter flights, catering.

WALES
CLWYD
MOTOR SAFARI. Treetops, Mold, Clwyd CH7 4SS (0352) 770439 or 770769
Quads, Pilots and 4x4's - Leisure driving to professional training.Vehicles supplied or bring your own.

PARTS & SPARES
(Manufacturers/Distributors)
CROSS REFERENCE: See also INDEPENDENT 4WD SPECIALISTS

ENGLAND

AVON
BRISTOL LAND ROVER CENTRE. Old Gaol Workshops, Cumberland Road, Bristol BS1 6XW
(0272) 294896 FAX: (0272) 294495
Land Rover, Range Rover, Discovery parts and accessories. Sales & service, engines/gearboxes, full
rebuilds, mail order - send SAE for parts catalogue.

BUCKINGHAMSHIRE
DINGOCROFT. High Street, Downley, High Wycombe, Bucks HP13 5XJ
(0494) 448367 FAX: (0494) 459964 TELEX 84962 TELFAC G ATTN DINGO
Land Rover Genuine Parts stockist. Comprehensive stock from '58 to date some Series I parts.
Accessories/manuals/books etc. Range Rover, Discovery, military.
E.V.E. COMPONENTS LTD. 11-17 High Street, Iver, Bucks SL0 9QT (0753) 653330
New & secondhand parts and accessories for Land Rover - 1949 onwards.
AUTOMEC EQUIPMENT & PARTS LTD. 36 Ballmoor, Buckingham, Bucks MK18 1RQ
(0280) 822818/823117 FAX: (0280) 823140
Manufacturers of thick-walled copper brake pipe sets, clutch and fuel lines. Suppliers of silicone
D.O.T.S. brake fluid and ABA hoseclips.

CHESHIRE
LAND RANGER SERVICES LTD. 1c Brooks Lane Industrial Estate, Middlewich,
Cheshire CW10 0JG (0606) 734981 FAX: (0606) 736124
Vast stock of Land Rover & Range Rover parts/accessories at extremely competitive prices. Family
business established 1979.

CO. DURHAM
AUTOSERVICE. Fair View Garage, Beamish Street, Stanley, Co. Durham DH9 8AH
(0207) 231898/231108
Range Rover & Land Rover parts specialists all at extremely competitive prices. Open 7 days, Mon-Fri
9am-5.30pm Sat 9am-5pm Sun 10am-12.30pm

DERBYSHIRE
AEW PADDOCK MOTORS LTD. The Showground, The Cliff, Matlock, Derbys DE4 5EW
(0629) 584499 FAX: (0629) 584498
The most competitive and one of the largest dealers for Land Rover & Range Rover spares and
accessories. Nationwide delivery, export and shipping.
D L S. Water Lane, Wirksworth, Matlock, Derbys DE4 4AA (0629) 822185 FAX: (0629) 825683
Land Rover/Range Rover specialists in parts, mail order or export. Accident repairs, recovery, service,
MOT station, servicing to makers specification.
LAND ROVER CENTRE. Bay 115 Circular Road, Storforth Lane Trading Estate, Chesterfield,
Derbys (0246) 211043
New & used parts/accessories for Land/Range Rover. Engines/gearboxes/ starters/alternators/clutches/
brakes/springs/shocks/body panels etc.

ESSEX
J.A. 4x4. Station Approach, Harwich, Essex CO12 3NA (0255) 240623 FAX: (0255) 241814
Land Rover & Range Rover mail order/collect parts, spares & accessories. Also servicing, repairs and
M.O.T. preparation.
LAND SPARES LTD. 3 Woodside Parade, 261 Woodside, Leigh on Sea, Essex SS9 4SS
(0702) 512110
Comprehensive stocks of replacement for all Land Rover models. Prompt international & nationwide
deliveries arranged.

GLOUCESTERSHIRE
FOREST LANDROVERS. Newton Road, Cinderford, Glos GL14 3JE
DAY: (0594) 822606 MOBILE (Anytime): (0831) 198814
Over 7,000 new & used spares at competitive prices. Full workshop. Proper gearbox reconditioning.
Mail order and free friendly advice.

HERTFORDSHIRE
AYLMER THE LAND ROVER SPECIALISTS. The Old Coach Station, Great North Road, Bell Bar, Hatfield, Herts AL9 6NA (0707) 665588 FAX: (0707) 665206
Servicing, repairs, welding, advice, accessories and parts, parts and more parts for Mail Order around the world.

KENT
DANESMEAD MOTORS. r/o Danesmead Terrace, Margate, Kent CT9 1RF (0843) 295858
Thanet's independent Rover 4x4 specialists. Good stocks of new/used parts/accessories - Competitive prices backed up by our friendly service.
DELGRAH CROSS COUNTRY ROVERS. Unit 11, Victory Park, Trident Close, Medway City Estate, Strood, Rochester, Kent ME2 4ER (0634) 717713
Land Rover/Range Rover/Discovery parts & accessories. Discount prices. Shop open 7 days a week. Mail order service, large stock, export service.
FAWKHAM FORGE LTD. 4 Clearways Business Estate, London Road, West Kingsdown, Kent TN15 6ES (0474) 852427 FAX: (0474) 852478
Full parts and service facilities for Land Rover/Range Rover/Discovery. Distributor for Rancho suspension. Fully equipped workshops.
K.A.S. Unit 8, New Road Business Estate, New Road, Ditton, Aylesford, Kent ME20 6AF (0732) 871186/840617 FAX: (0732) 870491
Wholesale and export sales of new Land Rover, Range Rover and Discovery spares. Suppliers of original and replacement parts to the motor trade.
LINGLEY ROVERS. Unit 9, Rochester Court, Anthonys Way, Stood, Kent ME2 4NW (0634) 717653
Land Rover/Range Rover mail order parts. Export specialists.
OASIS. House, Barfrestone, Nr Dover, Kent CT15 7JH (0304) 831685 FAX: (0304) 830737
Trade distributors, specialists in four wheel drive accessories.

LEICESTERSHIRE
A M D FOUR WHEEL DRIVE. Unit 22 Merrylees Industrial Estate, Nr Desford, Leics LE9 9FS (0530) 230023
Land Rover/Range Rover accessories, new & used spares, vehicles for sale, repairs for all years/models.
PANJETANI MOTOR SPARES. 282 Narborough Road, Leicester LE3 2AQ (0533) 630367
We stock a comprehensive range of Land Rover parts/accessories incl r/racks body panels/wheel bearings/ engine parts/clutches/radiators & s/absorbers.

LANCASHIRE
TAYLOR BROTHERS. Canal Mill, Botany Bay, Chorley, Lancs PR6 8XA (0257) 232881
New/used Land Rover parts, genuine parts, MOT failures bought for cash.

LINCOLNSHIRE
4 WHEEL DRIVE TRUCK CENTRE. Risegate, Nr Spalding, Lincs PE11 4EZ (0775) 750223 FAX: (0775) 750223
Parts supplied worldwide. Mk I, II, III, FC, 90, 110, RR - overnight service. New/used spares 1948 to date. Military 4x4 spares LR & Bedford.
BAILEY'S GARAGE. Main Road, Theddlethorpe, Mablethorpe, Lincs LN12 1NS (0507) 338426
Land Rover spares & repairs. Large stocks carried, injectors serviced etc.
BINBROOK MOTORS. Grimsby Road, Binbrook, Lincoln LN3 6DH (0472) 398248 FAX: (0472) 398614
Land Rover parts and accessories specialists. Expert service and top quality spares.

LONDON
AUTOPOST LTD. Unit 21, Zennor Road Trading Estate, Off Cavendish Road, London SW12 081-673 1298 FAX: 081-673 4287
London's leading Land Rover/Range Rover parts centre. Counter service. Mail order - next day delivery available. Export sales welcomed.

MANCHESTER, GREATER
LAND RANGER SERVICES LTD. 278 Adswood Road, Stockport SK3 8PN 061-483 4313
Large range of Land Rover/Range Rover/Discovery replacement parts, spares and accessories.

MERSEYSIDE
AINTREE OFF ROAD CENTRE. 23 Topham Building, Racecourse Industrial Estate, Ormiskirk Road, Liverpool L9 5AL 051-525 0399 FAX: 051-929 3413
Land Rover + Range Rover new and used parts.

LAND RANGER SERVICES LTD. 65 High Street, Newton-La-Willows WA12 9SL (0925) 229988
Land Rover/Range Rover/Discovery parts & accessories.
MERSEYSIDE LAND ROVER SERVICES LTD. Bridge Industrial Estate, Speke Hall Road, Speke,
Liverpool L24 9HE 051-486 8636/0066 FAX: 051-486 5986
Worldwide suppliers of Land Rover/Range Rover parts & accessories back to 1960, mail order/trade
counter. Tel for free catalogue (state model)

MIDDLESEX
AJD LANDROVERS. 166 Lincoln Road, Enfield, Middlesex EN1 1LN
081-364 4874 MOBILE: (0860) 551541
Land Rover sales, servicing, repairs. New and secondhand spares/tyres for all makes of Land Rover &
Range Rover. LHD Land Rovers also available.

NORFOLK
ALLPART. Mill Yard, High Street, Methwold, Thetford, Norfolk IP26 4NX (0366) 727055
Suppliers of brake & clutch components.

NORTHAMPTONSHIRE
SKINNER LANDROVERS. 1 Thornton Road, Kingsthorpe, Northants NN2 6LS (0604) 720968
Land Rover Series 2/2A/3/90/110/Range Rover/Discovery - new parts on the shelf, some Genuine Parts.
Some s/hand parts available. Ring for a quote.

NOTTINGHAMSHIRE
ASHFIELD LANDROVER SPARES. Unit 2a, Wigwam Lane Industrial Estate, Hucknall,
Nottingham NG15 7TA (0602) 632435
Spares, parts and accessories.
JOHN MILNER LAND ROVERS. The Bungalow, Haggonfield, Worksop, Notts S80 3HW
(0909) 486741
Comprehensive stocks of genuine and non-genuine parts for Land Rover & Range Rover. Telephone for
quote on any part. Carriage charged at nett.

OXFORDSHIRE
BANBURY 4x4 SUPPLIES. Unit 9, Overthorpe Industrial Estate, Thorpe Way, Banbury,
Oxon OX16 8SP (0295) 271270
Land Rover, Range Rover body panels and spares new & secondhand. Nudge bars, books, hi-lift jacks
and off-road accessories.
F.B. COMPONENTS. 36-41 Edgeway Road, Marston, Oxford OX3 0HF
(0865) 724646 FAX: (0865) 250065
Land Rover, Range Rover and Discovery parts for home market and export. Mail order specialists.
Credit cards welcome.

SHROPSHIRE
LAND RANGER SERVICES. Unit E4, Greenwood Court, Cartmel Drive, Harlescott,
Shrewsbury SY1 3TB (0743) 236335
Suppliers of Land Rover & Range Rover spares and accessories at discount prices. Call for prices and
information Mon-Sat 9.00-5.30, Sat 9.00-1.00
McDONALD ENGINEERING SERVICES. Units 4, Mile Oak Industrial Estate, Maesbury, Road,
Oswestry SY10 8HA TEL/FAX: (0691) 657705
Land Rover/Range Rover/Discovery parts and accessories. Reconditioned engines and gearboxes also
available.

SOMERSET
BROOKWELL (TAUNTON) LTD. r/o 56 Station Road, Taunton, Somerset TA1 1NX
(0823) 254630 FAX: (0823) 323351
Specialists in Land/Range Rover parts & accessories - competitive discounted prices. Agents for
Superwinch, P.W.S. nudge bars etc.

STAFFORDSHIRE
R.K. AUTOMOTIVE. Unit 5, Tamworth Enterprise Park, Mariner, Lichfield Road Industrial Estate,
Tamworth, Staffs B79 7UL (0827) 63866 FAX: (0827) 63865
Parts, accessories, panels, used parts, engines, gearboxes, conversions, handling kits, workshop facilities,
performance exhausts.

JOHN CRADDOCK LTD. 70-76 North Street, Bridgtown, Cannock, Staffs WS11 3AZ
(0543) 577207 or 505408 FAX: (0543) 504818
Mail order specialists for Land Rover/Range Rover/Discovery parts, spares, accessories & used spares.
Open 7 days a week (Sun 10am-12 noon).

SURREY
MUDDYTRAX - LAND ROVER SPARES & ACCESSORIES. Abbey Business Park, Monks Walk,
Farnham, Surrey GU9 8HT (0252) 717922
Authorised stockist of Bearmach spares and accessories. Land Rover genuine parts for Land Rover
(all series), Range Rover and Discovery.
PREMIER SUPPLY CO. Perram Works, Merrow Street, Guildford, Surrey GU4 7BP
(0483) 34346 FAX: (0483) 303992
Manufacturers and distributors worldwide of the County range of spare parts for Land Rover and Range
Rover vehicles. Wholesale enquires welcomed.

SUSSEX, EAST
CYRIL G GROOMBRIDGE. 'Meadowside', Newick Lane, Heathfield, East Sussex TN21 8PY
(0435) 863228 FAX: (0435) 867580
Land Rovers, Range Rovers, Discoverys - all spares stocked. Reconditioned Land Rovers exported to all
parts of the world (established since 1964)
ROBERTS RANGE ROVERS. Ninfield Garage, Bexhill Road, Ninfield, Battle, East Sussex TN33 9EE
(0424) 893280 FAX: (0424) 892178
Range Rover specialist - parts/accessories, servicing, repairs, breaking all vehicles, diesel conversions,
vehicle sales, export welcome.

SUSSEX, WEST
SC PARTS GROUP LIMITED. 13 Cobham Way, Gatwick Road, Crawley, W Sussex RH10 2RX
(0293) 547841/4 FAX: (0293) 546570
Parts specialists for Range Rovers, principally up to 1985. Catalogue available on request.

TYNE & WEAR
ACE AUTOPARTS. 1 Jubilee Terrace, Crawcrook, Ryton NE40 4HL 091-413 7414
Specialists in Land Rover & Range Rover quality parts and accessories. Number plates while-u-wait.
All British & foreign car parts & accessories.

WARWICKSHIRE
AUTOMOTIVE PRODUCTS PLC. Tachbrook Road, Leamington Spa, Warwicks CV31 3ER
(0926) 470000 FAX: (0926) 472000
Manufacturers of Borg & Beck clutches and brake components.

WEST MIDLANDS
BIRMINGHAM LAND ROVER SERVICES LTD. 480 College Road, Erdington,
Birmingham B44 0HL 021-373 7425 FAX: 021-384 7412
Huge discounts on chassis & body parts, springs, exhausts, seats & trim, wheels, tyres, parts and
accessories. Send for our free price list.
J.L. SERVICES. 47/48 Stafford Street, Willenhall, West Midlands WV13 1SJ (0902) 634000
Land Rover & Range Rover spare parts from stock.
LONGBRIDGE 4x4. Rear of Spot Garage, 1163 Bristol Road South, Longbridge,
Birmingham B31 2SL 021-475 2190
Specialists in Land Rover/Range Rover spares and accessories.

YORKSHIRE, NORTH
R.A.T's REPLACEMENT PARTS AND ACCESSORIES. Brook Farm, Weaverthorpe,
Nr Malton, N Yorks YO17 8EY (09443) 513
Land Rover owners ... for all your requirements call R.A.T's, East Yorkshire's latest outlet of parts, all at
competitive prices.

YORKSHIRE, SOUTH
SOUTH YORKSHIRE LANDROVERS. Hall Farm, Upper Hoyland Road, Hoyland, Barnsley,
S Yorks S74 9NL (0226) 747014
Motor factors - Land Rover parts, spares & accessories.

YORKSHIRE, WEST
A.E. AUTOPARTS LTD. PO Box 10, Legrams Lane, Bradford, W Yorks BD7 INQ
(0274) 723481 FAX: (0274) 308746
Manufacturers of short and full engines. Trade only.

NORTHERN IRELAND
BELFAST
LANDROVER SALES & SPARES. 22 Moss Brook Road, Carryduff BT8 8AJ (0232) 812385
Suppliers of new & used parts, plus vehicles.

SCOTLAND
GRAMPIAN, HIGHLAND & ISLANDS
R.D.H. LAND-ROVERS. Castletown Farm, Ballindalloch, Banffshire AB3 9AJ
(0807) 500354 or (0807) 590406
All new replacement parts for Land Rovers and Range Rovers. Everything from mechanical & body to
luxury parts.

LOTHIAN AND BORDERS
LENG LANDROVER LTD. Juniperbank, Walkerburn, Peebleshire, Borders EH43 6DE
(089687) 519 FAX: (089687) 411
Suppliers of Original Equipment and top quality spare parts for Land Rovers. Now in our SEVENTH
year, we stock over 1500 different lines.

WALES
CLWYD
LAND RANGER SERVICES LTD. Queensferry Industrial Estate, Chester Road East, Pentra, Deeside,
Clwyd CH5 2EB (0244) 520127
Replacement parts & accessories for Land Rover/Range Rover at discount prices inc bull bars, wheels,
carpets, seats, roof racks and much more.
NORTH WALES LAND ROVER CENTRE. 8 Vale Road, Rhyl, Clwyd LL18 2BS (0745) 337623
Series I, II & III, 90/110 & R/Rover, the most comprehensive stock of parts, equipment and accessories at
competitive prices in North Wales.

GWENT
ALL TERRAIN ROVERS. Unit 8b, Mill Street Industrial Estate, Abergavenny, Gwent NP7 5HE
(0873) 858085 FAX: (0873) 858085 <fax only between 9am - 5pm>
Land Rover/Range Rover parts & quality accessories incl. engine, gearboxand chassis parts/winches/
polybush kits/bull bars etc. Also Mail Order.

POWYS
FORGE FOUR WHEEL DRIVE. The Strand, Builth Wells, Powys LD2 3BL (0982) 553105
8500 lines of L/Rover, R/Rover, Discovery parts/accessories. Services incl. export, specialist
manufacture, packaging, shipping documentation.
SHARN GARAGE. Newtown, Powys SY16 4EW (0686) 88718/626765
2.5/2.25 diesel engines, 5/4 speed Range Rover and late type Series III gearboxes, 5 speed transfer boxes,
cylinder heads, fitting service avail.

WEST GLAMORGAN
SWANSEA 4x4 CENTRE. Unit 2, St Katherine's Court, Winch Wen Industrial Estate, Llansamlett,
Swansea, W Glamorgan SA1 7ER (0792) 792522
8500 lines of L/Rover, R/Rover, Discovery parts/accessories. Services incl. export, specialist
manufacture, packaging, shipping documentation.

ENGLAND

BEDFORDSHIRE
AUTO TECHNIQUE. Kingsway Industrial Estate, Kingsway, Luton, Beds LU1 1LP
(0582) 414000 FAX: (0582) 419690
Engine tuning using our 4 wheel drive rolling road, fuel injection and carburettor specialist. Turbo sales and service. Auto electrical repairs.

DEVON
BOXER ENGINEERING. 13 Ernesettle Crescent, Higher Street, Budeaux, Plymouth, Devon PL5 2ET
(0752) 361434
Designers and distributors of the 'Boxer RV8 Inlet Manifold' and associated performance aftermarket accessories for Rover V8 engines.

ESSEX
CHAMPION MOTORS. Units 5 b c & d, West Station Industrial Yard, Maldon, Essex CM9
(0621) 857444
Complete with the latest Sun diagnostic equipment and 4WD Rolling Road Dyno, we can help from a tune-up to a full rebuild.
ESSEX TURBOCHARGERS LTD. The Causeway Industrial Estate, Galliford Road, Maldon, Essex CM9 7XD (0621) 850111/850112 FAX: (0621) 854964
Land Rover/Range Rover/Discovery supplies, spares and service. Specialists in all aspects of turbochargers.

HAMPSHIRE
OVERFINCH LTD. Unit 7, Newman Lane Ind. Est, Alton, Hampshire GU34 2QR
(0420) 542877 FAX: (0420) 543693
Range Rover enhancement specialist since 1975. Hi performance 5.7 & 5.0 GM engines, steering, suspension (including air), interior and exterior improvements for Range Rovers up to 5 years old.

HEREFORDSHIRE
BENGRY'S SPECIAL TUNING CENTRE. Southern Avenue, Leominster, Hereford HR6 0QF
(0568) 615641/612337
Performance tuning for road/race/rally. 4 wheel drive Sun XII rolling road to 480 bhp & 125 mph, producing computer power graph printouts.

KENT
AMERICAN SPEED SPECIALTIES. Unit 1, Thayers Farm Road, Beckenham, Kent BR3 4RH
081-650 9733 FAX: 081-663 3551
Chevy, Ford, Chrysler and Jeep race engines. Performance parts, suspension lift kits, wheels, tyres, winches, 4x4 sales & servicing.
B.D. ENGINEERING. Unit G1, Newington Industrial Estate, London Road, Newington, Nr Sittingbourne, Kent (0795) 843980
2WD & 4WD 400 BHP rolling road tuning with the latest diagnostic equipment. Electronic Fuel Injector testing/servicing. Also alloy wheel polishing.

LEICESTERSHIRE
T.R.M. 56 Scalford Road, Melton Mowbray, Leics LE13 1LD (0664) 63241 FAX: (0664) 69029
The Lichfield Range Rover: 220 bhp/4.3 litre TVR & 275 bhp/4.5 litre TVR units as part of the Viceroy service, including suspension upgrade etc.

LINCOLNSHIRE
WARWICK BANKS HANDLING. West Farm, Witham-on-the-Hill, Bourne, Lincs PE10 0JN
(0778 33) 275 or 484 (0778 33) 466
Land Rover Tdi diesel modifications (140+ bhp). Suspension kits/synthetic oils/shock absorbers/tarox brake/noise control kits/S.E.T. devices etc.

MIDDLESEX
THINK AUTOMOTIVE LTD. 292 Worton Road, Isleworth, Middlesex TW7 6EL
081-568 1172 FAX: 081-847 5338
Mocal oil cooler kits/remote oil filter installations inc Rover V8 oil pump cover take-off's/oilstats etc. Aeroquip hoses/fittings for oil/fuel/brakes.

NORFOLK
COURTENAY TURBO. Folgate Road, North Walsham, Norfolk NR28 0AJ (0692) 404313
Suppliers of 'The Simmer Switch', an accessory allowing turbochargers to cool down after use thus preventing damage. Simple DIY installation.

NORTHAMPTONSHIRE
TURBO TECHNICS. 17 Galowhill Road, Brackmills, Northampton NN4 0EE
(0604) 764005 FAX: (0604) 769668
Turbocharging systems for V8 Efi Range Rover and Discovery.Upgraded suspension systems.

NOTTINGHAMSHIRE
MIDLAND TURBO. Unit 3, 70 Meadow Road, Netherfield, Nottingham NG4 2FR (0602) 614516
Turbo exchange, overhaul, spares, waistgates, blue printing, pressure testing, all makes, intercoolers. Setting the pace in turbo technology.

OXFORDSHIRE
OSELLI POWER & PERFORMANCE ENGINEERING. Ferry Hinksey Road, Oxford OX2 0BY
(0865) 248100
4 Wheel Drive Rolling Road. Up to 750 bhp, diagnostics, re-calibration work, emissions testing, computer print-outs; free Rolling Road brochure

SURREY
SPEED & SPARES AMERICA. Unit 4, Epsom Business Park, Kiln Lane, Epsom, Surrey KT17 1JF
(0372) 745747 FAX: (0372) 728485
Huge inventory of American performance and replacement parts available. Manifolds/carbs/headers/brakes/exhaust/ignition/pumps/suspension & trim.

WILTSHIRE
JANSPEED ENGINEERING LTD. Castle Road, Salisbury, Wiltshire SP1 3SQ
(0722) 321833 FAX: (0722) 412308 TELEX: 47540
Manufacturers of high performance exhaust manifolds and systems, modified cylinder heads. Suspension, carburettor and turbocharger conversions.

SCOTLAND
LOTHIAN
INCH DIESEL INJECTION LTD. 9-11 Old Dalkeith Road, Edinburgh EH16 4TE 031-458 5456
Lothian's only official diesel diagnostic centre. Specialists in removal, reconditioning & re-timing of diesel fuel injection systems.

WALES
GWENT
ALLARD DIESEL TUNE. P.O. Box 19, Monmouth, Gwent NP5 4XW
(0600) 772527 FAX: (0989) 66697
Land Rover/Discovery/Range Rover, diesel tuning for performance/economy. Full range of turbocharger services. Intercoolers. Gas/air tuning.

SOUTH GLAMORGAN
LLYSWORNEY GARAGE LTD. Llysworney, Nr Cowbridge, South Glamorgan (0446) 772348
We are the specialists in performance/executive cars. Crypton tuning & electronic fuel injection, diagnostic service, performance/rally prep.

CROSS REFERENCE: See also ELECTRICAL PARTS, ACCESSORIES & SERVICES PERFORM-
ANCE & TUNING

ENGLAND

AVON
    HOOPERS. 1 Maypole Square, Church Road, Hanham, Bristol BS15 3AA (0272) 676563
Motorsport shop/mail order. Extensive range of equipment. Engine rebuilds and dyno facilities available.

BUCKINGHAMSHIRE
    AERO TEC LABORATORIES INC. 37 Clarke Road, Mount Farm, Bletchley,
Milton Keynes MK1 1LG (0908) 270590 FAX: (0908) 270591
ATL fuel cells - essential equipment for Cross Country Rally Raids.FIA approved. Custom cells and
bladders, any size, any shape.

CAMBRIDGESHIRE
    JAYBRAND RACEWEAR. 363 Dogsthorpe Road, Peterborough, Cambs PE1 3RE
(0733) 68247 MOBILE: (0860) 649199 FAX: (0733) 68249
Flameproof overalls, crash helmets, embroidered logos (includingLand Rover), sweatshirts, poloshirts and
team clothing.
    ROLLCENTRE. Somersham Road, St. Ives, Cambs PE17 4LY (0480) 64052 FAX: (0480) 494547
Roll cages, hoops and bars for race & rally.

CHESHIRE
    ABP MOTORSPORT. Units 5 & 9, Weston Court, Shavington, Crewe, CheshireCW2 5AL
(0270) 67177 FAX: (0270) 68177
Motorsport shop and mail order service. 26 years involvement in race and rally, benefit from our
experience - advice is free!
    DEMON TWEEKS. High Street, Tattenhall, Nr Chester, Cheshire CH3
(0829) 70625 FAX: (0829) 71002
Proban/Nomex racewear, helmets, seats, harnesses, fire extinguishers, trip computers etc - virtually
everything race'n'rally. Open Mon-Sat 9-5
    EARS MOTORSPORT & 4x4 CENTRE. Buxton Road, Macclesfield SK10 1LZ
(0625) 433773 FAX: (0625) 433614
Motorsport/off-road accessories. Wheels, tyres, competition seats, fire extinguishers, harnesses, helmets,
lighting, light guards, bull bars etc

CO.DURHAM
    A C MOTORSPORT. Unit 15, Nestfield Industrial Estate, Albert Hill, Darlington DL1
(0325) 362876 MOBILE: (0831) 463387 Anytime
Secondhand parts & spares including Facet fuel pumps, 3/4 point harnesses, 2.5kg/5kg fire extinguishers,
high back racing seats, Facet fuel pumps etc.
    SWIFT MOTORSPORT. 8 Armstrong Road, N.E. Industrial Estate, Peterlee,Co. Durham SR8 5AJ
091-586 7311 FAX: 091-518 0433
Motorsport shop. Wheels, coil springs, shock absorbers etc.

DERBYSHIRE
    TERRATRIP (UK) LTD. Ship Farm, Horsley, Derby DE2 5BR (0332) 882640 FAX: (0332) 882640
Rally time/speed/distance computers, intercoms, map lights etc. Suppliers to Land Rover for Camel
Trophy vehicles.

DEVON
    GOODRIDGE (UK) LTD. Exeter Airport, Exeter, Devon EX5 2UP (0392) 69090 FAX: (0392) 66956
Brake, fuel, oil and hydraulic hoses in braided steel. Oil coolers,clutches etc.

ESSEX
    BURTON PERFORMANCE CENTRE LTD. 623/631 Eastern Avenue, Ilford, EssexIG2 6PN
081-554 8507 FAX: 081-554 4828
Motorsport shop/mail order service. Stockists of Weber carbs, Mintex brake pads, K & N filters,
Janspeed exhausts and varied rally equipment.
    OWEN ENGINEERING. Unit 6, Quest End, Rawreth Lane, Rayleigh, Essex SS6 (0268) 782416
Specialised automotive modifications. Race car fabrication, roll cages, tube chassis, narrowed axles,
suspension systems. S.A.E. for catalogue.

TORQUE DEVELOPMENTS. Unit 6, Riverside Industrial Estate, 27 Thames Road, Barking, Essex IG11 0NZ 081-591 0552 FAX: 081-591 2427
4 Wheel Drive rolling road, printout of power & torque. Engine Dyno facilities. Turbo & injection specialists, engine, suspension & brakes.

GLOUCESTERSHIRE

COTSWOLD WINDSCREENS. Hooks Lane, Malswick, Newent, Gloucester GL18 (0531) 822424
Windscreen specialists for Trials machines, Competition Safari racers and 4x4 specials.
CITY SPEED LTD. Woodrow Way, Bristol Road, Gloucester GL2 6DX
(0452) 415848 FAX: (0452) 308672
Leading suppliers of quality motorsport parts & accessories for 25 yrs. Large stocks held including racewear, helmets. Helpful friendly service.

KENT

FORMULA ONE ACCESSORIES. Main Road, West Kingsdown, Sevenoaks, Kent TN15 6EU
(047485) 2271 FAX: (047485) 3808
Nomex & Proban racesuits, helmets, seats/harnesses and a full range of competition accessories inc fuel pumps/oil coolers/hoses/oils etc.

LANCASHIRE

PRO-TEC PERFORMANCE LTD. 192b Emmanuel St., Plungington, Preston, Lancs PR1 7NQ
(0772) 822898 MOBILE: (0860) 387537 FAX: (0772) 8822898
Used rally spares including bucket seats, harnesses, plumed-in and hand-held fire extinguishers, tachometers/gauges, switches etc.
RT PERFORMANCE CENTRE. Power House, Bridge Street, Freetown Bury, Lancs BL9 6HH
061-761 1177/8
8,000 sq.ft. of purpose-built, Machine Shop, Retail motorsport equipment showroom & workshop. Rover V8 engine specialists, preparation/rebuilds.

LEICESTERSHIRE

PRO-SPORT. 14 Granville Road, Melton Mowbray, Leics LE13 0SN
(0664) 501982 FAX: (0664) 501762
Retail performance/motorsport shop.

LONDON

CROYDON RACE & RALLY CENTRE. 279/283 Portland Road, South Norwood,
London SE25 4QQ 081-656 7031
South London's leading motorsport and specialised accessories superstore. Racewear, helmets, fire systems & assorted rally equipment.
RIPSPEED. 54 Upper Fore Street, Edmonton, London N18 2SS 081-803 4355 FAX: 081-807 7495
The largest motorsport and styling centre in the UK. Large range of racewear and equipment. 88 page full colour catalogue £2.50 on request.

MIDDLESEX

MOCAL AEROQUIP. 292 Worton Road, Isleworth, Middx TW7 6EL
081-568 1172 FAX: 081-847 5338
Oil cooler installations/remote filter kits for V8 conversions/Aeroquip fuel pipes & brake lines/temp gauge adaptors. Catalogue £1.50 refundable.
REAL STEEL. Unit 9, Tomo Industrial Estate, Packet Boat Lane, Cowley, Uxbridge, Middx UB8 2JP
(0895) 440505 FAX: (0895) 422047
The place to buy V8 performance parts, Huffaker V8 intake manifolds, Holley carbs, instruments, engines: Rover V8/Ford & Chevy/Pontiac/Mopar.
R.R. RACING. R.R. House, 52 Unwin Road, Isleworth, Middx TW7 6HX 081-847 4913
"Ironman" snatch bumpers, ratchet jack bumpers, winch bumpers, quick release tow bars, roll cages, bullbars etc.

NORFOLK

S.C.A. RACE & RALLY CENTRE. Unit 12, Page Road, Sweet Briar Industrial Estate,
Norwich NR3 2BX (0603) 789909 (2 lines)
Total 3/4/5/6 point safety harnesses from £34, ½ layer proban racesuits from £46.81, 2½kg plumed-in fire extinguishers c/w gauge £65 (all + VAT)

NOTTINGHAMSHIRE
ROADRUNNER. 379 Nuthall Road, Aspley, Nottingham NG8 5BU
(0602) 781173 FAX: (0602) 423054
1st for performance parts in the East Midlands. Rally lighting, suspension, filters, exhausts, seats, electronic ignition etc.

OXFORDSHIRE
AUTOMOTIVE DEVELOPMENTS. Oddington Garage, Oddington, Oxford
(0867) 33226 FAX: (0867) 33332
4WD rolling road * DynoPlot power/torque analysis * Weber, Dellorto, SU and fuel injection specialists * Quality engine conversions & servicing.

SHROPSHIRE
W.A.R.S. MOTORSPORT. Units G5,G6,F3, Bank Top Industrial Estate, St Martins, Oswestry, Salop SY11 3PL (0691) 774163 FAX: (0691) 773888
Welsh Area Rally Spares stock many essentials such as fire extinguishers, harnesses, seats, hoses + fibreglass battery boxes, bonnet louvres etc.

STAFFORDSHIRE
EUROPA. Fauld Camp, Tutbury, Burton-upon-Trent, Staffs DE13 9HR
(0283) 815609 FAX: (0283) 814976
Massive selection of motorsport/performance parts, spares and accessories. Retail shop, telephone & mail order.

SUFFOLK
SAFETY DEVICES. 176 Exning Road, Newmarket, Suffolk CB8 0AF (0638) 661421
Land Rover/Range Rover/Discovery roll cages, bars & safety equipment.

SURREY
AVONBAR OFF-ROAD PERFORMANCE. 219 Haw Road, Addlestone, Surrey KT15 2DP
(0932) 842024/840058 FAX: (0932) 858317
Quality 4x4 performance parts: Janspeed exhausts, harnesses, roll bars, Pacet/Kenlowe fans, uprated suspension, etc.

SUSSEX, EAST
LUKE RACING SYSTEMS LTD. Unit 6, Diplocks Buildings, Diplocks Way, Hailsham, E Sussex BN27 3JF (0323) 844791 FAX: (0323) 844046
LUKE harnesses for comfort, safety & value. Latest 'three inch wide' design. 3/5/6 point belts. Send A5 24p SAE for catalogue/dealer list.

WILTSHIRE
MERLIN MOTORSPORT. Castle Combe Circuit, Chippenham, Wilts SN14 7EX
(0249) 782101 FAX: (0249) 782161
Comprehensive range of motorsport spares and accessories.
SPEEDEX AUTOSPARES LTD. 150 West Wilts Trading Estate, Westbury, Wilts BA13 4JN
(0373) 826334 FAX: (0373) 858052
Suppliers of performance and specialist parts for Fast Road, Rally, Race, Kit Car and 4x4 in the West Country. Mail order/counter service.
TOTAL RESTRAINT SYSTEMS LTD. Unit 2, St Martin's Workshops, Fifield Bavant, Broad Chalke, Salisbury, Wilts SP5 5HT (0722) 780192 FAX: (0722) 780195
Manufacturer of competition harnesses, ratchet tie downs, tow straps and specialist motorsport equipment.

YORKSHIRE, SOUTH
BETTAWELD. Churchill Buildings, 4b Churchill Road, Doncaster DN1 2TF (0302) 351264
LR/RR internal & external roll bars plus one-off's/specials/space frames to exceed ARC/AWDC specifications. Full workshop facilities & fitting.

YORKSHIRE, WEST
AIREDALE RACE COMPONENTS. 29 Springfield Road, Guiseley, Leeds LS20 9AN (0943) 878986
Manufacturers of perspex and polycarbonate windows for off-road vehicles.
LARKSPEED. Arndale Centre, Crossgates, Leeds LS15 8NW (3 branches)
LEEDS: (0532) 643231 ROTHERHAM: (0709) 361105 CLECKHEATON: (0274) 877787
Retail motorsport & performance centres. Range Rover Bilstien/Spax shock absorbers, heavy duty coil springs, Cibié & KC Daylighters, etc.

WEST MIDLANDS

JAMES LISTER HOSES. Sandwell Industrial Estate, Spon Lane South, Smethwick, Warley, W Midlands B66 1QJ 021-525 7733
Comprehensive range of braided steel hoses & fittings. High pressure oil coolers, brake lines & fuel couplings.

SCOTLAND

GRAMPIAN, HIGHLAND AND ISLANDS

DEESIDE MOTORSPORT. North Deeside Road, Banchory AB3 3YR (03302) 3833
Specialist performance equipment at competitive rates. Piper cams/K & N Filters/Spax/Hella/Bilstien/ Erskine Fire/Luke Harnesses/Aleybars etc.

WALES

GLAMORGAN, MID

PETER LLOYD RALLYING. 18 Oxford Street, Pontycymmer, Nr Bridgend, South Wales CF32 8DE (0656) 870538
All types of motorsport equipment. Fast mail order specialists. Shop open 7 days per week.

REFURBISHMENT/RENOVATION

CROSS REFERENCE: See also VEHICLE SALES

ENGLAND

CHESHIRE

FROGGATT'S RANGE ROVER SALES. Unit 2 Whirley Quarry, Sandy Lane, Whirley, Macclesfield SK10 4RJ (0625) 425524 MOBILE (0860) 479462 FAX (0625) 619494
Specialists in overhauled and refurbished petrol & diesel Range Rovers.Please telephone (0625) 425524 for all your requirements.

ESSEX

GRATECH ENGINEERING. The Common, East Hanningfield, Essex CM3 8AH (0245) 400485
Fully refurbished Series III Land Rovers. Chassis restored and corrosion treated, all parts repaired or replaced, interior retrimmed, guaranteed.
LAND ROVER SERVICE CENTRE. Grafton Farm, Curtis Mill Green, Stapleford Abbotts, Nr Romford, Essex RM4 1RT (0708) 688502 FAX: (0708) 688678
Nr Chigwell in Essex, full or partial L/Rover restorations (all models).Elderly motors cared for with emphasis on quality & genuine enthusiasm.

KENT

SITE SERVICES. 132 London Road, Sittingbourne, Kent ME10 1QB (0795) 426360 MOBILE: (0836) 542070
Land Rover/Range Rover total repair service; engines and gearboxes reconditioned, MOT repairs, renovations, breakdowns, new & used spares.

LANCASHIRE

FYLDE LANDROVER SERVICES. Wharfedale Works, 8 Dock Road, Lytham, Lancs FY8 5AQ (0253) 739401
Specialists in the restoration of pre-1984 Land Rovers. Also repairs, servicing, new & used parts.

LINCOLNSHIRE

4 WHEEL DRIVE TRUCK CENTRE. Country Workshops, Risegate, Nr Spalding, Lincs PE11 4EZ TEL/FAX: (0775) 750223
Specialist engineers. Land Rover new and used parts service 1948 to date.Retail/trade exports. UK 24 hour delivery. Access & Visa.

LONDON

CHAMBERLAIN'S SEAT COVERS. 2 Tremaine Road, London SE20 7T2 081-778 7997
More practical than a re-trim, machine washable seat covers. All models tailor-made in authentic Land Rover-type fabric. 80 designs, samples sent.
REARRANGED ROVERS. Unit 14F, Stonehill Business Park, Angel Road, London N18 1RT 081-807 9806 (24 hour answerphone) MOBILE: (0831) 474654
We know Landy's inside out. Major rebuilds & restorations. All models refurbished. Series I specialists - replacement mech/body parts available.

WARWICKSHIRE
MIDLAND LAND ROVER SERVICES. Unit 1, Station Road Industrial Estate, Higham On The Hill, Warwicks CV13 6AG (0455) 212332
Specialists in refurbished Land Rovers. We believe a finer longer lasting Land Rover cannot be found elsewhere. Also Range Rover/Discovery.

WEST MIDLANDS
NATIONWIDE TRIM. Unit 6, Sloane House, Sloane Street, Hockley, Birmingham B1 3BX
021-233 9410 FAX: 021-233 9429
Cloth/leather retrims, R/Rover & Discovery. Carpets, fibreglass headlinings, casings, accessories. Full fitting service. Free brochure on request (See our main advertisement front inside cover).

WILTSHIRE
THE WILTSHIRE LAND ROVER CO. LTD. Snarlton Lane, Melksham, Wilts SN12
(0225) 700975 MOBILE: (0831) 277048 24 Hours.
Fully reconstructed vehicles hand built for your personal needs and requirements.

YORKSHIRE, WEST
LAND ROVER CENTRE. Bridge Street, Lockwood, Huddersfield HD4 6EL
SALES: (0484) 542092 24 hrs Mail Order: (0484) 513604 FAX: (0484) 545534
Land Rover 88"/109" refurbishment specialists inc. chassis, mechanical, interior and bodywork. Also servicing/repairs/parts/accessories/exports.

SCOTLAND

LOTHIAN & BORDERS
W.A. RAMSEY. Unit 11, Pentland Industrial Estate, Loanhead, Edinburgh EH20 9QH 031-440 0555
Car & commercial seats repaired. Leather re-conollising to any vehicle. Carpets. Vinyl roofs.

WALES

GWENT
ALCHEMY RESTORATIONS LIMITED. Lower Trostra Farm, Glascoed, Pontypool,
Gwent NP4 0TX (0495) 755004
Range Rover specialists: Refurbishment & full restoration of 2 door vehicles. New/used body & chassis parts/diesel conversions/export/LHD.
G. U. PRODUCTS. Unit 9, Abersychan Industrial Estate, Pontypool NP4 7BA TEL: 0495 774953
Lumiweld process. Welds all aluminium/Birmabright (Land Rover bodies).Diecast at 730°f (380°c) using Buthane/Propane, 4 x stronger than base metal. 5 rod kit: £13.90 10 rod kit: £21.90 including p+p. Credit cards accepted. Please send S.A.E. for details and free sample.

ENGLAND

DORSET

PAR INDUSTRIES LTD. St Andrews House, St Andrews Industrial Estate, Bridport, Dorset DT6 3DB (0308) 23414 FAX: (0308) 421872
Convert your storage well area into a flat deck with a lockable secure drawer - "The Bootbox".

HAMPSHIRE

EQUESTRIAN SAFETY PRODUCTS LTD. Unit 1a, Mainline Business Centre, 74 Station Road, Liss, Hants GU33 7AD (0730) 895668
A range of products to protect both horse and owner. Fire extinguishers, first aid kits, anti-attack horse alarms, etc.

ISLE OF WIGHT

LIFELINE FIRE & SAFETY LTD. New Barn Business Park, Merstone, Newport, Isle of Wight PO30 3BT (0983) 521921 FAX: (0983) 522951
Suppliers of vehicle fire protection systems, electrically and mechanically operated. Used in numerous rallies including Paris-Dakar.

LONDON

RICHBROOK INTERNATIONAL LTD. 2 Munro Terrace, 112 Cheyne Walk, London SW10 0DL 071-351 9333 FAX: 071-351 7732
Manufacturer and distributors of the 'Dis-Car-Nect' battery isolation device preventing battery drain, electrical fires and deters thieves.

MANCHESTER, GREATER

WM HEALTHCARE. Park Mill, Royton, Oldham 0LT 6PZ 061-624 5641
Compact winter security packs known as 'Sno-Pac Survival Kits'. Kits contain body/foot warmers, aluminium survival suits, lightsticks etc.

NORFOLK

GUARDIAN FIRE LTD. Britannia Works, Hurricane Way, Airport Industrial Estate, Norwich NR6 6EY (0603) 787679 FAX: (0603) 787996
Manufacturers of a range of BS5423 portable fire extinguishers suitable for car, caravan, boat and domestic use. Call for your nearest distributor.

OXFORDSHIRE

HELLA LTD. Wildmere Industrial Estate, Banbury, Oxon OX16 7JU (0295) 272233
Manufacturers of the "Gloria" range of refillable 1kg and 2kg dry powder fire extinuishers.

SURREY

QUADRANT CORPORATION LTD. F2 Kingsgate Business Centre, Kingsgate Road, Kingston upon Thames KT0 5AA 081-541 3210 MOBILE: (0831) 212206 FAX: 081-541 3142
Fire extinguishers with powder, Halon, CO_2 or foam. UK made c/w gauge& mountings. For vehicle use, caravans, homes etc. to British standards.

SUSSEX, EAST

FIRESTEM LTD. The Enterprise Centre, Eastbourne, E Sussex BN21 1BD (0323) 416831
Portable hand-held extinguishers and fire blankets designed for home/car/caravan etc - also home/office security products.

YORKSHIRE, SOUTH

HEATH ENTERPRISES. 171 Manchester Road, Deepcar, Sheffield S30 5QY (0742) 830514
Anti-theft units secure your overdrive from underneath. Robust steel construction, locks onto chassis, removable for servicing clutch etc.

WEST MIDLANDS

AMENDOLA ENGINEERING. 80 Hewell Road, Barnt Green, Birmingham B45 8NF 021-445 1085
'Plumbed-in' fire fighting system. Activated by a simple dash-mounted handle, BCF Halon 1211 is propelled instantly over the engine via two jets. Hand-held Halon & powder units also available. Phone for details.

CAR FURNISHINGS LIMITED. 4th Floor, 33 Great Charles Street, Birmingham B3 3JN
021-236 9582 FAX: 021-236 2587
The "Country Cabinet", in beautiful mahogany, effectively adds a boot to your 4x4 keeping valuables (inc. guns) out of sight in locked drawers.
LOW-LOC SECURITY SYSTEMS. Manor Farm, Chadwick Lane, Knowle, Solihull B93 0AS
(0676) 535388 FAX: (0676) 534572
Anti-theft security device for Discoverys & Range Rovers. Situated in the driver's footwell, the lockable device clamps around all 2/3 pedals.

SCHOOLS (4x4 TUITION)
CROSS REFERENCE: See also OFF-ROAD DRIVING CENTRES

ENGLAND

BEDFORDSHIRE
DRIVE-IT-ALL. 50 High Street, Leighton Buzzard, Beds LU7 7EA (0525) 384903
Activities include rally driving with full tuition + quads.

CAMBRIDGESHIRE
VENTURE TRAINING. 4x4 OFF-ROAD DRIVING CENTRE Eastern Grove, Three Holes, Wisbech, Cambs PE14 9JY (0945) 772270
4x4 courses daily, half day or by the hour. Individual/Corporate groups, Dealer/Club days. Quad bikes/ clay shooting/horse driving; novice or exp.

CUMBRIA
THE LAKELAND 4x4 DRIVING EXPERIENCE. Oaklea, Low Wood, Haverthwaite, Ulverston, Cumbria LA12 8LY (05395) 30030 FAX: (05395) 30030
The ultimate 'Experience' in 4WD tuition, set in 100 acres of beautiful fellside and woodland in the English Lake District. Land Rover approved instruction. Please phone, fax or write for our full colour brochure.
LAKELAND FOUR WHEEL DRIVE SAFARI. "Duddon View", Kirkby-in-Furness, Cumbria LA17 7UW (0229) 89333 MOBILE: (0831) 874646 (24 hour answerphone)
Experience genuine off-roading whilst exploring the natural beauty of the English Lake District. Individual tuition, group & corporate events.

DEVON
DAVID BOWYER'S OFF-ROAD CENTRE. East Foldhay, Zeal Monachorum, Crediton, Devon EX17 6DH (0363) 82666 FAX: (0363) 82782
Britain's longest established professional off road school offers the best value in 4x4 tuition for both novices and business users.

HERTFORDSHIRE
FRESH TRACKS. Haultwick Farm, Haultwick, Ware, Herts SG11 1JQ
(0920) 438758 MOBILE: (0831) 247775 FAX: By arrangement
Off-road driving centre/Britain's largest course. Tuition from qualified instructors and Land Rover's own demo team. Prices from £65 per person.

HUMBERSIDE
EAST YORKSHIRE 4x4 CENTRE. Rysome Garth, Holmpton, Nr Withernsea, E Yorks HU19 2RQ
(0964) 630481
10 acre site offering every type of obstacle likely to be encountered - deep water/rocks/sand/incline. Individual/group tuition including lunch

KENT
BRANDS HATCH 4 WHEEL DRIVE AND OFF ROAD SCHOOL. Brands Hatch Circuit, Fawkham, Longfield, Kent DA3 8NG (0474) 872367 FAX: (0474) 874766
The nearest thing a motorist can get to a commando course. Tuition for novice and experienced drivers in Suzuki Samurais over exciting terrain.

NORTHAMPTONSHIRE
THE ADVENTURE VEHICLE COMPANY. 22 York Road, Northampton NN1 5QG
(0604) 603641 FAX: (0604) 21485
Various courses for public and corporate entertainment. Novice to advanced driving, management training, Third World surviving/driving etc

ROUGH TERRAIN TRAINING LTD. 36 Hinton Road, Woodford Haise, Daventry, Northants NN11 6TR (0295) 788414
Training courses in our specially-equipped Land Rovers cover all aspects of off-road driving. Corporate hospitality includes Quads/ Ex military tanks/Hovercraft/ATV vehicles/JCB driving/Paint Ball games/ Microlights.

SOMERSET
HASELBURY PARK ADVENTURE DRIVING CENTRE. Near Yeovil, Somerset
Andy Raison (0935) 825314 evening or Nick Ground (0202) 822065
Non damaging site for all types of 4x4. Suit beginners or experts. Group tuitions (£40 per vehicle), 1:1 tuition (£85), Open Days (£15 per vehicle)

SUSSEX, EAST
OFF ROAD ADVENTURE. Gotwick Wood Farm, Holtye Road, Hammerwood, East Grinstead, E Sussex RH19 3PP (0342) 315504
Set in 8 acres, full days or hourly instruction in your own vehicle. Vehicles for hire if required. Group tuition. Open 7 days per week.

WARWICKSHIRE
WARWICKSHIRE COLLEGE OF AGRICULTURE. Off Road Driving School, Moreton Morrell, Warwick CV35 9BL (0926) 651367 ex. 224
Professional tuition - private or corporate. Vehicles include LR 110 diesel, Lightweight, Range Rover. Also clay shooting/go-karts/quads.

WEST MIDLANDS
THE LAND ROVER EXPERIENCE. Lode Lane, Solihull, West Midlands B92 8NW 021-742 7964
Land Rover professional off-road tuition.

YORKSHIRE, NORTH
NORTH YORKSHIRE OFF ROAD CENTRE. Bay Ness Farm, Robin Hoods Bay, Whitby, N Yorks YO22 4PJ TEL/FAX: (0947) 880371 MOBILE: (0831) 694294
Open every day. Expert tuition in your own 4x4 or a school four wheel drive vehicle. Drive your own 4x4 @ £15.00 per day - quads etc.
YORKSHIRE 4x4 EXPLORATION. West Pasture, Bedale, N Yorks DL8 1TT (0609) 770710
Expert Land Rover trained instruction on our 35 acre adventure training ground. 1 day course or 2 day trek & overnight luxury accommodation.

SCOTLAND

DUMFRIES AND GALLOWAY
THE BARONY COLLEGE OFF-ROAD DRIVING SCHOOL. Parkgate, Dumfries DG1 (0387) 86251 FAX: (0387) 86395
Basic and advanced driving, recovery and maintenance courses, using our own dedicated off-road course and workshop facilities.

GRAMPIAN, HIGHLAND AND ISLANDS
HIGHLAND DROVERS. Kincardine, Boat-of-Garten, Invernesshire PH24 3BY (0479) 83329 FAX: (0479) 83216
Driving school, 1 on 1 tuition, own vehicle or our own. Industrial driver training, Scottish 4x4 holiday expeditions.
THE OFF-ROAD EXPERIENCE/GLEN TANAR OFF-ROAD CENTRE. The Balnacoil Hotel, Rhu-Na-Haven Road, Aboyne, Grampian AB3 5JD (03398) 86806
Half/one/two/three day tuition with qualified instructors in either your own or school vehicles: Range Rover/Land Rover/Discovery/Jeep/Suzuki.

LOTHIAN & BORDERS
RONNIE DALE DRIVING SCHOOL. Whiteburn, Abbey St Bathans, Duns, Berwickshire TD11 3RU (0361) 4244 FAX: (0361) 4239
Britain's biggest privately owned on & off road facility. Vehicles:-Mercedes G-Wagen, Foers Ibex, LR 90TD, Suzuki Vitara, Toyota Landcruiser

TAYSIDE, CENTRAL AND FIFE
TAYTRAX 4x4 OFF-ROAD TRAINING CENTRE. 48 Graystane Road, Invergowie, Dundee DD2 5JQ (0382) 562567
112 acres of scenic hill and woodland in Perthshire. Non damaging trails and personal tuition at all levels. Accommodation available.

WALES

GWYNEDD
LANDCRAFT OFF ROAD TUITION & DRIVING CENTRES. Plas-yn-dre, Top Floor, 23 High Street, Bala, Gwynedd LL23 7LU (0678) 520820 FAX: (0678) 520152
With several sites in the UK, we offer the ultimate in off-road driving. The main centre is in Bala, Wales. We also offer a specialist equipment service.

POWYS
TUFF TERRAINS 4x4 OFF-ROAD SCHOOL. Abbey Cwmhir, Llandrindod Wells, Powys LD1 6PG (0597) 851551 FAX: (0597) 851551
Unforgettable off-road action, one to one tuition from £49 + VAT per day. Land Rovers/quads/country pursuits/corporate, fun & promotion days

STEERING

ENGLAND

CHESHIRE
NATIONAL TYRES AND AUTOCARE. 80-82 Wellington Road North, Stockport, Cheshire SK4 1HR 061-480 7461 FREEPHONE: (0800) 626666 FOR NEAREST BRANCH
Steering, 4x4 tyres, wheels, other tyres, exhausts, batteries & range of auto services. Check for service before travelling, 400 branches
nationwide.

DEVON
T.I. MOTOR ENGINEERS (STEERING SPECIALISTS). Plymouth - Moving - Please phone for new address (0752) 772209
Manual steering boxes and rack & pinions reconditioned. All models catered for, any age of box or rack reconditioned. LHD equipment also supplied.

LEICESTERSHIRE
NATIONAL POWER STEERING. Computer Centre, 21 Church Avenue, Leicester LE3 6AJ (0533) 514706 FAX: (0533) 628959
Nationwide distribution of L/Rover R/Rover & Discovery power steering units, single items & quantity to trade & public delivered overnight to your door.

LONDON
ADVAR ENGINEERING. Unit 17, Marlowe Business Centre, Batavia Road, New Cross, London SE14 6BQ 081-692 3930 FAX: 081-692 3930
Power and manual steering boxes reconditioned using genuine parts. Tested and guaranteed for 12 months. Nationwide exchange service.
LIONES. 124 Merton High Street, South Wimbledon, London SW19 1BD 081-543 2100 FAX: 081-543 9722
Reconditioned power and manual steering boxes. Track rod ends and ball joints. Mail order service. Trade enquires welcome.

WEST MIDLANDS
POWER STEERING SERVICES. Grinells Business Park, Sandy Lane, Stourport, West Midlands (0299) 879281
Power & manual steering boxes, pumps, drop arms, pipe sets, idlers etc. All Land Rover/Range Rover models. Fully guaranteed, next day delivery.
STEERING COMPONETS LTD. Unit 16, 1615 Pershore Road, Stirchley, Birmingham B30 2JF TEL & FAX: 021-433 3550
Highest quality reconditioned PAS boxes & pumps, also manual boxes from stock or recon & return. All models Land Rover and Range Rover serviced.

SUSPENSION

ENGLAND

CHESHIRE
NATIONAL TYRES AND AUTOCARE. 80-82 Wellington Road North, Stockport, Cheshire SK4 1HR 061-480 7461 FREEPHONE: (0800) 626666 FOR NEAREST BRANCH Suspension, 4x4 tyres, wheels, other tyres, exhausts, batteries & range of auto services. Check for service before travelling, 400 branches nationwide.

CORNWALL
4 WAY SUSPENSION UK. PO Box 444, Falmouth, Cornwall TR11 3YS (0326) 376745 FAX: (0326) 313448 Revolutionary stabiliser shock absorber. Greatly improved handling and braking, eliminates excessive roll & nosedive. Please ring for details.

DERBYSHIRE
HARVEY BAILEY ENGINEERING LTD. Ladycroft Farm, Kniveton, Ashbourne, Derbys DE6 1JH (0335) 346419 FAX: (0335) 346440 Suspension specialists - Range Rover, Land Rover, Discovery, Isuzu Trooper- suspension improvement packages, Bilstein shock absorbers.

LINCOLNSHIRE
WARWICK BANKS HANDLING. West Farm, Witham-on-the-Hill, Bourne, LincsPE10 0JN (0778 33) 275 or 484 FAX: (0778 33) 466 Excellent handling improvement systems for all Land Rover, Range Rover & Discovery models. DeCarbon/Koni shock absorbers. Springs specially made.

NORTHAMPTONSHIRE
BOGE (UK) LTD. Britannia House, Long March, Daventry, Northants NN11 4NR (0327) 300353 FAX: (0327) 300363 OE suppliers of L/Rover & R/Rover levelling units (hydromats). Full range of replacement shock absorbers & suspension coil springs available ex-stock

NOTTINGHAMSHIRE
MANSFIELD LAND ROVERS. Unit 3, Westfield Industrial Estate, Bellamy Road,Mansfield, Notts NG18 4LN (0623) 27340 MOBILE: (0860) 880262 Trail Master Suspension: We cater for all vehicles from Series I Land Rover to the very latest 4x4 models. Shock absorbers/coils/leaf springs.

YORKSHIRE, SOUTH
ARROW SERVICES. Unit 4, Churchill Buildings, Churchill Road, DoncasterDN1 2TF DAY: (0302) 341154 EVENING: (0831) 409343 Coil spring conversion specialists for Series II & III. Also Land Rover, Range Rover and Discovery parts & service.
SUSPENSION SUPPLIES LTD. 92 Burton Road, Sheffield S3 8AD (0742) 753723 FAX: (0742) 738503 Distributors of coil springs to the automotive aftermarket. Please contact your local distributor on our range of standard & specialist applications.
TURTON TONKS SPRINGS LTD. Burton Road, Sheffield S3 8DA (0742) 701577 FAX: (0742) 756947 Trade only manufacturers of coil springs for Land Rover 90 & 110, all models of Discovery and Range Rover including diesel conversions.

YORKSHIRE, WEST
SHOCKTATICS LTD. Unit 1, Livingstone House, Howard Street, Batley, W Yorks WF17 (0924) 459595 Suspension and brake component specialists. Retail shop/mail order.

TOOLS/GARAGE EQUIPMENT

ENGLAND

CORNWALL

BOTT LIMITED. Kings Hill Industrial Estate, Bude, Cornwall EX23 8PW
(0288) 355666 FAX: (0288) 352692
Tool storage systems comprising shelving, cabinets/draws, wall-mounted Toolboards, static/mobile workbenches & aluminium transport containers.

DEVON

TOOLS INTERNATIONAL. East Foldhay, Zeal Monachorum, Crediton, Devon EX17 6DH
(0363) 82666 FAX: (0363) 82782
Complete selection of quality hand tools to carry on board vehicles or for use in the workshop. Choose from colour catalogues. Up to 25% off.

HERTFORDSHIRE

MOTIVAIR COMPRESSORS LIMITED. Victoria House, Britannia Road, Waltham Cross,
Herts EN8 7NU (0992) 714444 FAX: (0992) 710533
Air compressors, sprayfinishing systems, air tools, installations, service.Work on all types of compressors. 6 branches UK branches, No 1 in the UK.

LANCASHIRE

SYKES-PICKAVANT LTD. Kilnhouse Lane, Lytham St Annes, Lancs FY8 3DU (0253) 721291
Tool manufacturers, Diagnostic equipment & garage services.

LEICESTERSHIRE

SIP (INDUSTRIAL PRODUCTS) LTD. Gelders Hall Rd., Shepshed, Loughborough,
Leics LE12 9NH (0509) 503141 FAX: (0509) 503154
SIP - one of Europe's largest manufacturers of air compressors, welding equipment and pressure washers. Contact us for your local distributor.
TOOLWISE LTD. 174 Catherine Street, Leicester LE4 6GA (0533) 681175 FAX: (0533) 611973
Retail/trade workshop and garage equipment.

LONDON

GO-T-EL LANDROVERS. Office: 14 Cliffsend House, Normandy Rd, London SW9 6HE
071-820 0959 Workshop: 55 Woolwich Church St, Woolwich SE18 081-855 3201
A comprehensive range of new, low-priced tools available. Please send a SAE for our current price list.

NORTHAMPTONSHIRE

WALTER-BROADLEY MACHINES LTD. Gladstone Road, Northampton NN5 7RX
(0604) 583191 FAX: (0604) 751517
Challenger range of floor cleaning machinery including power sweepers and scrubber driers.

NOTTINGHAMSHIRE

MACHINE MART LTD. 211 Lower Parliament Street, Nottingham NG1 1GN
(0602) 411200 FAX: (0602) 483117
Suppliers of quality garage and workshop equipment for the professional and car enthusiast.

WALES

GWYNEDD

R H ENGINEERING SERVICES. The Meads, Llechwedd, Conwy, Gwynedd, LL32 BDX
(0492) 573320 FAX: (0492) 573320
'Bushwaka' - a range of tools to take the pain out of the difficult jobs. Drop arm pullers, steering wheel & ball joint seat extractors. Suspension bush kits for spring & chassis, radius arms & panhard rods.

CROSS REFERENCE: See also WINCHES VEHICLE RECOVERY/TRACTION AIDS

ENGLAND

AVON
BRYCRAFT LTD. Unit 9, Riverside Business Park, St Annes Road, St Annes Park, Bristol BS4 4ED
(0272) 724906 FAX: (0272) 724906
Webbing equipment manufacturers. Transporter/recovery ratchet lashing straps/tow lines/tree strops/horsebox breech straps/car dolly etc.

BUCKINGHAMSHIRE
BIAS TOWBARS. Unit 14, Woodways Farm Industrial Estate, Long Crendon, Bucks
(0844) 237110 FAX: (0844) 237075
Sales of vehicle transportation trailers inc. Quad & Pilot. Towing and trailer accessories. Mobile towbar fitting service available.
PULLMAN ENGINEERING. P.O. Box 1538, Marlow, Bucks SL7 1GT
(0628) 473938 FAX: (0628) 898060
Manufacturers of the Pullman Powered Tow Hitch. An independently powered 1-ton line-pull cable integrated with the standard tow-ball.
SCOTTORN TRAILERS LTD. Chartridge, Chesham, Bucks HP5 2SH (0494) 782631
Manufacturers of powered axle trailers for 90/110/Defender Land Rovers, fitted with Land Rover "High Capacity" pick-up back body shell.

CAMBRIDGESHIRE
ASHLEY BANKS LIMITED. 5 King Street, Langtoft, Peterborough PE6 9NF (0778) 560651
For all your vehicle suspension problems relating to towing. Air shock ride levellers, load-a-justers/load levellers, coils, airsprings, etc.

CHESHIRE
BATESON TRAILERS. Doodfield Works, Windlehurst Road, Marple, Stockport, Cheshire SK6 7EN
061-426 0500 FAX: 061-426 0245
Manufacturers and suppliers of galvanised hydraulic tilt recoverytrailers.
PETER J. LEA CO. LTD. Lavenders Brow, Churchgate, Stockport, Cheshire 061-480 2377
Manufacturers of an infinitely variable coupling carrier for fitting of a tow ball/jaw.
TOWBARS UK. 11 Aston Court, Woolston, Warrington, Ches WA1 4SG
(0925) 814700 MOBILE: (0831) 391090 FAX: (0925) 826060
Towbars, winches, nudge bars, roll cages etc. Nationwide supply and fitting service. Competitive prices, phone head office for quote.
WITTER TOWBARS. 18 Canal Side, Chester, CH1 3LL (0244) 341166 FAX: (0244) 341243
Towbars and adjustable couplings for Land Rover/Range Rover. Towbars for most 4x4 vehicles. Nationwide network of stockists listed in Yellow Pages.

CORNWALL
CARNKIE GARAGE. Carnkie, Wendron, Nr Helston, Cornwall TR13 0DY (0209) 860370
Front tow hitch for Discovery. Ideal for manouvering boats, caravans, trailers etc.

DEVON
TOR TRAILER TENT HIRE. Highland Barn, East Wallabrook, Tavistock, Devon PL19 0LB
(0822) 810846
Trail away our complete hire package and enjoy freedom and comfort in our easy to erect, simple to tow fully equipped 4/6 berth trailer tents.

ESSEX
TOWSPEC. Unit 1, Fordview Industrial Estate, New Road, Essex RM13 8ET (0708) 550375
Buy direct from the manufacturer. Builder's trailers, campers, tippers, car transporters. Indespension Challenger stockists.

GLOUCESTERSHIRE
D.R.W. TRAILERS. The Woodlands, Ross Road, Longhope, Glos GL17 0RA
(0452) 830403 (0452) 831176
All types of trailer. Tow bars, fitting & trailer spares. Manufactureand hire.
SHOCKLINK (U.K.) LTD. Forum Buildings, Minsterworth, Glos GL2 8JS
(0452 75) 708 FAX: (0452 75) 770
Manufacturers of the Shocklink system of trailer-towing shock reduction device.

HAMPSHIRE
THE ASSOCIATION OF TRAILER MANUFACTURERS LTD. Surety House, Old Redbridge Road, Southampton, Hants SO1 ONE (0703) 705985 FAX: (0703) 705444
Trade association representing a reasonable proportion of the light trailer industry.

HERTFORDSHIRE
GT TOWING. 6-12 Hatfield Road, Potters Bar, Herts EN6 1HP (0707) 52118/58312
Our vast stock of Witter towbars are ready for immediate free dispatch. Indespension trailers for hire - D.I.Y. - or ready assembled.

LANCASHIRE
LEYLAND LEISURE SALES (TRAILER CENTRE). 314-316 Preston Road, Clayton le Woods, Nr Chorley, Lancs PR6 7HZ (0257) 268488
With over 25 years experience behind us, we can manufacture any size & weight or trailer including boat, flat bed, box van or car transporter.

LEICESTERSHIRE
KING TRAILERS LTD. Rockingham Road, Market Harborough, Leics LE16 7PX (0858) 467361 FAX: (0858) 467161
Specialists in transport equipment: Trailers, lowloaders, stepframes-200t., cabling equipment, skid steer loaders. Fabrication/spares/service.

LONDON
LONDON TOWBAR CENTRE LTD. 40 High Street, Colliers Wood, London SW19 2AB 081-540 6815
Over 5,000 towing brackets for over 1,000 different models of cars, 4x4's, trucks and lorries. Also winches and nudge bars.

MANCHESTER, GREATER
INDESPENSION LTD. Belmont Road, Bolton BL1 7AQ (0204) 309797
Trailer manufacturers. Suspension parts, towbars and accessories. Also trailer hire: car transporters, van trailers, goods trailers & tippers.

MIDDLESEX
FEENY & JOHNSON LTD. Alperton Lane, Wembley, Middx HAO 1JJ 081-998 4458/9
Vacuum power brake operating systems for trailers. For retro fitting.
R.R. RACING. R.R. House, 52 Unwin Road, Isleworth, Middx TW7 6HX 081-847 4913
"Ironman" bullbars, bumpers and 3-pin quick release tow bars for allRange Rover and Discovery models. One-off's made to order.

NORTHAMPTONSHIRE
BRIAN JAMES TRAILERS. Woodford Halse Industrial Estate, Nr Daventry NN11 8PZ (0327) 60733/61811 (All hours)
New galvanised car transporter trailers. Also extra wide-bed commercialduty, wheels under deck recovery trailers. Best quality and value.

OXFORDSHIRE
BANBURY TRAILER CENTRE. Thorpe Way Industrial Estate, Banbury, Oxon OX16 8SP (0295) 251526 (0295) 269163
All types of trailers/services: Vans, goods, car transporters, vending & exhibition units, specials. Hire or buy. Caravan accessories & towbars.

SUSSEX, WEST
PAUL RUTTER. Haybourne Engineering Works, Blackgate Lane, Pulborough, W Sussex RH20 1DE (0403) 700941 MOBILE: (0831) 460475
Horsebox and trailer hire.
UNIVERSAL TRAILERS. Johnsons Yard, Coneyhurst, Billingshurst, W Sussex RH14 9DG (0403) 782862 FAX: (0403) 783528
Ifor Williams Trailers main dealer for the south. Sales/spares/repair/hire,used trailers always available. Canopies and toolboxes for pick-up trucks.

WARWICKSHIRE

AL-KO B & B LTD. Queensway, Royal Leamington Spa, Warwicks CV31 3JP
(0926) 452828 FAX: (0926) 316626
Manufacturers of all types of trailer parts and accessories. All parts of German design and origin.
BLT TRAILER HIRE. Station Works, Claverdon, Warwick CV35 8PE
(092684) 2448 FAX: (092684) 3398
Car transporters, horse trailers, box/van trailers. general purpose, all terrain trailers, service, spares, repair and hire.

WEST MIDLANDS

McARDLE FABRICATIONS. Unit 3, Shilton Industrial Estate, Coventry CV7 9JY (0203) 612463
Manufacturer/supplier of 2000 Kgs capacity 2-wheel Carporter, 2 ton capacity 'A' frames and full size 4-wheeled car transporters.

YORKSHIRE, SOUTH

DISCOUNT TOWING. Discount Towing, PO Box 130, Sheffield S6 4HZ (0742) 330344/330131
Discount tow bars, wiring kits, tow balls, spring assistors, Cycle Master bike racks, caravan mains kits.
Send for free colour brochure.
TOWSURE PRODUCTS LTD. 152-153 Holme Lane, Hillsborough, Sheffield S6 4JR
(0742) 341656/340542
Britain's leading value towing brackets. Easy fitting, strong designs, neat appearance. Send for our free colour catalogue.

YORKSHIRE, WEST

BRADLEY DOUBLELOCK LTD. Victoria Works, Bingley, W Yorkshire BD16 2NH
(0274) 560414 FAX: (0274) 551114
Towing equipment and trailer components: Towballs, jaws, hooks, couplings, props and jockeys.
Stockists throughout the UK.

WALES

CLWYD

DIXON-BATE LTD. Unit 45, 1st Avenue, Clwyd CH5 2LG (0244) 288925 FAX: (0244) 288462
Towing brackets and accessories for Land Rovers, Discoverys and Range Rovers - and most 4WD vehicles.
IFOR WILLIAMS TRAILERS LTD. Cynwyd, Corwen, Clwyd LL21 0LS
(0490) 2527 FAX: (0490) 2770
Britain's largest trailer manufacturer. Full range up to 3500 kg GVW, also pick-up canopies. Nationwide distributor network.

GLAMORGAN, MID

BRAMBER TRAILERS. Trailer Works, Treorchy Industrial Estate, Treorchy, Rhondda,
Mid Glamorgan CF42 6ET (0443) 440666 FAX: (0443) 431986
Trailer parts - flexiride, bramberide, rubber suspension axles. Boat trailers, commercial and specialist trailers.

FRANCE

ALAIN COURNIL. 42 Avenue des Voltaires, 15000 Aurillac, France TEL: (1) 71.48.23.15.
Manufacturers of a high quality trailer suitable for off-road use.
RALI. Les Fontaines, 73400 Ugine, France TEL: 79.37.53.13
Producers of high quality off-road trailers.
REMORQUES BOUCHEZ. 73 Rue de Beauvais, 60200 Margny-Les Compeigne, France
TEL: (1) 44.83.42.91
Manufacturers of off-road and heavy duty trailers.
SCIFA. B.P. 64, 43110 Aurec, France TEL: 77.35.24.55
Robust, compact, high payload all terrain trailers.

SOUTH AFRICA

CUTS MANUFACTURING. 7 Oscar Nero Road, Marburg, Port-Shepstone 4240,
P.O. Box 10013, Natal, R.S.A. TEL: (0391)-20693 FAX: (0391)-21923
Manufacturers of heavy duty all terrain Safari Trailers of 750 & 1000kg payload, various body configurations produced.
VENTER LEISURE & COMMERCIAL TRAILERS LTD. 4th Floor, 6 Sandown Valley Crescent,
P.O. Box 783424, Sandton, 2146 Johannesburg, R.S.A. TEL: 27 (011) 883-2171 FAX: 27 (011) 884-6008
Manufacturers of all types of configurations of 2, 4 & 6 wheel trailers of excellent design and high quality build.

TRAVEL

CROSS REFERENCE: See also CLOTHING (for outdoor clothing), INDEPENDENT 4WD SPECIALISTS (for safari vehicle preparation), TOWING (for trailer tents etc.)

Due to its large content, this category has been divided into separate headings & sub headings. Please refer to the 'Quick Reference Guide' below for speedy use:-

Text Copyright © 1993 B. Waloff (Author).

OVEX.
Basil M.A. Waloff F.R.G.S.
6 Pickets Close,
Bushey Heath,
Herts WD2 1NL
Tel : 081-950-2977 (E&OE.)

1. TRAVEL (INDEPENDENT & OVERLAND)

ENGLAND

BEDFORDSHIRE
   WILDLIFE EXPEDITIONS LTD. Christchurch House, Upper George Street, Luton LU1 2RD Northwest Africa, East Africa, Southern Africa, Malaga-Nairobi £1375+ £400 food kitty, Nairobi-Harare £615 + £110 food kitty.

BERKSHIRE
   WORLD EXPEDITIONS LTD. 8 College Rise, Maidenhead, Berkshire SL6 6BP
   (0628) 74174 FAX:(0628) 74312
   Worldwide adventure/trekking holidays, camel trips, Southern India by bicycle, Gorillas, Tibet, Patagonia, China.

BUCKINGHAMSHIRE
OVERLAND SAFARI. c/o D.W. Percy, 32 Swallow Close, The Badgers, Bucks MK18 7ER (0280) 815928
From £1270 plus food kitty for 24 week London to Zimbabwe via North Western, Central, Eastern, and Southern Africa.

CHESHIRE
MORROCH LETTINGS. c/o ABC, Grafton Place, Grafton Street, Hyde, Cheshire SK14 2AX
061-368 0085 FAX: 061-368 5894
Private bay, South West Scotland: Beach cottage/smallholding in superb isolated location, accessible only down cliffside by L/Rover or similar.

CUMBRIA
AFRICAN ENCOUNTER EXPEDITIONS. 18 Roper Street, Grasslot, Maryport, Cumbria CA15 8DJ (0900) 817046
20-26 week trips via West/Central Africa £1600-1850 inclusive of food kitty.
DICK PHILLIPS. Whitehall House, Nenthead, Alston, Cumbria CA9 3PY (0434) 381440
Specialised Icelandic travel service. Detailed maps, sea passages. Information on lesser known routes through Iceland.

DERBYSHIRE
TRANSAFRIQUE EXPEDITIONS. 47 Long Row, Belper, Derbys DE5 1TD
(0703) 822061 or (0509) 216814
5-14 week East and Southern Africa expeditions from £400 to £1,150 plus flight.

DEVON
EPIC ADVENTURES. 1 Hillside Cottage, Wilmington, Honiton, Devon EX14 9JX TEL/FAX: (0404) 831259
18 week African Highlights Malaga-Nairobi £1575 + £280 food kitty,Namibia- Tanzania 10 weeks £1040 + £150.

DORSET
JOURNEY INTO AFRICA. 20 Brisbane Road, Christchurch, Dorset BH23 2HP (0202) 480198
Kenya to Southern Africa via Uganda, Zaire, pygmees, Tanzania, Lake Malawi, Victoria Falls, Namibia, Zambia: £1650 + £300 food kitty including single flight to Mombasa.
LANDSCAPE ADVENTURE HOLIDAYS. 30 Livingstone Road, Christchurch, Dorset BH23 1HL (0202) 480198.
49 day Kenya-Zimbabwe £799, 15 week Gambia-Kenya £1150 + £200 food kitty.

ESSEX
PIONEER OVERLAND LTD. Graylings, Clavering Mills, Saffron-Walden, Essex CB11 4RL (0799) 550352 FAX: 081-365 0849
16-26 week Trans Africa or Trans Africa slowly, £1536 (26 week) food kitty £420 Via W. Sahara , Mauritania and West Africa to Uganda and Kenya.

GLOUCESTERSHIRE
OVERLAND LATIN AMERICA. 8 Ormond Terrace, Regent Street, Cheltenham, Glos GL50 1HR TEL & FAX: (0242) 226578
Expeditions from 19 days to 15 weeks through the Amazon, over the Andes and across Patagonia. Small groups, specialised OLA overland vehicles.

HAMPSHIRE
EXPLORE LTD. 1 Frederick Street, Aldershot, Hants GU11 1LQ (0252) 319448 FAX: (0252) 343170
4WD/walking/trekking holidays to Europe/Middle East, Africa, The Americas, Asia/China/Pacific i.e. 15 day Egyptian Saraha Adventure in Landcruisers.

HERTFORDSHIRE
OVEX. c/o Basil M.A. Waloff F.R.G.S. 6 Pickets Close, Bushey Heath, Herts WD2 1NL 081-950 2977
Independent and Overland travel advisor, Personal and Vehicle Equipment selection specialist, Route Planning.
ROBERT WATT F.R.G.S. 14 Brocket Road, Welwyn Garden City, Herts AL8 7TY
(0707) 260163 FAX: 071-580 8560
Expeditionary Advisor, Rainbow Rovers to Saharwi Democratic Arab Republic (former Spanish Sahara).

KENT
SAGA HOLIDAYS LTD. The Saga Building, Middelburg Square, Folkestone, Kent CT20 1A7
FREEPHONE: 0800 414 383 (For advice & reservations)
The international leader in holidays for people over 60. 23 day Australian 'Wilderness Experience'
travelling in air-conditioned Land Rover 110's.

LEICESTERSHIRE
AFRICA JACK, OVERLAND TRAVEL ADVICE. Ye Olde Red Lion Hotel, Market Bosworth,
Leicestershire (0455) 291713
Trans Africa special advice and information weekends. 18 Trans Africa trips completed - supplied or
equipped over 400 Land Rovers for Africa Trips.
PHOENIX OVERLAND. 52 Roydene Crescent, Leicester LE4 0GL
(0533) 626899 FAX: (0533) 535766
Overland African safaris and expeditions. Transport by specially extended Bedford four wheel drive
trucks with 5 rows of seats above cab height.
ROVAROUND HOLIDAYS. P.O. Box 23, Leicester LE4 8NZ (0533) 693849
Self drive Land Rover holidays to Kenya, Turkey and Scotland.

LINCOLNSHIRE
K&J SLAVIN (QUEST) LTD. Cow Pasture Farm, Louth Road, Hainton, Lincoln LN3 6LX
(0507) 313401 24 hr phone FAX: (0507) 313609
All types of expedition preparation incl. roll bars/cages, winches, etc. Maintenance/service courses for
Defender. Expedition consultancy service.

LONDON
ACACIA EXPEDITIONS LTD. 5 Walm Lane, London NW2 5SJ 081-451 3877 FAX: 081-451 4727
Acacia run the best overland safaris in Africa for 18-40's. Please phone for brochure (24 hours).
AFRICA TRAVEL SHOP - SKYWAY TRAVEL LTD. 4 Medway Court, London WC1 9QX
071-387 1211 FAX: 071-383 7512
Shop specialising in overland and independent travel particularly Africa.
ASIA TRAVEL SHOP. 4 Medway Court, London WC1 9QX 017-387 1211 FAX: 071-383 7512
Specialising in Asian Travel.
ABSOLUTE AFRICA. 17-19 King Street, Hammersmith, London W6 9HW
TEL/FAX: 081-748 1154 or (0372) 842839 FAX: (0372) 844297
4-10 week East & southern Africa expeditions (10 week) £775 + £150 food kitty.
THE ADVENTURE TRAVEL CENTRE. Top Deck House, 131-135 Earls Court Road,
London SW5 9RH 071-370 4555 FAX: 071-373 6201
Specialist travel agents for overland, adventure travel, Africa, short tours, S America, S.E. Asia.
AUSTRALIAN PACIFIC TOURS (UK) LTD. 2nd Floor, William House, 14 Worple Road,
Wimbledon, London SW19 4DD 081-879 7322 FAX: 081-879 7763
AAT King's - Australia's premier overland adventure tour operator. 4-15 day wildlife tours/outback
safaris in purpose-built 5.7 litre Mercedes Unimog.
BUKIMA AFRICA. 55 Huddlestone Road, London NW2 5DL
081-451 2446 MOBILE: (0860) 345929 FAX: 081-451 2446
22 week trans Africa £1350 + £295 food kitty, 10 week Livingstone trail £895 + £170, 25 day Gorilla
safari £495 + £90 by 8 litre M.A.N. 4x4 truck.
ENCOUNTER OVERLAND. 267 Old Brompton Road, London SW5 9JA
071-370 6845 FAX: 071-244 9737
Africa, South America and Asia overlands up to 29 weeks.
EXODUS EXPEDITIONS. Weir Road, London SW12 0LT 081-673 0859 FAX: 081-673 0779
18 years experience of Africa, Asia & South America overland expeditions from 4-24 weeks. Departures
every month, Bedford & Merc expedition trucks.
JOURNEY LATIN AMERICA. 16 Devonshire Road, Chiswick, London W4 2HD 071-747 3108
Southern America Specialist travel agents/tour operators.
KUMUKA. 42 Westbourne Grove, London W2 5SH 071-221 2348 FAX: 071-792 9204
Trans Africa 16-20 weeks, Southern Africa 45 days, Gorilla safaris 4 weeks. South America overlands
by purpose-built Mercedes 6x4 overland vehicle.
OKAPI AFRICA. 131/133 Curtain Road, London EC2A 3BX 071-729 3299 FAX: 071-729 6186
6-25 week Trans Africa expeditions.
SAFARI AFRICA. Meridian House, Royal Hill, Greenwich, London SE10 8RT
081-858 1370 FAX: 081-305 1782
6 month trans Africa via West Africa £1650.
SAFARI DRIVE LTD. 104 Warriner Gardens, London SW11 4DU 071-622 3891 FAX: 071-
498 0914
Self-Drive Land Rover safaris around Botswana, Zimbabwe, Namibia, South Africa. All vehicles
fully equipped.

THE ONE STOP OVERLAND SHOP - SAFARI AFRICA. 7a Davids Road, Forest Hill, London SE23 081-291 9904
Trans Africa through Mauritania, Vehicles, equipment for sale and Overland information.
TOP DECK. 131-135 Earls Court Road, London SW5 9RH 071-244 8641 FAX: 071-373 6201
Adventure tours in Europe/Russia & East Europe/SE Asia/Africa/South America and Australia by Mercedes/M.A.N. 4x4 trucks & overland double decker buses!
TRACKS. 12 Abingdon Road, London W8 6AF 071-937 3028/29/30 FAX: 071-937 3176
Tracks have operated African tours for over 20 years. Our new free colour brochure includes 30 trips from 8 days - 18 weeks.
TRAILFINDERS. 194 Kensington High Street, London W8 7RG 071-938 3303
U.K.'s No 1 company for low/budget priced airfares & overland holidays, worldwide, book shop and medical vaccination centre.
TRAVELLERS INTERESTS. 77 Oxford Street, London W1R 1RB
071-287 1642 or 071-439 1188 FAX: 071-287 1645
Red Sea & Turkey. Tours/expeditions incl. snorkelling, learning to dive, dive safaris, trans Africa and South America overlands.
TRUCK AFRICA. 37 Ranelagh Gardens, London SW6 3UQ 071-731 6142 FAX: 071-371 7445
5-7 month Trans Africa overland expeditions. 6 weeks Nairobi- Zimbabwe,4 week Eastern Africa explorer.

MIDDLESEX
AFRICAN TRAILS. British Rail Goods Yard, Lionel Road, Brentford, MiddxTW8 0JA 081-747 8093
4 week Gamepark & Gorilla trips to 22 week Trans African overland safaris.Transport by specialised 16 ton Leyland trucks. Phone for free brochure.
ECONOMIC EXPEDITIONS. 28 Trimmer Walk, Brentford, Middx TW8 0RL
081-994 0841 or 081-995 7707
London-Johannesburg via Sahara, West, Central and East Africa for £1,580.
TWICKERS WORLD LTD. 22 Church Street, Twickenham, Middlesex TW1 3NW
081-892 8164/7606 FAX: 081-892 8061
Wildlife, cultural and wilderness journeys, South and Central America, New Guinea, Madagascar, Trans Sahara, S.& E. Africa. 6WD/4WD Australian tours.

SUFFOLK
DRAGOMAN. 100 Camp Green, Debenham, Suffolk IP14 6LA (0728) 861133 FAX: (0728) 861127
Explore Africa, Asia & South America on overland expeditions of 3-31 weeks. Transport by a fleet of Mercedes purpose-built overland vehicles.
EASTRAVEL. 79 Norwich Road, Ipswich, Suffolk IP1 2PR
(0473) 214305 or 210770 FAX: (0473) 232740
United Arab Emirates excursions, safaris or individual tailor made self-drive itineraries in Toyota Landcruisers. Desert driving courses available.(According to Eastravel's brochure, desert driving in the United Arab Emirates is known locally as "wadi-bashing"! - Ed)
HOBO TRANS-AFRICA EXPEDITIONS (HALESWORTH) LTD. Wisset Place, Norwich Road, Halesworth, Suffolk IP19 8HY (0986) 873124 FAX: (0986) 872224
20/21 weeks £1,295 + £310 food kitty, London-Nairobi. Nairobi-Harare, add £225 + £30 food kitty.
SAFARI CONSULTANTS LTD. Orchard House, Upper Road, Workhouse Green, Little Cornard, Sudbury, Suffolk CO10 0NZ (0787) 228494 FAX: (0787) 228096
Independent and specialist safari tour operator offering high quality travel to East and Southern Africa.

SURREY
ARCTIC EXPERIENCE LTD. 29 Nork Way, Banstead, Surrey SM7 1PB
24 hour brochure line. (0737) 362321
U.K.'s leading holiday specialist to Iceland. Fully inclusive "package" or basic travel arrangements. Ask for our 4WD information pack.
HANN OVERLAND LTD. 2 Ivy Mill Lane, Godstone, Surrey RH9 8NH
(0883) 744705 FAX: (0883) 744706
Worldwide adventure holidays by Bedford, Magirus Deutz or Mercedes trucks.
Borneo/Burma/India/Laos/Russia/Sulawesi/Tibet/Thailand/Vietnam + Africa.
INTO AFRICA (EXPEDITIONS & SAFARIS) LTD. 70 Windmill Road, Croydon, Surrey CRO 2XP 081-683 4744 FAX: 081-689 0253
Land Rover Trans Africa 15 weeks £1845 + £300 food kitty, 22 weeks £2450+ £430, Gorillas, East and South Explorer.

SUSSEX, EAST
TRAILBLAZERS. 25 Oriental Place, Brighton, East Sussex BN1 2L (0273) 748333
Moroccan safaris in your own or hired Land Rover including the High Atlas mountains & Sahara desert. Contact us for a comprehensive safari dossier.

WARWICKSHIRE
MANTEC SERVICES. 21 Oldbury Road, Hartshill, Nuneaton, Warwicks CV10 0TD (0203) 395368
Manufacturers & suppliers of 4x4 equipment, specialising in long range desert and overland travel.

WILTSHIRE
GUERBA EXPEDITIONS LTD. 101 Eden Vale Road, Westbury, Wilts BA13 3QX
(0373) 826611/826689 FAX: (0373) 858351
The Rolls Royce of the Overland companies. Extensive range of overland and localised tours up to 33
weeks, transport by Bedford 4x4 expedition trucks.
HEWAT, THERESA & JOHN. 46 Wine Street, Bradford-on-Avon, Wilts BA15 1NS
Co-writers of the Roger Lascelles publication *"Overland & Beyond"* (see Books category, Middlesex,
England). Welcome correspondence regarding overland travel. Please enclose an S.A.E.
NOMAD AFRICA. 7 High Street, Marlborough, Wilts SN8 1AA (0672) 515737 FAX: (0672) 512153
Trans-Africa expedition organisers. Consultation for private expeditions in your own vehicle. Please
phone for details.
OVERLAND LTD. Link Road, West Wilts. Trading Estate, Westbury, Wilts BA13 4JB
(0373) 858272 FAX: (0373) 824525
Specialist outfitters of Overland Vehicles, Steyr-Puch Pinzgauer suppliers, Self Drive Overland travel
packages.
WORLDSAWAY LTD. 101 Eden Vale Road, Westbury, Wilts BA13 3QX
(0373) 858956 FAX: (0373) 858351
Backpacking, trekking to Himalayas, Morocco, Turkey, Iceland, Greenland, South America, East Africa.

YORKSHIRE, EAST
BUTTERFIELDS INDIAN RAIL TOUR. Burton Fleming, Driffield, East Yorkshire (026 287) 230
All India, and South India Rail Tours from 18-29 days in a privately converted private railway carriage.

WALES

GWENT
AFRICA EXPLORED. 126 Stow Hill, Newport, Gwent NP9 4GA
(0633) 222250 FAX: (0633) 214979
Trans-African overland expeditions from 5 weeks to 22 weeks. Please phone for brochures (24 hours)
EXPLORER EXPEDITIONS. 65 Blewitt Street, Newport, Gwent NP9 4DB (0633) 257561.
Trans-African overland expeditions aboard specially converted Bedford 4x4. From 6 weeks @ £395 - 27
weeks @ £1494. Free brochure available.

AUSTRALIA

GUIDES TO ADVENTURE. P.O. Box. 450, Smithfield, Cairns, Queensland 4878, Australia.
12/14/18 day guided safaris from bush to rainforest. Modified 4x4's hired locally. Groups of 4-12
vehicles. Write for details.
GLEN, SIMON & JAN. P.O. Box. 711, Aitkenville, Townsville 4814, Australia TEL: 077/754 586
Co-writers of the *"Sahara Handbook"*, (Roger Lascelles book publishers, Middlesex, England) for advice
and information on overland travel.

CANADA

GREEN ROAD WILDERNESS EXPEDITIONS LTD. 3396 Marine Drive, West Vancouver, British
Columbia, Canada V7C 1M9 TEL: (604) 925-1514 FAX: (604) 922-8340
Escape to the mountains of Western Canada. Six-day expeditions in our fully equipped Land Rovers.
Please send for brochure.

FRANCE.

4X4 STAGES PASSION. Bob Wiles, La Croix du Sud, 73150 Val d'Isère, France.
4x4 off-road driving days in Val d'Isère, Eastern France.The highest location in Europe reserved for
4x4's - rock, gravel, snow and mud.
CRTT. 55 rue Liancourt, 75014 Paris, France 010 331 4279 8322 FAX: 010 331 40476428
Organisers of long distance off-road holidays in France, Spain, Portugal and North Africa. English guide
and full back-up provided.
LA MAISON DE L'AFRIQUE. 2 Rue de Viarmes, 75001, Paris, France.
TEL: (1)45.08.35.51 FAX:(1) 45.08.38.51
Operators of Safaris in Benin, Bourkina Fasso, Niger and Togo.

GERMANY

ROTEL TOURS-GEORG HOLTL. 8391 Tittling/Passau, Germany.
(08504) 4040 FAX: (08504) 4926.
A unique concept of lorry and coach mounted coach seat and sleeping compartments in trailers unusual trips worldwide, i.e. China, Tibet, Ethiopia, Angola etc.

HOLLAND

KERSTEN, PIETER & IDA. Palmstraat 79, Amsterdam, Holland. 020/252556.
Pieter Kersten, a real authority on the Sahara welcomes the opportunity to give restrained and practical advice.

KENYA

BUSHBUCK ADVENTURES. P.O.Box 67449, Nairobi, Kenya.
(254-2) 212975/6, 218478 (office), 521554 (home) FAX: (254-2) 218735/212977
Offering high quality camping safaris in and around Kenya and East Africa at reasonable price, visiting interesting and unusual parts, off the beaten tourist track.
HABIB'S CARS LTD. Agip House, Haile Selassie Avenue, P.O. Box 48095, Nairobi, Kenya. Nairobi 20463, 23816 & 20895.
Go-anywhere self drive Suzuki, Land Rover, Land Cruiser campers all with sleeping bags, utensils, crockery, cutlery, stoves, lamps, jerry cans, roof top tents etc.
SAFARI CAMP SERVICES LTD. P.O. Box 44801, Nairobi, Kenya.
Nairobi 28936 or 330130 (after hours 891348).
Offering camping safaris by 4 wheel drive truck including the famous Turkana Bus plus many non package tourist destinations.

RUSSIA

AUTOKAM TOURS LTD. 22A Tverskaya Street, 103050, Moscow, Russia
(095) 299 3183 FAX: (095) 299 3827
Autokam Tour five day four wheel drive holidays.

SOUTH AFRICA

AFRICA UNLIMITED. P.O. Box 68880, Bryanston, Johannesburg R.S.A.
(011) 886-2281 FAX: (011) 787 6678
24 week South Africa to Morocco in Bedford and Land Rover Us$ 2900.
BED'N BREAKFAST & STAY ON A FARM (PTY) LTD. P.O. Box 91309, Aukland Park 2006 R.S.A. (011) 482-2206 FAX: (011) 726 6915
20. 8th Avenue, Melville, Johannesburg R.S.A.
Offering accommodation at reasonable prices in private homes & farms on a bed and breakfast basis at several hundred locations throughout South Africa (U.K. Agent:- Safari Consultants of Suffolk, see above).
DRIFTERS. P.O. Box 48434, Roosevelt Park 2129, Johannesburg R.S.A.
(011) 888-1160 FAX: (011) 888-1020
40 days Overland Safari Cape to Kenya, S.A.Rand 5,995.
KARIBU SAFARI. P.O. Box 35196, Northway, 4065, Durban R.S.A.
(031) 83 9774 or (011) 792 1810 FAX:(031) 83 1957
22 day South Africa to Kenya Safari, S.A. Rands 2800 + US$ 250.
WHICH WAY ADVENTURES. 34 van de Merwe Street, Somerset West, 7130, Cape Province R.S.A.
(024) 852 2364 FAX: (024) 852 1584
Overland safaris through Africa Cape to Kenya 46 days S.A. Rands 3299 (approx £660) + food kitty.
WILD FRONTIERS. P.O. Box 844, Halfway House, 1685, Johannesburg, R.S.A
(011) 707 2132 FAX: (011) 702 1131
5 week overland journeys ex Zimbabwe-East Africa. S.A. Rands 4635 + food kitty US$ 230, Heart of Africa. S.A. Rands 4325 + food kitty US$ 250.

SPAIN

QUATTRO FOUR. 110a Pani, Ampuriabrava, Castello D'Ampuries, Gerona, Spain
010 34 72 452134 FAX: 010 34 72 451387
1 week guided breaks in Catalunya, N. Spain. Drive your own 4x4 or hire locally, parties of 4-12, vehicles travel defined routes. Send for info.

Sub Heading: Travel Books

BUCKINGHAMSHIRE
BRADT PUBLICATIONS LTD. 41 Nortoft Road, Chalfont St Peter, Bucks SL9 0LA
TEL/FAX: (02407) 3478
Publishers of some of the best in-depth travel guides specialising in Africa and South America plus *"Through Africa- The Overlanders Guide"*.

HAMPSHIRE
GEO CENTER UK. The Viables Centre, Harrow Way, Basingstoke, Hants RG22 4BJ
(0256) 817987 FAX: (0256) 817988
Publishers/distributors of *"Apa Insight"* and *"Nelles Guide"* books on travel worldwide.

KENT
ODDESEY GUIDES. Mill Road, Dunton Green, Sevenoaks, Kent TN13 2YA
Publishers of excellent travel guides to many third world countries.

LEICESTERSHIRE
CORDEE. 3a DeMontfort Street, Leicester LE1 7HD (0533) 543579 FAX: (0533) 471176
Publishers of a comprehensive range of travel books, camping, backpacking.

LONDON
COLUMBUS BOOKS. 19-23 Ludgate Hill, London EC4M 7PD 071-248 6444
Publishers of the well known *"Rough Guide"* series.
LONELY PLANET PUBLICATIONS. Devonshire House, 12 Barley Mow Passage, Chiswick, London W4 4PH TEL/FAX: 081-742 3161
Publishers of the *"On a Shoestring Guides"*, indispensable to nearly all travellers, virtually worldwide coverage.
STANFORDS. 12-14 Long Acre, London WC2E 9PL 071-836 1321
Possibly the world's best supplier of maps and travel books.
THE TRAVEL BOOKSHOP LTD. 13 Blenheim Crescent, London W11 2EE 071-229 5260
An outstanding bookshop covering all aspects of worldwide travel including historical travel books.

MIDDLESEX
ROGER LASCELLES. 47 York Road, Brentford, Middx TW8 0QP 081-847 0935 FAX: 081-568 3886
Worldwide Cartographic and Travel book publisher, including the outstanding *"Sahara Handbook"*.

SOMERSET
HAYNES PUBLISHING GROUP. Sparkford, Nr Yeovil, Somerset BA22 7JJ
(0963) 40635 FAX: (0963) 40001
Publishers of motoring and transport related books plus the well-known *"Haynes Workshop Manuals"*.

AUSTRALIA
LONELY PLANET PUBLICATIONS. P.O.Box. 617, Hawthorn, Victoria 3122, Australia
Publishers of the Lonely Planet range of *"Shoestring"*, *"Travel Survival Kits"*, *"Trekking Guides"* and *"Phrasebooks"*.

Sub Heading: Magazines

ENGLAND

AVON
"B.B.C. WILDLIFE" **Magazine.** Broadcasting House, Whiteladies Road, Bristol, Avon BS8 2LR
FAX: (0272) 467075
A wildlife magazine featuring, natural history, travel, Bush Talk, W.W.F. events and Eco/Environmental Off the Beaten Track holiday adverts.

BERKSHIRE
WANDERLUST PUBLICATIONS LTD. P.O. Box 1832, Windsor, Berks SL4 5YG
TEL/FAX: (0753) 620426
"Wanderlust", a new travel magazine for the independent-minded traveller.

LONDON

GOLDCITY COMMUNICATIONS UK LTD. Suite M9, Shakespeare Commercial Centre, 245A Coldharbour Lane, London SW9 8RR 071-737 5933 FAX: 071-738 3613
Publishers of the quarterly travel and tourism review magazine on Africa, *"Safara"*.
WEXAS LTD. 45-49 Brompton Road, London SW3 1DE 071-589 0500
Part of Wexas International Ltd., the travel club specialising in worldwide, longhaul and independent travel; publishers of the quarterly magazine *"Traveller"* and annual *"Traveller's Handbook"*.
CENTURION PUBLICATIONS LTD. 52 George Street, London W1H 5RF
071-487 4248 FAX: 071-224 0547
Publishers of the Royal Geographical Society's monthly magazine *"Geographical"*.

NORFOLK

"INTERNATIONAL OFF-ROADER and 4x4". Milebrook Ltd., April Cottage, Botesdale, Diss, Norfolk IP22 1BZ (0379) 890250 FAX: (0379) 898244
Encompassing most marques of all wheel drive vehicle, IOR includes products, equipment tests, overland vehicle travel.
"LAND ROVER OWNER INTERNATIONAL". LRO Publications Ltd., The Hollies, Botesdale, Diss, Norfolk IP22 1BZ (0379) 890056 FAX: (0379) 898244
The No. 1 magazine for all Land Rover buffs, featuring overland travel articles, products, vehicle rebuilds etc.
SOMETHING OF VALUE PTY LTD. 2 Sidney Road, Old Costessey, Norwich, Norfolk NR8 5DR (0603) 749124
"African Safari" - the 1st magazine solely devoted to safaris and travel in all parts of Africa.

SURREY

LINK HOUSE MAGAZINES LTD. Dingwall Avenue, Croydon, Surrey CR9 2TA
081-686 2599 FAX:081-781 6042
Publishers of *"Off Road and 4 Wheel Drive"* magazine featuring 4x4 products, manufacturers, Safari Quests travel articles.

FRANCE

"4x4 MAGAZINE". 122 Champs Elysees, 75008, Paris, France (1) 42.25.31.62.
The No.1 French 4x4 magazine featuring travel, accessories, equipment reviews, historical articles, raids and rallies.

SOUTH AFRICA

RAMSAY, SON and PARKER (PTY) LTD. Uitvlugt, Howard Drive, Pinelands 7405 Cape R.S.A.
(021) 531 1391 FAX: (021) 5313846
Southern Africa's premier travel magazine *"Getaway"* featuring most of Africa below the Sahara, safaris, vehicle and equipment reviews.

U.S.A.

GREAT EXPEDITIONS INC. 242 W Millbrook, Suite 102-A, Raleigh, North Carolina 27609.
(919) 846 3600 FAX: (919) 847 0780
Excellent independent and long distance travel magazine, features unusual destinations.

Sub Heading: Travel Clubs/Associations

ENGLAND

HERTFORDSHIRE

153 CLUB. c/o Ruth Page (Secretary), 94 Sebright Road, Barnet, Herts EN5 4HN 081-440 6539
A club for the desert traveller, particularly Sahara.

LONDON

GLOBETROTTERS CLUB. BCM Roving, London WC1N 3XX
A worldwide club for the independent traveller publish a quarterly news letter *"Globetrotter"* and have bi-monthly meetings.
THE ROYAL GEOGRAPHICAL SOCIETY. 1 Kensington Gore, London SW7 2AR
071-581 2057 FAX: 071-584 4447
A must for any traveller, Map Room, Expedition Advisory Centre, Geographical Magazine, Independent travellers conferences, lectures, publications.
WEXAS LTD. 45-49 Brompton Road, London SW3 1DE 071-589 0500
Club/association providing reasonably priced airfares, adventure type holidays.

MIDDLESEX

A.I.T.O. The Association of Independent Tour Operators, P.O.Box 180, Isleworth, Middx TW7 7EA
081-569 8092
Trade association representing large number of the best tour operators in the independent travel market.

GERMANY

SAHARA CLUB B.V. Geschaftsstelle: Bockweg 15, 7900 Ulm 10, Germany.
Club for trans-Saharan travellers.

SWITZERLAND

TOURING CLUB SUISSE. Information Touristique, 9 rue Pierro-Fatio, CH-1211, Geneva 3,
Switzerland.
Publishers of the book *"Transafrique"* (French language) and *"Durch Africa"* in conjunction with Darr
Expedition service (German language). Complete overland route notes of most African roads.

3. CAMPING EQUIPMENT, CLOTHING & PERSONAL SUPPLIES, CARAVANNING

Sub Heading: Camping Equipment, Clothing & Personal Supplies

ENGLAND

AVON

COLEMAN UK LTD. INC. Unit 2, Parish Wharf Estate, Harbour Road, Portishead, Bristol BS20 9DA
(0272) 845024
Manufacturers of pressure lamps, fridges, coolboxes, gas lights and stoves.

BEDFORDSHIRE

ELECTROLUX LEISURE APPLIANCES. Oakley Road, Luton, Beds LU4 9QQ
(0582) 491234 FAX: (0582) 490197
Portable 12v fridges, paraffin freezers.

BERKSHIRE

CAMPING GAZ (G.B.) LTD. 9 Albert Street, Slough, Berks SL1 2BH
(0753) 691707 FAX: (0753) 691671
Manufacturers of portable gas stoves, barbecues, 12v/240v gas fridges, coolboxes, flasks, gaslights.

BUCKINGHAMSHIRE

ANTIFERENCE LTD. Bicester Road, Aylesbury, Bucks HP19 3BJ (0296) 82511
Suppliers of Melaware and Campus Picnicware.
FRAMET LTD. 8 Rendlesham, Little Woolstone, Milton Keynes, Buckinghamshire
Manufacturers of Camp Beds.
JOY & KING. 6 Wooburn Industrial Park, Wooburn Green, High Wycombe, Bucks HP10 0PF
(06285) 30686 FAX: (0628) 810446
Suppliers to trade of Towing, chassis, trailer, water, heating, sanitation, kitchen, gas, refrigeration, safety,
electrical, awnings, furniture and just about any item you can think of for the camping/caravanning trade.
UNIMATCO MISSION AID. Beta Works, Oxford Road, Tatling End, Gerrards Cross,
Bucks SL9 7BB (0753) 886105 FAX: (0753) 889378
Suppliers of vehicles, generators, domestic equipment, cookers, fridges, etc. for use in third world
situations.

CORNWALL

BIVVY BAG. Boscarhyn, Syra Close, St Kew, Highway, Cornwall PL30 3ED (0208) 84649
Producers of Bivouac Bags.
CLOTHTEC LTD. 92 Par Green, Par, Cornwall PL24 2AG (0726) 813602
Manufacturers of Aerial Walkways, Bivouac bags, materials for D.I.Y. tents, hammocks.

CUMBRIA

JACK WOLFSKIN (ADVENTURE CAMPING LTD). Kingstown Broadway, Kingstown Industrial
Est. Carlisle, Cumbria CA3 0HA (0228) 27624 FAX: (0028) 512835
Backpacks, bags, tents, sleeping bags, outdoor clothing.
LOWE (EUROPA SPORT). Ann Street, Kendal, Cumbria LA9 6AB (0539) 24740
Suppliers of high quality rucksacks, back packs & accessories.
SURVIVAL GROUP LTD. Morland, Penrith, Cumbria CA10 3AZ
(0931) 714444 FAX: (0931) 714450
Suppliers throughout UK shops: survival equipment, backpacks, water filters, sleeping bags, clothing,
boots.

TRAVELLING LIGHT. Morland House, Morland, Penrith, Cumbria CA10 3AZ
(0931) 4488 FAX: (0931) 4555
Suppliers of all types of clothing for safari and tropical travel, plus useful lightweight wear and
equipment.

DERBYSHIRE
ILKESTON CAMPING & LEISURE. 11 Nottingham Road, Ilkeston, Derbys DE7 5RF
(0602) 309457
Awning, tent and canvas repairs/alterations. Sun canopies, groundsheets, skirts, tent spares, lightweight
tarpaulins and boat covers.
SAFARIQUIP. The Stones, Castleton, Derbys S30 2WX (0433) 620320 FAX: (0433) 620061
All types of top quality lightweight travel accessories for safaris and tropical travel.

ESSEX
FIELD & TREK. 3 Wates Way, Brentwood, Essex CM15 9TB (0277) 233122 FAX: (0277) 260789
Suppliers of footwear, tents, cooking, clothing, sleeping-bags, tents, climbing equipment.

GLOUCESTERSHIRE
COTSWOLD. Broadway Lane, South Cerney, Cirencester, Glos GL7 5UQ
(0285) 860612 FAX: (0285) 860483
Small chain of shops supplying clothing, tents, rucksacks, sleeping bags, water filters, books, guides,
maps, plus Travel Information Desk (free).

HERTFORDSHIRE
CULVERHOUSE. 96 The Parade, High Street, Watford, Herts WD1 2AW (0923) 244100
Tents, sleeping bags, rucksacks, travel essentials, boots, performance clothing.
IRVIN (GB) LTD. Icknield Way, Letchworth, Herts SG6 1EW (04626) 6262
Manufacturers of special jungle hammocks.
NOMAD. 4 Potter Road, New Barnet, Herts EN5 5HW TEL/FAX: 081-441 7208
Suppliers of all types of lightweight equipment for independent and overland travel, plus travel
information service (free).
PORTASTAT LIMITED. 6 Hodwell, Ashwell, Baldock, Herts SG7 5QG (0462) 742854
Take your Satellite TV on holiday. Small, 4 kg foldaway antenna/dish erects in minutes using only a
simple compass. Astra/Eutelstsat II etc.

KENT
DOLPHIN ASSOCIATES. 109 Central Parade, Herne Bay, Kent CT6 5JL (02273) 3581
Manufacturers of Twizelpeg, a glassfibre reinforced tent peg.

LANCASHIRE
JIM WATSON. 2 St Johns Church, Hartford Square, Featherstall Road South, Oldham,
Lancs OL9 7AG 061-624 6623
Tent & awning repairs. Specialists in zips, mesh plastic windows, alterations, awnings extended etc.
KARRIMOR INTERNATIONAL LTD. Petre Road, Clayton-le-Moors, Accrington, Lancs B85 6PR
(0254) 385911
Rucksacks - amongst the world's highest quality, plus Karrimat high density close celled mats, footwear
and small portable cookers.
MVS. Unit P3, Roe Lee Industrial Estate, Whaley New Road, Blackburn, Lancs BB1 9SU
(0254) 662096
Help avert a possible disaster with a gas detector/alarm. Detects the presence of propane, butane, methane
or natural gas. 12 volt operation.

LONDON
BROWNCHURCH (LAND-ROVERS) LTD. Hare Row, off Cambridge Heath Road, London E2 9BY
071-729 3606
Land Rover conversions for overland use. Suppliers of roof-racks, roof-top tents, jacks, jerry-cans, water
filters, winches, sand ladders, etc.
SILVERMAN'S. 2-8 Harford Street, Mile End, London E1 4PS
071-790 5585 (For information) 071-790 5257 (For free catalogue)
`Government surplus kit: Marquees/bell tents/ridge tents/lightweight dome tents/jungle clothing/water
carriers/mosinets/jungle boots/jerrycans/etc
TARPAULIN & TENT MANUFACTURING CO. 101-103 Brixton Hill, London SW2 1AA
081-674 0121 FAX: 081-674 0124
Expedition and safari outfitters: tents, ex W.D. ammo boxes, pierced steel mud/sand mats, cooking &
tropical equipment.

WILSTOW LTD. Gardiner House, Broomhill Road, London SW18 4JQ
081-871 5184/5/6 FAX: 081 877 0759
Distributors of the Maggiolina roof-top tent, luggage boxes, heavy duty roof racks and bicycle racks.

MANCHESTER, GREATER
TENT VALETING SERVICES LTD. 2 Joseph Street, Farnworth BL4 7LH (0204) 708131
Awning/tent/trailer tent repair, alteration, extension/reduction, PVC welding, reproofing. New panels,
zips, windows, mudwalling. SAE/brochure

MIDDLESEX
ANTHONY GOLDSMITH AND CO LTD. York House, Empire Way, Wembley, MiddxHA9 OPG
081-902 8730
Manufacturers of Markill food storage boxes and jars.
CAMPING & OUTDOOR LEISURE ASSOCIATION. Morrit House, 58 Station Approach, South
Ruislip, Middx HA4 6SA 081-842 1111
Trade association representing a major proportion of manufacturers and retailers of camping and outdoor
equipment, clothing, footwear etc.

NORFOLK
LEISURE ACCESSORIES LTD. Britannia Works, Hurricane Way, Airport Industrial Estate,
Norwich NR6 6EY (0603) 414551
Manufacturers of 12 volt water pumps and dual battery isolators for split charging of additional batteries.

NORTHAMPTONSHIRE
CURVER LTD. Willowbrook Estate, Corby, Northamptonshire.
Manufacturers of cool boxes.
KELLY KETTLE COMPANY. Rectory Farmhouse, Eydon, Nr. Daventry, Northants NN11 6PP
Manufacturers of the Volcano kettle for fast water heating.

STAFFORDSHIRE
CANVAS REPAIR CENTRE. 121 Branston Road, Burton-on-Trent, Staffs DE14 3DD (0283) 41721
Awnings extended/reduced. Repairs & reproofing to all makes of awning, tent or trailer tent. Fast
nationwide collection & delivery service.

SURREY
FJALL RAVEN LTD. Unit 5, Waterside, Hamm Moor Lane, Weybridge, Surrey KT15 2SN
(0932) 57319 FAX: (0932) 54491
Innovative designs in high quality outdoor clothing, tents, rucksacks, sleeping bags, waterproofs.
MISSION SUPPLIES LTD. Alpha Place, Garth Road, Morden, Surrey SM4 4LX
081-337 0161 FAX: 081-337 7220
Suppliers of solar panels, generators, tropicalised equipment VAT free, water filters, vehicles, export/
shipping.

SUSSEX, EAST
SCOUT SHOPS LTD. Churchill Industrial Estate, Marlborough Road, Lancing, E Sussex BN15 8UG
(0903) 755 352 FAX: (0903) 750993
Countrywide chain of camping and outdoor leisure equipment - footwear, clothing, tents, rucksacks,
sleeping bags.
SUPREME SPORTS & LEISURE. 20-22 Boundary Road, Hove, E Sussex BN3 4EF
(0273) 417455 FAX: (0273) 418776
Suppliers of all types of camping and outdoor equipment.
ELSAN LTD. Buxted, Nr Uckfield, E Sussex TN22 4LW (0825) 813291
Manufacturers of portable W.C.'s and accessories.

TYNE & WEAR
BERGHAUS. 34 Dean Street, Newcastle upon Tyne NE1 1PG (091) 232 3561 FAX: (091) 261 0922
Manufacturers of very high quality outdoor/winter sports climbing clothing, backpacks.
CIMEG UK LTD. 8 Sedling Road, Wear End Ind. Est. Washington, Tyne & Wear NE38 9BZ
091-415 0268 FAX: 091-415 3801
Suppliers of Gas, electrical, cooking, heating, w.c.'s, camping and caravanning equipment.

WARWICKSHIRE
FIAMMA UK. 17 Wentworth Drive, Nuneaton, Warwicks CV11 6LZ
(203) 344960 FAX: (203) 370558
Suppliers of awnings/blinds, w.c.'s, pumps, vents, tanks, roof top boxes, caravan jacks.

THETFORD (AQUA) PRODUCTS LTD. Centrovell Industrial Estate, Caldwell Road, Nuneaton, Warwickshire (0203) 341941
U.K. distributors of the "Porta-Potti" portable w.c.

YORKSHIRE, NORTH
COLCLOUGH TRADING COMPANY. New York Industrial Estate, Summerbridge, Harrogate, N Yorks HG3 4BW (0423) 781589
Manufacturers of the "TRAVEL POD" combined roof top box and tent.

SCOTLAND
STRATHCLYDE
CARANEX. Cuan Ferry, Seil Oban, Argyll PA34 4RB (08523) 258
The tent that fits to the rear of your 4x4 in minutes. Please write or phone for a colour catalogue.

WALES
SOUTH GLAMORGAN
B.C.B. INTERNATIONAL LTD. Clydesmuir Road Industrial Estate, Cardiff, S Glamorgan, Wales (0222) 464463 FAX: (0222) 491166
Suppliers of all types of small lightweight personal equipment for survival and outdoor use.

NORTHERN IRELAND
MUNSTER SIMMS ENGINEERING LTD. (WHALE) Old Belfast Road, Bangor, Northern Ireland BT19 1LT (0247) 461531
Manufacturers of caravan and motorhome water pumps, taps, mixers and accessories.

BELGIUM
L. BRUTSAERT ACCESSORIES N.V. Kortrijkstraat 343, B-8930 Menen, Belgium
00-32/56/51 56 74 (51) FAX:00-32/56/51-02 05
Omnistor suppliers, vents, awnings/blinds, levellers, steps, roof boxes, bike carriers, wheel carriers, jacks.

FRANCE
ALCAR B.P. 581. 06010 Nice, Cedex, France TEL: 93.96.68.95
Manufacturer of the 'Blivouac' roof-top tent.
I.D.C. s.a. B.P. No.1. Chatuzange-Le-Goubet, 263000 Bourge-de-Peage, France TEL: 75.72.23.30
Manufacturers of Geminy Tente Gallerie Goelette roof-top tents.
LANDO PARANA. 60 Rue de la Liberation, 38610 Gieres, France TEL: 76.89.38.06
Manufacturers of roof-top tents.
MAP-HOME. 220 quai Stalingrad, 92130 Issy-les-Moulineaux, France TEL: 558.55.77
Equipment for trans-Africa/Sahara journeys, as well preparing vehicles.
ROGANEL. 23 rue des Archives, 75004 Paris, France TEL: 40.29.02.20
Camping equipment, safari/tropical clothing, footwear, backpacks, tents.

GERMANY
BERND WOICK GmbH. Gutenbergstresse 14, 7302, Ostfildern 4, Germany
TEL: 0711-455038 FAX: 0711 4560526
Supplier of overland caravans, books, maps, vehicle/trailer equipment, tents, vehicle export service, roof-top tents, camping equipment.
DARR EXPEDITION SERVICE GmbH. Thereisenstrasse 66, D-8000, Munich 2, Germany
TEL: 0049-89-282023 FAX: 0049-89-282525
An unequalled shop supplying books, clothing, medical, camping, cooking, storage, fuel-tanks, maps, navigation, water-filters, roof-top tents, roof racks, snake bite kits, air-filters, p.s.p. sand mats, fridges, vehicle equipment.
GLOBETROTT ZENTRALE. Bernd TESCH, Karlsgraben 69, D-5100 Aachen-Centrum, Germany
TEL: 0241-3-36-36
Supplier of all types of equipment essential to the overland traveller on foot, by motorbike or vehicle.
SEAWARE-DEPOT GmbH. Zur Eisernen Hand 25, D-6109 Muhltal-Triasa, Germany
TEL: 06151 147794
Stockists of a large range of travel books and are campervan specialists.

SOUTH AFRICA
ARMOUR STEEL. Little Lumley, Main Road, Hout Bay, Nr Cape Town, R.S.A.
TEL: (021) 790 1980 FAX: (021) 790 5138
Manufacturers of 4x4 accessories incl. roof-top tents, roof racks, long range petrol tanks, split-charge 12v systems.

BORN FREE. P.O. Box 137, Pinetown, Durban, Natal, R.S.A.
Manufacturers of a complete range of back-pack and free standing frame tents.
CADAC (EDMS) BPK/(PTY) LTD. P.O. Box 43196, Industria 2042, Johannesburg, R.S.A.
TEL: (011) 474-1466 FAX: (011) 474-2985
Manufacturers of a full range of camping gas bottles, stoves, lights, cookers, and Braai (the South African barbecue).
CAMPERS CORNER. Johannesburg, R.S.A. TEL: (011) 789-2327 FAX: (011) 787 6900
Blaze-A-Trail with a SABONAZI Cross Country Rental. Toyota Hi-Lux double cab pick-up fitted for rough terrain. Sleeps four in two roof-top mounted tents. Camp kitchen, 100 litre deep freezer, air-con, radio/tape player, Hi-Lift jack.
CAMPING FOR AFRICA (PTY) LTD. P.O. Box 1938, Randburg 2125, Johannesburg, R.S.A. (the Hill Street Mall/Oak Avenue - Nr Post Office) TEL: (011) 787-3524 or (011) 787-3498
Suppliers of new and used camping/hiking gear for sale and hire.
COWLEY EXHAUST SYSTEMS. 72 Acacia Road, Primrose East, Germiston, Johannesburg, R.S.A.
TEL: (011) 828-8848/9 FAX: (011) 828-5548
The Apollo 20 Lightweight stainless steel Paraffin Geyser for Campers. Capable of heating 20 litres of water to boiling with 250ml paraffin in 10 minutes.
EEZI-AWN. Johannesburg, R.S.A. TEL: (011) 792 1731
Manufacturers of high quality Awnings, roof-top tents and tents.
MOBILE ADVENTURE CC. P.O. Box 102. Schagen 1207, R.S.A.
4x4 fully equipped off-road campervans for hire.
MINUS 40. P.O. Box 1492, Dassenberg 7350, R.S.A. TEL: (0226) 73033 FAX: (0226) 73620
Manufacturers of portable 12 volt operation fridges and chest freezers.
SAFARI CENTRE. Main Road, Bryanston, Johannesburg, R.S.A. P.O. Box 1883, Randburg 2125, R.S.A. TEL: (011) 465 3817 FAX: (011) 465-2639
Suppliers and installers of all types of overland and safari equipment: roof racks, jacks, winches, sand ladders, roof-top tents, spare wheel carriers, tanks, filters.
STORM ACCESSORIES CC. 13 Bundo Road, Sabenza, Edenvale, P.O. Box 8522, Edenglen, Johannesburg 1613, R.S.A. TEL: 452 6719 FAX: 609 4728.
Supply and manufacture of plastic tanks, roof racks, bush bars, Hi-Lift jacks, spare wheel carriers.
TESCON ENERGY SYSTEMS (Pty) LTD. Johannesburg, R.S.A.
TEL: (011) 452-5438 FAX: (011) 452-5263
Manufacturers of 12 volt fridges and freezers.

SWITZERLAND.

MAGASIN GLOBE TROTTER. 150 Route de St Julien, 1228 Plan des-Ouates, Geneva, Switzerland
TEL: 022/944747
Suppliers of equipment for overland travel.

Sub Heading: Caravanning

ENGLAND

AVON
SAS PRODUCTS. Chestnut House, Chesley Hill, Wick, Nr Bristol BS15 5NE
(0272) 564908 MOBILE: (0860) 657990
In a Practical Caravan survey of '91, 86% of stolen caravans had been fitted with a hitchlock. Don't be a statistic, fit an SAS Wheelclamp.

BEDFORDSHIRE
FRANK'S CARAVANS. 27 Wigmore Lane, Stopsley, Luton, Beds (0582) 32168
Caravan breakers - Used windows, doors, towing brackets, suspension units, awnings, lights, cookers/ fridges, catches/latches/locks etc. + new spares.

BUCKINGHAMSHIRE
CARALEVEL. Wood End House, Little Horwood, Milton Keynes, Bucks MK17 0PE
(0296) 712992 FAX: (0296) 712875
The only fully automatic caravan levelling system.

CAMBRIDGESHIRE
BCS MOULDINGS LTD. Unit 1, Wiffen Industrial Estate, Brigstock Road, Wisbech, Cambs PE13 3JJ
(0945) 581855
Towing/caravan accessories. Protecta Plate towball cover & Eezi-Pull awning aid. Please telephone for details.
STRETCH COVER CENTRE. 50 Hereward Shopping Centre, Peterborough, Cambs PE1 1TQ
(0733) 61305
Caravan stretch covers. Large range of patterns, zip or tape fastening. Send today for free patterns.

DERBYSHIRE
CARALUX UPHOLSTERY. Amber Buildings, Meadow Lane, Alfreton, Derbys DE5 7EZ
(0773) 831242 FAX: (0773) 520142
Is your caravan ready for refurbishing? Caravan & boat upholstery specialists to the trade and public.

SURREY
CARAVAN ABROAD LTD. 56 Middle Street, Brockham, Surrey RH3 7HW (0737) 842735
Flights/first night hotels/rental of fully equipped caravan/car/tent etc. to Canada, S.Africa, Germany,
New Zealand, USA, Malaysia, Australia.
BARNFIELD CONVERSIONS. Barwell Court, Off Leatherhead Road, Chessington, Surrey KT9 2LZ
(0372 470737
Motor caravan conversions, repairs, parts. We offer a quality service at realistic prices whether it be DIY,
part or full conversions.

SUSSEX, WEST
TOUCHSTONE HOLIDAYS. The Caravan Club, East Grinstead House, East Grinstead,
W Sussex RH19 1UA (0342) 326944
A range of 79 holidays taking your own caravan, m/caravan or trailer tent. Childrens holiday care
leaders. Non-members accepted.

YORKSHIRE, WEST
LOWBRIDGE UPHOLSTERY. 46 Parkwood Street, Keighley, W Yorks BD21 4DH (0535) 665010
Top quality car, caravan & boat upholstery. Complete replacements, re-covers, made to measure
upholstery in zipped cover form, curtains.

SCOTLAND

CENTRAL
JOHNSTON KICZUN. The Old Laurie Trailer Works, Bankside, Falkirk FK2 7XF (0324) 36500
All makes of touring & static caravans repaired. Re-sprays, sales, servicing. Manufacturer of mobile
units and refurbishment.

4. CAMPERVANS, DEMOUNTABLES & VEHICLE CONVERSIONS

ENGLAND.

CHESHIRE
M.M.B. INTERNATIONAL. Unit A, Calamine Street, Macclesfield, Ches SK11 7HU
(0625) 615025 FAX: (0625) 511513
GRP roof extensions for 110 & 109, also ambulance and special extensions. Export worldwide.

DEVON
MURVI. Coombe Park, Ashprington, Totnes, Devon TQ9 7DY (0803) 732246 FAX: (0803) 723815
Conversion of 4x4 Bedfords and Fiats to all terrain motorhomes.

HAMPSHIRE
E.V. ENGINEERING LTD. 6A Aysgarth Road, Waterlooville, Portsmouth, Hants PO7 7UG
(0705) 241215 FAX: (0705) 254231
Manufacturers of the Barouche large-bodied living vehicle conversion ofthe Land Rover 130. Also fully
demountable interior conversion allowing 3 different uses for your LWB :- 1 = 10-seater 2 = 7-seater/
cooker 3 = 6-seater/two berth bed/etc.

HUMBERSIDE
LOWN. Holme Industrial Estate, Holme-on-Spalding Moor, Humberside YO4 4BA
(0430) 861007 FAX: (0430) 861001
Demountable conversions to VW, Mercedes Unimogs and various chassis's.

ISLE OF WIGHT
ISLAND PLASTICS LTD. Edward St., Ryde, Isle of Wight PO33 2SJ
(0983) 64911 FAX: (0983) 811200
Producers of demountable body shells and motor-caravans for the Land Rover LWB/110. Can be
completed as mobile workshops, site huts etc.

KENT
ALDINGTON CARAVANS. Aldington, Ashford, Kent TN25 7DH (0233) 72462
The Clip Car vehicle-mounted caravan body for installation on pick-ups.

CONTINENTAL MOTOR CAMPERS LTD. (REIMO) Unit 4, Lympne Industrial Park, Lympne, Kent CT21 4UR (0303) 261062 FAX: (0303) 261063
Suppliers of parts and equipment to carry out conversions to VW and other vehicles to produce motorhomes/campervans.

AUSTRIA

ACTION MOBIL. Leogangerstrasse 53, A-5760, Saalfelden, Austria
TEL: 06582 27120 FAX: 01582 5123
Land Rover 130 Campervan conversions, 4 wheel & all wheel drive conversions i.e. Unimog, Mercedes, MAN, truck conversions to all terrain motor homes.

FRANCE

BEJY. BP35 84110, Vaison-La-Romaine, France TEL: 90-35-1586
Manufacturers of vehicle mounted campervan bodies for fitting to Land Rovers and Toyota Land Cruiser pick-ups.
MAP HOMES. 220 Rue Stalingrad, 92130, Issy-Les-Moulineaux, France TEL: 558 5577
Manufacturers of campervan bodies for fitting to pick-ups.

GERMANY

AIGNER. Buro Di FR, Biblesbach 9, D-8301 Hohenthann, Germany TEL: 08784-696
Expedition vehicles and all wheel drive living-vehicle conversions.
GEO SERVICE-W.LIETZAU GmbH. Industriestrasse 35/39, 7521 Hambrucken, Germany
TEL: (07255) 4794 or 2792
Daimler-Benz-Unimog Expedition vehicle body conversions.
HARTMANN. Carl-Zeiss Strasse 2, 6320 Alsfeld, Germany
TEL: (0 66 31) 60 71 FAX: (0 66 31) 47 48
Conversion of all wheel drive vehicles to all terrain motor homes.
SPECIAL MOBILS. Ulrich Phillipps, Hoher Steg 2, D-7128 Lauffen, Germany
TEL: (071 33) 12200 FAX: (071 33) 17007
Camping car conversions to Land Rovers, Land Cruisers, VW's, Mercedes G-wagens etc.
TISCHER FREIZEITFAHRZEUGE GmbH. Frankenstrasse 1, D-6983 Kreuzwertheim, Germany
TEL: (09342) 8159
Manufacturers of demountable cabins to fit VW single and double cab pickup VW Transporter versions.
VARIOMOBIL FAHRZEUGBAU GmbH. 4508, Bohmte, Postfach, Germany TEL: (05471)-1131
Vehicle mounted campervan bodies.

ITALY

GRAND ERG LINEA CIRANI. Via Dante 19, 20039, Varedo, Milano, Italy.
Manufacturers of superb and luxury camping conversions based upon 4 wheel drive chassis of trucks i.e. MAN, Renault, Fiat.

SOUTH AFRICA.

C.I. LOFTUS SPRITE. P.O. Box 77290, Fontainbleau, 2032 Randburg, Johannesburg, R.S.A.
Suppliers of the CI Caravans "Bakkie Mate" (pick-up) accommodation unit demountable body shell.
GULF INDUSTRIES CC. P.O. Box 633, Randburg, 2125 Johannesburg, R.S.A. TEL: (011) 886-5637
4x4 safari motorhome conversions of Land Rover Forward Control (i.e. SIIB 109 & 110).

5. DOCUMENTATION, INSURANCE, MAPS & NAVIGATION

Sub Heading: Documentation

ENGLAND

HAMPSHIRE
AUTOMOBILE ASSOCIATION DEVELOPMENTS LTD. Fanum House, Basingstoke,
Hants RG21 2EA (0256) 20123 FAX: (0256) 460750
Similar to the RAC, the AA can issue Carnet documents in the UK for vehicles transmitting countries where customs import duties are levied. (Document exempts vehicle owner from paying duty).

LONDON
VISA SHOP WORLDWIDE. 194 Kensington High Street, London W8 7RG 071-938 3848
Specialists in obtaining visas for just about any country worldwide.
WORLDWIDE VISAS LIMITED. 9 Adelaide Street, Charing Cross, London WC2
071-379 0419/0376 FAX: 071-497 2590
Specialists in urgent visa acquisition & new passport processing/amendments plus embassy liason in UK & Europe, U.K. & U.S.A. immigration consultancy.

SURREY
ROYAL AUTOMOBILE CLUB. (Touring Information). RAC House, P.O. Box 100, South Croydon, Surrey CR2 6XW 071-686 2525
Along with the AA, the RAC is the only other issuer of Carnet documents in the UK.

FRANCE
AUTOMOBILE CLUB DE FRANCE. 6 Place de la Concorde, Paris 8e TEL: 4265 3470 or 265 6599
Issuers of the Carnet document in France.

GERMANY
AUTOMOBILCLUB VON DEUTSCHLAND. Neiderrad, Lyonstrasse 16, D-6000 Frankfurt, Germany.
Issuers of the Carnet document in Germany.

Sub Heading: Travel Insurance

GLOUCESTERSHIRE
FENNELL TURNER AND TAYLOR LTD. Southway House, South Way, Cirencester, Glos GL7 1HL (0285) 659685
Providers of trailer tent, folding caravan or camping equipment insurance.

HAMPSHIRE
ALEXANDER STENHOUSE UK LTD. Richmond House, College Street, Southampton, Hants SO9 4BZ (0703) 225616 FAX: (0703) 631055
Arrangers of The Expeditions Travel Insurance Scheme prepared in consultation with The Expedition Advisory Centre at The Royal Geographical Society, London.

LONDON
TRAILFINDERS. 194 Kensington High Street, London W8 7RG 071-938 3303
Travel insurance service.
WEXAS LTD. 45-49 Brompton Road, London SW3 1DE 071-589 0500
Travel insurance service.
CAMPBELL IRVINE. 42-48 Earls Court Road, Kensington, London W8 6EJ 071-938 3366
Issuers of the Carnet Indemnity Insurance Bond Guarantee required by the AA/RAC plus personal, vehicle and baggage insurance worldwide.
R.L. DAVIDSON. Bury House, 31 Bury Street, London EC3A 5AH
071-816 9876 FAX: 071-816 9880
Provide Carnet Bond Guarantees in relation to AA/RAC carnet documents. Also offer personal and baggage insurance for overland travel.

LINCOLNSHIRE
STEER & CO. 11 The Crescent, Spalding, Lincs PE11 1AE (0775) 768581 FAX: (0775) 725516
Specialists in arranging overseas insurance for expeditions, aid projects, commercial ventures, political/credit risks, cargo & transit.

MANCHESTER, GREATER
BRITISH MOUNTAINEERING COUNCIL. Crawford House, Precinct Centre, Booth Street East, Gtr Manchester M13 9RZ 061-273 5835
BMC Insurance for Climbers, Hillwalkers, Mountaineers & skiers.

WORCESTERSHIRE
A.C.C.E.O. INSURANCE SERVICES. Blair House, 67 High Street, Bewdley, Worcs DY12 2DJ (0299) 405489 FAX: (0299) 403141
Special caravan insurance rates for members of The ARC (Association of Rover Clubs Ltd.) and discounts on ferry bookings.

KENYA
HEMISPHERE INSURANCE CO. 1st Floor, Rooms 129 & 130 Mutual Building, Kimathi Street, P.O. Box 44228, Nairobi, Kenya. Nairobi 333501 & 337342
Providers of competitive insurance for the overland traveller having previously obtained short term insurance to transit to Nairobi.

ENGLAND

HAMPSHIRE
CHUTE MAP COMPANY LTD. Valance Cottage, Upper Chute, Nr Andover, Hants SP11 9EH
(0264) 70392
Lamination of maps and charts.
ORDNANCE SURVEY. Romsey Road, Maybush, Southampton, Hants SO9 4DH
(0703) 792792 FAX: (0703) 792404
Directorate of Overseas Surveys sells and produces maps for numerous countries in the following areas.
Mediterranean, Asia, Indian Ocean, Africa, Atlantic Ocean, Central & South America, Caribbean, Pacific
Ocean.

HERTFORDSHIRE
THE GOAD MAP SHOP. 8-12 Salisbury Square, Old Hatfield, Herts AL9 5BJ
(0707) 271171 FAX: (0707) 274641
Map sales for all leading publishers including Ordnance Survey. Maps for the whole of the U.K. and IGN
maps of France.

LONDON
THE ROYAL GEOGRAPHICAL SOCIETY. 1 Kensington Gore, London SW7 2AR
071-581 2057 FAX: 071-584 4447
Expedition Advisory Centre and Map Room open to the general public.
ROBERTSON, McCARTA LTD. 17 Angel Gate, 320 City Road, London EC1V 2PT 071-278 8278
Specialists in maps of France and Africa.
STANFORDS. 12-14 Long Acre, London WC2E 9PL 071-836 1321 FAX: 071-836 0189
The world's largest map shop - mail order service.

MIDDLESEX
MICHELIN TYRE PUBLIC LTD COMPANY. Tourism Sales Department, Davy House, Lyon Road,
Harrow, Middx HA1 2DQ 081-861 2121 FAX: 081-863 0680
Producers of Michelin range of maps and guides covering Europe, Africa etc.
ROGER LASCELLES. 47 York Road, Brentford, Middx TW8 0QP 081-847 0935 FAX: 081-568 3886
Worldwide cartographic publisher/stockist.

OXFORDSHIRE
BLACKWELL'S MAP & TRAVEL SHOP. 53 Broad Street, Oxford (0865) 792792
We stock a large range of maps, atlases, travel guides & travel writing. Books on cars are stocked next
door at BLACKWELL'S 50 Broad Street, Oxford

WORCESTERSHIRE
THE MAP SHOP. 15 High Street, Upton upon Severn, Worcs WR8 0HJ
(0684) 593146 FAX (0684) 594559
Maps and guide books. Comprehensive stock of international maps including highly detailed satellite
desert charts used by Rally/Raid navigators in top events such as Paris-Dakar. Agents for many
country's large scale official mapping worldwide.

SCOTLAND

LOTHIAN & BORDERS
THOMAS NELSON & SONS LTD. 51 York Place, Edinburgh EH1 3JD 031-557 3012
Main agent for Ordnance Survey maps throughout Scotland.

WALES

SOUTH GLAMORGAN
LEAR'S BOOKSHOP. 13-17 Royal Parade, Cardiff CF1 2PR (0222) 395036
Ordnance Survey main agents. Full range of maps including Landranger, tourist, outdoor, leisure,
Michelin & Routemaster.

FRANCE

INSTITUTE GEOGRAPHIQUE NATIONAL (IGN). 107 Rue la Boetie, 75008 Paris, France.
Stockists/producers of a wide range of maps covering former French colonies many in very large scales.
L'ASTROLABE-LA LIBRARIE DU VOYAGEUR. 46 Rue de Provence, 75009 Paris, France
TEL: 285.42.95
A leading map shop, specialising in maps difficult to obtain.

GERMANY

DARR EXPEDITION SERVICE GmbH. Thereisenstrasse 66, D-8000, Munich 2, Germany
TEL: 0049-89-282023 FAX: 0049-89-282525
Stockist of all types of maps.
ILH GEOCENTER. Postfach 80, 0830, D-7000, Stuttgart 80, Germany TEL: 0711 735 3448.
BERND WOICK GmbH. Gutenbergstresse 14, 7302, Ostfildern 4, Germany
TEL: 0711-455038 FAX: 0711 4560526
Supplier of maps and navigation equipment.

HUNGARY

CARTOGRAPHIA. H-1149, Budapest, Bosnyak Ter 5. TEL: 163-3639 FAX: (36-1) 163-4639
Producers of large scale maps of Eastern European countries the former Soviet Union and many countries
with former communist leanings, ie. North Vietnam, Angola, Mozambique, Cuba, Ethiopia etc.

KENYA

SURVEY OF KENYA. The Public Maps Office, The Lands Department, off Harambee Avenue, City
Square, P.O. Box 30089, Nairobi.
Producer of an excellent selection of detailed maps, plus good quality Game Park maps.

SOUTH AFRICA

CARTE AFRIQUE (PTY) LTD. P.O. Box 1943, 2041 Houghton, Johannesburg, R.S.A.
TEL: (011) 728-1520 FAX: (011) 967-1186
Suppliers of difficult to obtain maps, special emphasis on Africa, from entire continent to local street
maps.
READERS DIGEST OF SOUTH AFRICA. 4th Floor United Towers, 160 Main Street, Johannesburg
2001, R.S.A. TEL: 27-11-230591 FAX: 21-11-230222
Producer of some excellent large scale maps of the Southern African continent.

SWITZERLAND

KUMMERLEY & FREY. Hallerstrasse 6-10, 3001 Bern, Switzerland
TEL: 031 23 36 66/23 51 11 FAX: 031 24 89 31
Producers of world maps, specialising in the Alps region of Europe.

Sub Heading: Navigation

ENGLAND

ESSEX
EUROVERSAL LTD. The Manor House, Little Square, Braintree, Essex CM7 7UT (0376) 327705
Navigation training courses for overland vehicles. Theory, practice, map reading scales, bearings,
compasses, landmarks, GPS, etc.

HAMPSHIRE
TRIMBLE NAVIGATION EUROPE LTD. Trimble House, Meridian Office Park, Osborn Way,
Hook, Hants RG27 9HX (0256) 760150 FAX: (0256) 760148
Manufacturers of the "Trimble-Ensign" GPS navigation system.

HERTFORDSHIRE
GLOBAL POSITIONING LTD. Greystones House, The Warren, Radlett, Herts WD7 7DS
(0923) 853322 FAX: (0923) 853926
Portable GPS in the palm of your hand. Gives latitude, longitude and altitude. 3 channel digital GPS
tracks up to 8 satellites. Only 397g.

KENT
S.I.R.S. NAVIGATION LTD. Swanscombe, Kent DA10 0BR (0322) 383672
The Navigator Auto-Compass - specially designed for accurate use within vehicles. A reliable, rugged
instrument @ only £49.50 + £2.50 p & p

LONDON
ELECTROTECH. Unit 6, Drury Way Industrial Estate, Laxcon Close, London NW10 0TG
081-451 6766
Europe's largest range of Global Positioning Systems (GPS) i.e. Hand held tracks up to 8 satellites,
Latitude / Longitude, accuracy to within 25 metres.

PUMKIN MARINE & LEISURE LTD. 100 The Highway, London E1 9BX
071-480 6630 FAX: 071-481 8905
Britain's biggest, brightest discount stores stocking fixed or handheld GPS systems, compasses, radar,
VHF radios etc. London/Poole/Southampton.

NORTHAMPTONSHIRE
ULTIMATE DESIGN. 37 Pytchley Road, Kettering, Northants NN15 6ND
(0536) 514400 24 hours FAX: (0536) 415050
Electronic vehicle compasses: Analogue display: £59 LCD Self-calibrating: £99.75 Electronic route
planner: £299 Please phone for colour brochure.

SUFFOLK
VIKING OPTICAL LTD. Unit 1C, Blyth Road, Industrial Estate, Halesworth, Suffolk IP19 8EN
Distributors of Suunto Compasses.

SURREY
SILVA (UK) LTD. Unit 10, Sky Business Park, Eversley Way, Egham, Surrey TW20 8RF
(0784) 471721 FAX: (0784) 471097
Silva produces the greatest range of magnetic compasses in the world for every type of navigator - GPS
also available.
STREAMLINE TECHNOLOGY LIMITED. 423A Ewell Road, Surbiton, Surrey KT6 7DG
081-241 8272 FAX: 081-241 8308
Manufacture & development of high performance GPS navigation receivers for marine and all other uses.
Phone for full details of products available.

WEST MIDLANDS
ZEMCO LTD. 509 Walsgrave Road, Coventry CV2 4AG (0203) 441428 FAX: (0203) 444197
Manufacturers of electronic compasses.

GERMANY
GPS. GESELLSCHAFT FUR PROFESSIONELLE SATELLITNNAVIGATION GmbH.
Thereisenstrasse 66, 8000 Munich 2, Germany
TEL: (089) 280 24 56 or (089) 28 20 33 FAX: (089) 28 25 25
GPS satellite navigation systems available from the following manufacturers: Garmin, Magellan, Trimble,
Hewlett Packard, Rockwell International and Sony.
BERND WOICK GmbH. Gutenbergstresse 14, 7302, Ostfildern 4, Germany
TEL: 0711-455038 FAX: 0711 4560526
Supplier of navigation equipment.

SOUTH AFRICA
OPTRON. P.O. Box 1462, Rivonia 2128, Johannesburg, R.S.A.
TEL: (011) 803-3136 FAX: (011) 803-4803
Distributors of Trimble Navigation GPS units.

6. MEDICAL, SAFETY & SECURITY

ENGLAND
AVON
THE EAST AFRICAN FLYING DOCTOR SERVICE (AMREF). 11 Waterloo Street, Clifton,
Bristol BS8 4BT (0272) 238424 FAX: (0272) 237607
Provide medical and aircraft rescue services throughout East Africa.

BERKSHIRE
BAYER (UK) LTD. Bayer House, Strawberry Hill, Newbury, Berks RG13 1JA (0635) 39000
Manufacturers of Autan insect repellant in aerosol, cream and stick form.
HOUSEMAN (BURNHAM) LTD. The Priory, Burnham, Slough, Berks SL1 7LS (06286) 4488
Manufacturers of 25 & 200 litre plastic drums.
WYETH LABORATORIES. Huntercombe Lane South, Taplow, Maidenhead, Berkshire (06286) 4377
Produce anti-venoms against poisonous snakes of the United States.

CUMBRIA
GREGSON PACK FIRST AID SYSTEM. Solway Trading Estate, Maryport, Cumbria CA15 8NF
(0900) 818276
First aid pack for mountaineers, canoeists and outdoors types.

HAMPSHIRE
SAFARI (WATER TREATMENTS) LTD. P.O. Box 56 Basing View, Basingstoke, Hampshire (0256) 29292
Water purifiers for portable, domestic, commercial and medical use.

KENT
PRE-MAC (KENT) LTD. Unit 1, 103 Goods Station Road, Tunbridge Wells, Kent TN1 2DP (0892) 34361 FAX: (0892) 515770
Manufacturers of PWP personal water purifiers. Tested to the highest possible standards and accepted by the M.O.D.
SIMMONSON & WEEL LTD. Heatherley House, Heatherley Road, Sidcup, KentDA14 4BR (0130) 01128 .
Manufacturers of portable splints.

LINCOLNSHIRE
KATADYN PRODUCTS LTD. 37 Town End, Wilsford, Grantham, Lincs NG32 3NX (0400) 30285
UK suppliers of the Katadyn system of water filters.

LONDON
HOSPITAL FOR TROPICAL DISEASES. 3 St Pancras Way, London NW1 OPE 071-387 4411
Recorded call/touchtone phone access:- (0898) 345081
Yellow fever vaccination centre and main UK hospital for treatment of tropical diseases; has an information service advising on requirements country by country.
JOHN BELL & CROYDEN. 54 Wigmore Street, London W1H OAU 071-935 5555
Suppliers of a wide range of pharmaceuticals and surgical supplies.Can advise and kit out overland medical kits.
MASTA. (Medical Advisory Service for Travellers Abroad), Keppel Street, London WC1E 7HT 071-631 4408
Can provide personal immunization schedules. Telephone 0891 224100 for free Health Brief for up to 6 countries.
NOMAD PHARMACY. 3-4 Wellington Terrace, Turnpike Lane, London N8 OPX 081-889 7014 FAX: 081-889 9529
North London Vaccination Centre. A travel pharmacy offering free consultations with resident pharmacist. Medical kits made to order at low cost.

MIDDLESEX
DENTAL PROJECTS LABORATORIES. Blakesley Lodge, Green Street, Sunbury-on-Thames, Middlesex (0932) 80303
Dentifix emergency dental kits.
HOECHST PHARMACEUTICALS. Salisbury Road, Hounslow, Middlesex.
Producers of anti-snake bite kits and serum for all areas of the world.

NORFOLK
OASIS. 1 High Street, Stoke Ferry, Kings Lynn, Norfolk PE33 9SF (0366) 500466 FAX: (0366) 501122
Suppliers of mosquito nets, insect repellents, DIY net re-treatment kits.

STAFFORDSHIRE
FAIRE INDUSTRIAL CERAMICS LTD. Filleybrooks, Stoney, Staffs ST15 0PU (0785) 813241 FAX: (0785) 818733
Manufacturers of Doulton and British Berkefeld Inline and portable water filters.

SURREY
SLANEYS. 40A Church Road, Richmond upon Thames, Surrey TW10 6LN 081-940 8634
Suppliers of Snake bite kits and medical expedition supplies.
TRUB ENVIRONMENTAL PRODUCTS. Dept 12, P.O. Box 29, Epsom, Surrey KT17 1XY 081-686 8896
Manufacturers of 12 volt mosquito killer lights.

SUSSEX, WEST
ARUN TRADING COMPANY LTD. Tripp Hill, Fittleworth, Pulborough, W Sussex RH20 1ER (0798) 82482
Distributors of Jungle Formula Insect Repellent.

FRANCE

INSTITUT PASTEUR. 25 Rue de Docteur Roux, 75724 Paris, Cedex 15, France
TEL: 306-22-63
Providers of anti-snake bite kits worldwide.

KENYA

THE EAST AFRICAN FLYING DOCTOR SERVICE. P.O. Box 30125, Wilson Airport, Nairobi, Kenya. Nairobi 501300 or 501123
British office located in Bristol - see above entry listed under Avon.

SOUTH AFRICA

PURE WATER CORPORATION. P.O. Box 413, Randburg, Johannesburg, R.S.A.
TEL: (011) 792-7109 FAX: (011) 792-6876
"PentaPure" portable water purification filter system.

7. MISCELLANEOUS ITEMS for OVERLAND & INDEPENDENT TRAVEL

ENGLAND

BUCKINGHAMSHIRE
ASSOCIATED OPTICAL. Unit 2, 64 High Street, Burnham, Bucks SL1 7JT (0628) 605433
Suppliers of Eschenback foldable prism binoculars.

HAMPSHIRE
DIRECT FOODS LTD. 20 Levant Street, Petersfield, Hants GU33 3LT (0730) 4911
Ranch House ready made meals and Protoveg products. Expedition discount 25%.
R. TWINNING & CO LTD. South Way, Andover, Hampshire SP10 5AQ
Foil tray packs of complete dinners cooked by immersion in boiling water. These are not dehydrated and do not need refrigeration.

LANCASHIRE
MAINAIR SPORTS LTD. Unit 2 Alma Industrial Estate, Regent Street, Rochdale, Lancs OL12 0HQ
(0706) 55134
Suppliers of Thommen altimeters.

LONDON
SWISS CUTLERY (LONDON) LTD. Victrinox House, 56/58 Crewys Road, London NW2 2AD
081-209 0123
U.K. Suppliers of the famous Swiss Army Knife and other assorted hunting knives etc.

MIDDLESEX
BAUSCH AND LOMB (UK) LTD. 74 Oldfield Road, Hampton, Middx TW12 2HR 081-979 7788
Suppliers of binoculars, telescopes and sunglasses.

NORTHAMPTONSHIRE
ALADDIN INTERNATIONAL INC. Warehouse 5, Westgate Interchange Estate, Saddleback Road, Northants NN5 5HL
Suppliers of the Grand Tornus French candle lamp.

SOUTH YORKSHIRE
HOTCAN LTD. Stadium Court, Parkgate, Rotherham, S Yorkshire S62 6EW (0709) 69856/9
Suppliers of self-heating meals in a can. Open the lid and the contents is self heated by a catalytic compound.

WORCESTERSHIRE
TYRENFIRE LTD. Unit 23 Bond Industrial Estate, Wickhamford, Nr Evesham, Worcs WR11 6RT
(0386) 860056
Manufacturers of a CO_2 tyre inflator (Carbon Dioxide).

SCOTLAND

PERTHSHIRE
ARDBLAIR SPORTS IMPORTS LTD. James Street, Blairgowrie, Perthshire PH10 8EZ (0250) 3863
Suppliers of Big Pack inflatable canoes.

WALES

MID GLAMORGAN
CHRONAR LTD. Unit 1, Waterton Industrial Estate, Bridgend, Mid Glam CF31 3YN (0656) 61211
Manufacturers of portable Solar Powered electrical panels.
RAVEN FOODS LTD. BCB International Ltd. Moorland Road, Cardiff, Mid Glam CF2 2YL
(0222) 464464
Dehydrated foods in day packs for 1, 2 or 10 persons.

CROSS REFERENCE: See also WHEELS

ENGLAND

BUCKINGHAMSHIRE
SINTON TYRES LTD. Unit 15, Broughton Manor Farm, Broughton, Milton Keynes,
Bucks MK10 9AA (0908) 665591 FAX: (0908) 604667
American General 4x4 tyre importers. Huge range of sizes and types. Available from over 400 retail tyre
specialists nationwide.

CHESHIRE
NATIONAL TYRES AND AUTOCARE. 80-82 Wellington Road North, Stockport,
Cheshire SK4 1HR 061-480 7461 FREEPHONE: (0800) 626666 FOR NEAREST BRANCH
4x4 tyres and wheels, other tyres, exhausts, batteries & range of auto services. Check for service before
travelling, 400 branches nationwide.

CORNWALL
BARRITTS. The National ATV Centre, Retallack Adventure Park, St. Columb, Cornwall TR9 6DE
(0637) 880080 FAX: (0637) 881464
U.K.'s leading ATV specialist for tyres/tubes/wheels/gaskets/batteriesbrake pads/shoes. ATV & Personal
Water Craft sales, hire, repairs, spares.

ESSEX
MICKEY THOMPSON PERFORMANCE TYRES. Unit B, Chelford Court, 37 Robjohns Road,
Chelmsford, Essex CM1 3AG (0245) 344170 FAX: (0245) 344172
4x4 tyre and wheel specialists.

HAMPSHIRE
CHESSINGTON TYRES LTD. Bordon Trading Estate, Bordon, Hants GU35 9HH
(0420) 477401 FAX: (0420) 477341
Tyre specialists * All brands * Huge stocks * Mail order facilities *Supply and fitting at 35 branches.
MICHELDEVER TYRE SERVICES. Micheldever Station, Winchester, Hants SO21
(0962) 89437 FAX: (0962) 89572
We're one of the largest tyre suppliers in the country: Avon, Dunlop, Firestone, Goodyear, Michelin,
Pirelli, Bridgestone, Yokohama etc.
NORTH HANTS TYRES. 10-30 Fleet Road, Fleet, Hants GU13 8QG (0252) 613261 (0252) 812225
American tyre & wheel importers. Please call for our free catalogue.

HEREFORDSHIRE
IAN JONES TYRES. Hatton Gardens, Kington, Hereford HR5 3DE (0544) 230 291
All major brands of import tyres for the complete range of truck/motor cycle/tractor/4x4 vehicle/A.T.V./
lawnmower/autograss mud & snow.

HERTFORDSHIRE
QUEENS PARK TYRES LTD. Baldock Tyres, Unit 22, London Road Industrial Estate, Baldock,
Herts SG7 6NG (0462) 894772/491315
Avon, Cooper, Merit, BF Goodrich. 1000's of tyres in stock, please ring for a quote.

HUMBERSIDE
INTA-TOWN TYRES. Hallgate, Pocklington, York YO4 2BT (0759) 30527
Wide range of 4x4 tyres. General, Marshal, Goodyear, Firestone, Mabor, Michelin, Powerguard, Bridgestone. Mail order next day delivery.

KENT
RUD CHAINS LTD. Units 10-12 John Wilson Business Park, Thane Way, Whitstable, Kent (0227) 276611 MOBILE: (0836) 276992
Non-skid chains for all types of vehicles.

MANCHESTER, GREATER
QUEEN STREET TYRE SERVICE. 47a Queen Street, Wigan WN3 4HX (0942) 46409
Four wheel drive specialist - General Grabber, Mickey Thompson, BF Goodrich, Dunlop, Bridgestone, Dick Cepek, Avon, Kumho Military etc.

MERSEYSIDE
KIRKBY (TYRES) LTD. Speke Hall Avenue, Speke, Liverpool L24 1UU
051-486 8800 FAX: 051-486 5391
Wholesale tyre distributors. Land Rover, 4x4, tractor, flotation, turf forestry, ATV tyres and tubes. Trade, OE and export enquires welcome.

MIDDLESEX
MICHELIN TYRE PLC. Davy House, Lyon Road, Harrow, Middx HA1 2DQ
081-861 2121 FAX: 081-863 0680
Tyres for Land Rover, Range Rover and virtually all 4x4 vehicles.

NORTHAMPTONSHIRE
TOYO TYRE (UK). Toyo House, Shipton Way, Express Park, Rushden, Northants N10 9GL
(0933) 411144 FAX: (0933) 410945
Manufacturers of a small but elite range of 4x4 tyres (including the '785' 205 R 15), suitable for Land Rover, Range Rover and Discovery.

OXFORDSHIRE
CHARLETT TYRES LTD. 81-89 Cassington Road, Yarnton, Oxon. OX5 1QB (0865) 842727
Michelin, Yokohama, Goodyear, Continental and more. New bargains, Nato ice-studded, military, part worn etc. Most sizes - please ring.

SHROPSHIRE
CHASE TYRES. Unit E1, Halesfield 23, Telford, Salop TF7 4NY (0952)684039
4x4 tyre specialist. For your on/off road vehicles including Land Rover, Range Rover and Discovery. Open Mon-Fri 8.30-5.30, Sat 9.00-4.00

STAFFORDSHIRE
J. WHIELDON TYRES. Regent Street, Leek, Staffs ST13 6LX (0538) 383324
4x4 tyres & wheels. Official BF Goodrich tyre stockist. Other makes include Kelly Safari, Goodyear, Pirelli, Toyo, Semperit. Carriage available.
NORTH STAFFS TYRE & BATTERY. Lightwood Road, Longton, Stoke-on-Trent, Staffs ST3 4JT (0782) 593091
Land Rover/Range Rover/Discovery tyre and wheel specialists with over twenty years in the business. We guarantee you won't find a better deal!
OLYMPIC TYRE CO. The Old Exchange, Fyfield Road, Staponhill, Burton on Trent, Staffs DE15 9QA (0283) 63004 FAX: (0283) 510787
Sole importer of Olympic brand from Australia. Large tyre stocks for Land Rover, farm, grassland, light truck etc. at our UK warehouse.

SUFFOLK
B.J.L. FIELDEN LTD. Starhouse Farm, Onehouse, Stowmarket, Suffolk IP14 3EL
(0449) 675071 MOBILE: (0836) 619479 FAX: (0449) 678282
Agents for Kelly, Goodyear & BF Goodrich. Budget tyres usually in stock. Information & help from friendly experienced staff. Free brochure.

WARWICKSHIRE
SOUTHAM TYRES LTD. Southam Drive, Southam, Warwicks CV33 0JH
(0926) 813888 MOBILE: (0831) 630571 FAX: (0926) 817724
B.F. Goodrich tyres; the largest range of patterns and sizes for Land Rover/Discovery/Range Rover. On and off-road applications.

Please mention MACK'S when you phone or fax.

TRELLEBORG LTD. 90 Somers Road, Rugby, Warwicks CV22 7ED
(0788) 562711/541147 FAX: (0788) 579959
Manufacturers/wholesalers of specialist tyres for forestry, agricultural, industrial machinery and grassland applications.

WEST MIDLANDS
BRIDGESTONE/FIRESTONE UK LTD. Bridgestone House, Birchley Trading Estate, Oldbury, Warley B69 1DT 021-552 3331 FAX: 021-552 5559
Manufacture and supply of all 4x4 tyres.
TYRE CARE (BIRMINGHAM). 70 Taylor Road, Kings Heath, Birmingham B13 0PG
021-441 2607
Tyres for 4x4 at competitive prices. If you want to fit them yourself, ask for my over the counter prices. Waxoil service available. Phone now.

WILTSHIRE
ARROW THE TYRE SUPPLIER. Elgin Drive, Swindon, Wilts SN2 6DN (0793) 51260
The major 4x4 stockist for the South and South West. Wheels & tyres supplied throughout the UK.
Bridgestone/Pirelli/Yokohama/BF Goodrich.
AVON TYRES LIMITED. Bath Road, Melksham Wilts SN12 8AA
(0225) 703101 FAX: (0225) 707880
Avon produces a range of high quality tyres for 4x4 vehicles and are also a recommended fitment for Land Rover.

SCOTLAND

STRATHCLYDE
COOPER BROS. Overtown Road, Newmains, Wishaw, Strathclyde ML2 7EH
(0698) 385477 FAX: (0698) 386673
Specialists in 4x4 tyres - BF Goodrich, Camac, Bridgestone, Kelly, Goodyear, Michelin, Avon. Exhausts and batteries.

N IRELAND

CO. TYRONE
TYRE SAFETY CENTRE (CO TYRONE) LTD. 2-8 Dungannon Road, Cookstown, Co. Tyrone, N Ireland BT80 (06487) 62528 FAX: (06487) 66634
BF Goodrich: Weather beating traction - world beating handling. Delivery anywhere in Ireland.

WALES

GLAMORGAN, SOUTH
A & A AUTO SERVICES. Leckwith Industrial Estate, Whittle Road, Cardiff CF1 8AT
(0222) 644178 3 lines FAX: (0222) 237252
For all your tyre requirements: BF Goodrich/Yokohama/Bridgestone/General Grabber/Michelin/ Toyo/Marshal/Kelly/Fulda/Goodyear. Mail order welcome. See our display advertisements in 'TYRE' CATEGORY or REAR INSIDE COVER.

GWENT
PONTHIR TYRE SERVICES. Unit 3, Boxer Trading Estate, Ponthir Road, Caerleon, Gwent NP6 1NY
(0633) 420211
Ponthir Tyre Services; tyre retailers and home of the Super Mud Plugga - aggressive remoulds.

POWYS
MOTORWAY REMOULDS LTD. Mill Green, Knighton, Powys LD7 1EE
(0547) 528525 (7 lines) FAX: (0547) 520470
Trade only remoulds manuf'd to BS AU144. 600.16/650.16/750.16 cross plys or dual traction, 195 R 15/ 215 R 15/205 R 16 M&S radials, 750 R 16 ZY radials.

A&A AUTO SERVICES

THE COMPANY THAT CARES

ENGLAND

AVON
RICHARD JAMES (BRISTOL) LTD. 48 Davis Street, Avonmouth, Bristol BS11 9JW
Tel: (0272) 828575 Fax: (0272) 826361 Telex: 449752 Chacom G
Suppliers of Land Rover & all motor vehicle spare parts, UK & overseas. Land Rover servicing & repairs. Large stock of new & s/h spares.

BERKSHIRE
ROVERTUNE READING. The Forge, Whitchurch Hill, Pangbourne, Berks RG8 (0734) 842777/842000
Many used parts/spares including body shells, gear/transfer boxes, chassis, axles, body panels, engines, interiors etc. Some new parts available.

CHESHIRE
FROGGATT'S RANGE ROVER SALES. Unit 2 Whirley Quarry, Sandy Lane, Whirley, Macclesfield SK10 4RJ (0625) 425524 MOBILE (0860) 479462 FAX (0625) 619494
Massive selection of used parts and accessories. Please telephone (0625) 425524 for all your Range Rover requirements.
RESCUE RANGERS. 18 Daneside Business Park, Riverdane Road, Congleton CW12 1UN (0260) 298787 MOBILE: (0831) 620476
Range Rover spares. Breaking 2 and 4-door vehicles. Far too many parts to list. Stock constantly changing, phone for current availability.

CUMBRIA
S.A. BURNE. Bonnie Mount, Edenhall, Penrith, Cumbria CA11 8SR (0768) 881624/881388
Vehicle breakers: Land Rovers, cars, vans & wagons.

ESSEX
G & L AUTO SPARES. Haven Road, Hythe Quay, Colchester, Essex CO2 8HT (0206) 790055
Specialists in secondhand Range Rover parts. Open 6 days per week.

HAMPSHIRE
B & H SERVICES. Unit 3, Beavers Yard, Pack Lane, Basingstoke, Hants RG22 5HR (0256) 810144 MOBILE: (0860) 509248 FAX: (0256) 810144
Range Rover new and used spares. Large selection including engines, gearboxes, body panels, interiors, etc.
FOUR BUY. Bordon Motors Industrial Estate, High Street, Bordon, Hants GU35 0AW (0420) 4777707 MOBILE: (0831) 270332
4-wheel drive recycling. Four wheel drive parts bought and sold.
KEITH GOTT LANDROVERS. Greenwood Farm, Old Odiham Road, Alton, Hants GU34 4BW (0420) 544330 MOBILE: (0860) 737925 FAX: (0420) 544331
We generally have a good selection of used spares for Land Rover. Series IIA, III and some 90 & 110. Mechanical and body parts available.

HEREFORDSHIRE
DOCKLOW LAND ROVER SERVICES. Lower Docklow Farm, Docklow, Hereford HR6 0RZ (056882) 248
Breakers of Land Rovers/Range Rovers. All parts available. Service Exchange engines & gearboxes. Also new spares and accessories.

KENT
ROVER RECLAIM. Unit 7A, Tech. Centre, Castle Road, Sittingbourne, Kent ME10 3RG (0795) 435029 MOBILE: (0860) 672285 FAX: (0795) 435029
Range Rover/Land Rover new & used spares inc body panels off the shelf(all guaranteed) C.O.D. possible. Wanted: LR's & RR's for dismantling.

LONDON
GO-T-EL LANDROVERS. Office: 14 Cliffsend House, Normandy Rd, London SW9 6HE
071-820 0959 Workshop: 55 Woolwich Church St, Woolwich SE18 081-855 3201
London's premier Land Rover breakers at the most competitive prices. See our advertisement for further details.

MILL HILL SPARES. 493-499 Watford Way, Mill Hill, London NW7 081-203 2111
British used spares specialist. Range Rovers/Discoverys/Rovers. Most parts off the shelf.

MANCHESTER, GREATER
MANCHESTER LAND ROVER & GYPSY BREAKERS. Hopes Carr Garage, 36 Upper Brook Street, Stockport, Gtr Manchester SK1 3BP 061-480 3165
New & used spares. Expert repairs, MOT preparation, chassis welding etc. MOT failures bought. Gearbox specialist. Always breaking Land Rovers.

NORFOLK
ROVER PART. Wayside Garage, Holt Road, Norwich NR10 3EE (0603) 891209 FAX: (0603) 890330
Rover SDi/800 breakers. SDi engines & spares - many parts compatible with Range Rover etc. Fast mail order service.

WEST MIDLANDS
AGRICULTURAL & CROSS COUNTRY VEHICLES. Drayton Mount Farm, Belbroughton, Stourbridge, West Midlands DY9 0BL
DAY: (0562) 730404 EVENING: (0562) 748862 FAX: (0562) 748862
Used Land Rover, Range Rover & Discovery spares. Breaking most models plus wide range of new & reconditioned spares. Friendly service.

WORCESTERSHIRE
PATHFINDER SUPPLIES. 79 Easemore Road, Redditch, Worcs B98 8EY (0527) 67476
Home-based friendly spares supplier; IIA specialist. Also off-road and recovery accessories, some new spares. Please send a S.A.E. for lists.

Have you got a shed full of 4x4 bits you don't want but would like to turn into instant cash?
  OR
Are you a trader looking for an easy way to reach those elusive customers?
OR
Are you still looking for that 'fluffer return pivot valve' for your twin overhead cam toolbox at a bargain price?

IF THE ANSWER IS YES

Then look no further than:

MIDLAND

4x4

AUTO JUMBLES

Events are held regularly throughout the country at proper sites with decent facilities for all the family and at a sensible price. For full details of our next event send a SAE to:

Midland 4x4 Auto Jumbles, P.O. Box 14, Tenbury Wells, Worcester
or Telephone: (0584) 810073

ENGLAND

BERKSHIRE
JAMES TAYLOR. Hollybush Lodge, South Stoke Road, Woodcote, Reading RG8 0PL (0491) 681915
Rover & Land Rover author and journalist.

KENT
BULLITT MINIATURE CARS. Pivington Works, Pluckley, Nr Ashford, Kent TN27 0PG
(0233) 84656 FAX: (0233) 84788
Mini electric Range Rover 1800mm x 1143mm, ideal for kids - or adults! 12V electrics/4hp motor/disc
brakes/coil springs. Also Jeep/Hi-Lux/buggy

LEICESTERSHIRE
PETE WILFORD. 56 Blunts Lane, Wigston Magna, Leicester LE18 2HA (0533) 881783
Land Rover cartoonist. Producer of calenders, Xmas cards etc. Commissions undertaken.

LONDON
MEDIAID. Headquarters, 102 Beaconsfield Road, London N15 4SQ 081-802 4625
Voluntary ambulance service comprising 3 fully equipped vehicles (including Land Rover).
Off-road/sports events, fêtes etc. Also first aid courses.

NOTTINGHAMSHIRE
AMBULINK INTERNATIONAL LTD. P.O. Box 7, Hucknall, Nottingham NG15 6EW
(0602) 638107 (24 hours) FAX: (0602) 632625
Range Rover ambulance available for national, international and club events. Units fully equipped.
Experienced Paramedic personnel.

SOMERSET
NICK DIMBLEBY. West View, Minehead Road, Bishop's Lydeard, Taunton, Somerset TA4 3BS
DAY: (0273) 696773 EVENING: (0823) 432787
Freelance motoring writer and photographer, Land Rover and off-road colour library, automotive PR
photography and text.

STAFFORDSHIRE
MARJORIE KING PHOTOGRAPHICS. 16 Holly Street, Cannock, Staffs WS11 2RU (0543) 423326
Club newsletters/membership forms, in fact any printed material designed or typeset/printed/distributed
incl. photography on site/location undertaken.
RAINBOW ROVERS. Stony Rock Farm, Waterhouses, Stoke on Trent, Staffs ST10 3LH
(0538) 308352
An independent organisation supplying vehicles/aid to Africa. Please contact Robert Ivins for further
information.

SURREY
ROGER CROWHURST MJI dip NEBSS. 'Windrush', 13 Eastlands Way, Oxted, Surrey RH8 0LP
(0883) 713079
Consultant Editor, freelance writer, car and industrial photographer and cartoonist. Member of The
Chartered Institute of Journalists and the Motoring Press Group.

TYNE & WEAR
LAND ACCESS AND RECREATION ASSOCIATION (LARA). P.O. Box 19,
Newcastle upon Tyne NE3 5HW TEL: 091 236 4082
The independent body to contact regarding Green Lane information.

WARWICKSHIRE
BRITISH MOTOR INDUSTRY HERITAGE TRUST. Gaydon, Warwickshire CV35 0BJ
(0926) 641188
The largest car collection in the world of British motor vehicles. The 300 exhibits include HUE 166, the
very first Land Rover ever made, and a 1971 Darien Gap Range Rover. There is also a small off-road
course available run by Land Rover Driving Experience. Please telephone for further details.

SCOTLAND

LOTHIAN
SCOTTISH RIGHTS OF WAY SOCIETY LTD. John Cotton Business Centre, 10/12 Sunnyside, Edinburgh EH7 5RA
Source of the publication - *Rights of Way: A Guide to the Law in Scotland.*

STRATHCLYDE
NORTHERN PARAMEDICAL SERVICES. 01/8 Leyden Court, Glasgow G20 9LY 041-945 5701
Safety & rescue units covering all types of off-road and sporting event. Range Rover-based Dakar Rapid Intervention Vehicle. 2/4 wheel drive rescue units/ambulances. RAC MSA licensed crews, paramedics, specialist equipment. The whole of Scotland & Northern England covered.

WALES

GLAMORGAN, SOUTH
c/o DAVIES COLOUR LAB. 168 Sloper Road, Cardiff CF1 8AA (0222) 230565 FAX: (0222) 221416
A unique vehicle available for hire - The Popemobile Range Rover. Please contact owner John Davies for further details.

VEHICLE SALES
CROSS REFERENCE: See also INDEPENDENT 4WD SPECIALISTS
MILITARY/EX-MILITARY REFURBISHMENT/RENNOVATION

ENGLAND

BEDFORDSHIRE
LW VASS LTD. Station Road, Amptill, Beds MK45 2RB (0525) 403255
Large selection of diesel SWB & LWB. All types available including ex M.O.D. vehicles from £800. Also full workshop facilities & spares service.

BERKSHIRE
BLUE GARAGE. 556-560 Reading Road, Winnersh, Nr Wokingham, Berks RG11 5HA
(0734) 774261 MOBILE: (0831) 301170 FAX: (0734) 891482
Largest selection of fully serviced & warranted 'A' to 'H'-plate Range Rover/Land Rover used vehicles in the south. Always 40 in stock.

CAMBRIDGESHIRE
R.J. LANDROVERS. 1 High Street, Sawtry, Huntingdon, Cambs PE17 5SR
(0487) 830813 MOBILE: (0860) 873958 FAX: (0487) 832300
Large selection of low milage civilian vehicles, plus ex MOD LWB, lightweights, ambulances & Forward Controls - LHD/RHD. Exports welcome.

CHESHIRE
FROGGATT'S RANGE ROVER SALES. Whirley Quarry, Sandy Lane, Whirley, Macclesfield SK10 4RJ (0625) 425524 MOBILE (0860) 479462 FAX (0625) 619494
Range Rover sales - large stocks of petrol & diesel Range Rovers, diesel conversion specialist. Massive stocks of new and secondhand parts.

CLEVELAND
STEVE GRAHAM SERVICES. Windsor Street, Haverton Hill, Stockton-on-Tees, Cleveland (0642) 564964
Tired of looking at rubbish? Then test drive one of our Land Rovers rebuilt using 90% new or reconditioned parts. Vehicles built to customer spec.

CO. DURHAM
J.D PATCHETT. Please telephone for address (0388) 730329
Land Rovers bought & sold. Always several in stock. Re-chassis service plus parts & spares. Open 7 days per week.

DERBYSHIRE
HIGH PEAK 4x4. The Bridge, Albion Road, New Mills, Derbyshire (0663) 741091
Land Rover sales including refurbished "High Peak Rovers". We usually have a choice of 15 vehicles for sale, most have 12 months MOT. Mon-Sat 9-5

DEVON

WINSTON PINCOMBE. The Garage, South Molton Street, Chumleigh, Devon EX18 7BW
DAY: (0769) 80900 EVENING: (0884) 860593
Land Rover/Range Rover and Discovery used vehicle sales. Also main distributors for Ifor Williams trailers in Devon.

DORSET

JOHN BENNS MOTOR COMPANY. Minster Garage, Wimborne Road, Walford, Dorset BH21 1NN
(0202) 883417
Range Rover and executive car specialists. Sales, service, car hire. Low mileage vehicles bought for cash.

ESSEX

THE 4x4 CENTRE. 56-58 Chigwell Road, South Woodford, London E18 081-518 8322
We buy and sell 4 wheel drive including Land Rover, Range Rover, Discovery, Lada, Suzuki, Mitsubishi, Daihatsu and much more.
BOUNDARY GARAGE. 343 London Road, Hadleigh, Essex SS7 2BT
DAY: (0702) 554586 EVENING <MOBILE>: (0860) 846101
Discovery and Range Rover desperately wanted for instant cash purchase. Highest prices assured, benevolent buyer calls nationwide.
ROGER M. BASS. Curtis Mill Green, Stapleford Tawney, Romford, Essex RM4 1RT
(0708) 688372 FAX: (0708) 688578
Land Rover, Range Rover, Discovery, Defender - worldwide vehicle sales. Full dealer facilities.

HAMPSHIRE

KEITH GOTT LANDROVERS. Greenwood Farm, Old Odiham Road, Alton, Hants GU34 4BW
(0420) 544330 MOBILE: (0860) 737925 FAX: (0420) 544331
Specialists in ex-M.O.D. and civilian Land Rovers, cheapies to fully reconditioned. Full workshop facilities. 25 years experience.
LOCKERLEY GREEN GARAGE. Lockerley, Nr Romsey, Hants SO51 0LU
(0794) 40406 FAX: (0794) 41318
Four x four sales. From 80" - 110", a varied selection of Land Rovers and assorted 4x4's always in stock.

KENT

ASHFORD CAR & 4x4 AUCTIONS. Romney House, Ashford Market, Ashford, Kent TN23 1PG
(0233) 622222 FAX: (0233) 646642
Regular auctions of 4x4 vehicles/spares plus special sections for boats and caravans. Low commission. Prompt payment. Café & restaurant/bar on site.
AUTOSOURCE INTERNATIONAL. Bournewood, Ham Street, Ashford, Kent TN26 2HJ
(0233) 732864
Any new 4x4 supplied at discounted prices including Range Rover, Discovery and Defender. All vehicles sourced and found via UK dealers.
B.H.M LAND ROVERS. Jail Lane, Biggin Hill, Kent TN16 3AU
(0959) 573644 or (0959) 575630 MOBILE: (0831) 454424 FAX: (0959) 540329
Land Rover/Range Rover specialists; always large numbers in stock. Private and authority vehicles, export and shipping, p/x and finance.
LION MOTOR COMPANY. Lion Garage, Rochester Road, Gravesend, Kent DA12
(0474) 533636/535009
Range Rover, Land Rover, Discovery, Daihatsu, Mitsubishi Shogun, Isuzu Trooper, Suzuki Vitara/ Samurai, Daihatsu etc. Usually 20+ 4x4's in stock.

LANCASHIRE

WINDMILL LANDROVERS. Preston New Road, Mellor, Blackburn, Lancs BB2 7NT
(0254) 813252 FAX: (0254) 814094
Land Rover sales specialist. Models from 1980 upwards all fully refurbished to a high standard. Petrol and diesel County types, Discovery, Range Rover.

LINCOLNSHIRE

NAVENBY 4x4 SALES. The Old Carpenters Shop, Clint Lane, Navenby, Lincoln LN5 0EX
(0522) 810947 MOBILE: (0836) 665536
Used Range Rover specialists. Vehicle sales and used spares available.

NORTHUMBERLAND
THROPTON MOTOR COMPANY. West End, Thropton, Northumberland NE65 7TL
(0669) 20043/21405
4x4 & diesel centre. Four wheel drive specialist sales include Land Rover, Range Rover & Discovery,
Isuzu/Subaru, Mitsubishi, Daihatsu, Toyota etc.

SHROPSHIRE
J.T. ROBERTS. Chellowdene, Heathgates Bank, Shrewsbury, Salop SY1 4BA (0743) 358416
Range Rover specialists.

SURREY
COUNTRY SPORT 4x4. Hindhead Road Garage, Hindhead Road, Haslemere, Surrey GU27 ILH
(0428) 643060 FAX: (0428) 642990 AFTER HOURS: (0428) 641027 MOBILE: (0831) 279350
Land Rover, Range Rover, Discovery and all makes of 4x4 (stock constantly changing). Open 6 days a
week, Sundays by appointment.
SHERE GARAGE LTD. Unit 1, Warren Court, Middle Street, Shere, Surrey GU5 9HF
(0483) 203525
Range Rover, Discovery, Land Rover, Shogun, Trooper, Suzuki, Daihatsu etc. Stock constantly
changing. Please phone for current availability.
WALTON MOTORS. 26 Sandy Way, Walton-on-Thames, Surrey KT12 1PG
(0932) 247176 or (0860) 239267
All models of Land Rover and Range Rover usually in stock, petrol & diesel with new M.O.T. 12 month
warranties available. Open 6 days a week.

SUSSEX, WEST
REID LAND ROVERS. Richmond Stud, A29 Bognor Road, Horsham, W Sussex RH12 3PY
(0403) 790518 MOBILE: (0836) 209208 FAX: (0403) 790946
7 days a week sales specialist. Large selection of privately owned SWB/LWB petrol/diesel Hard/Soft
Tops Safaris/Truck Cabs etc. £1,250-£10,000
SOUTHERN COUNTIES GARAGES. 13-15 London Road, Crawley, W Sussex RH10 2JD
(0293) 531222
Land Rover/Range Rover sales specialists & service.

WEST MIDLANDS
EX POLICE CAR CENTRE. 258 Delph Road, Brierley Hill, West Midlands DY5 2RP
(0384) 70662/480263
Well maintained cars up to police specifications. All makes and models including Land Rover & Range
Rover. Phone for availability.
WOODBRIDGE GARAGE. 25 Moseley Road, Birmingham B12 9BX 021-446 4929
Range Rovers wanted - all models - collect nationwide.

YORKSHIRE, NORTH
THE STABLES 4x4 CENTRE. Crag Lane, Beckwithshaw, Harrogate HG3 1QA
(0423) 505883 MOBILE: (0831) 569985
The North's leading suppliers of pre-owned Range Rovers. All vehicles fully prepared and serviced with
warranty and full MOT at a realistic price.

YORKSHIRE, SOUTH
CAWTHORNE CARRIAGE CO. 25 Church Street, Cawthorne, Barnsley S75 4HL
(0226) 790385 MOBILE: (0836) 653981 FAX: (0226) 790770
Range Rovers and other 4x4's in Yorkshire. Best selection at Cawthorne Carriage Co. Please telephone
for current availability.

YORKSHIRE, WEST
SIMMONITES (EST. 1963). 755 Thornton Road, Thornton, Bradford, W Yorks BD13 3NW
(0274) 833351 FAX: (0274) 835117
Land Rover/Range Rover sales, service, repairs, M.O.T., diesel engines, export, parts and accessories.
Please send S.A.E. for price lists.
STAMFORD GARAGE. 56 Wapping Road, Off Bolton Road, Bradford 3 (0274) 720471
Land Rover, Range Rover and Discovery sales. Also new and used parts department, servicing and
M..O.T. tests.

CO. DOWN
ROBINSONS OF HILLSBOROUGH LTD. 71 Moira Road, Hillsborough, Co. Down BT26 6DX
(0846) 682235 MOBILE: (0836) 551151 FAX: (0846) 682972
Ireland's leading 4WD specialists. We can supply most 4x4's including Land Rover, Range Rover &
Discovery. Over 50 4x4 vehicles in stock.

SCOTLAND
STRATHCLYDE
COUNTRY-SET VEHICLES. Low Gainford House, Stewarton Road, Fenwick, Ayrshire KA3 6AR
(05606) 736 MOBILE: (0836) 714859
We supply and deliver Land Rover, Range Rover and Discovery all over Scotland. Trade-in taken, HP
arranged. We are open 7 days a week.

WALES
MID GLAMORGAN
T.R.S. SPECIALIST VEHICLE SALES. Aberrhondda Road, Porth, Mid Glam CF39 0LD
(0443) 686688 FAX: (0443) 685587
4x4 vehicle sales and repairs. Land Rover specialist, ex-military vehicles in stock. New & used parts in
stock. M.O.T. testing carried out.

GERMANY
FWD GmbH. Markwinkel 3, D-3401 Waake, Germany
TEL: 49 5507 847 FAX: 49 5507 1565
New vehicle supply, especially the Defender range. Land Rover, Range Rover and Discovery spare parts.

VEHICLE RECOVERY/TRACTION AIDS

CROSS REFERENCE: See also WINCHES

ENGLAND

AVON

BRYCRAFT LTD. Unit 9, Riverside Business Park, St Annes Road, St Annes Park, Bristol BS4 4ED
(0272) 724906 FAX: (0272) 724906
Webbing equipment manufacturers. Transporter/recovery ratchet lashing straps/tow lines/tree strops/
horsebox breech straps/car dolly. Straps to customer specifications.

CHESHIRE

BRINDLEY CHAINS LTD. 1 Tatton Court, Kingsland Grange, Warrington, Cheshire WA1 1BR
(0925) 825555
'Pewag' snowchains: Easy to fit, superb grip in snow/mud, exchange scheme. Also 'Pewag' roofboxes -
aerodynamic/weatherproof/tough/secure.

HAMPSHIRE

NEW CONCEPT. P.O. Box 61, Winchester SO23 8XR (0962) 865996
The 'Easylift' Air Jack, a simple to use PVC bag inflated by exhaust gas. For use in mud or by the
roadside. Models to suit all 4x4's/vans/trucks

HEREFORDSHIRE

HEREFORD ROPE & TACKLE CO. Unit 11, Aydon Industrial Park, Holmer Road,
Hereford HR4 9UN (0432) 59334
Sales and repair of all types of lifting, lashing & winching equipment. Winches/tow ropes/Hi-Lift jacks/
slings/shackles/wheel chocks etc.

KENT

MGR UK. 42-43 Quarry Hill, Tonbridge, Kent TN9 2RS (0732) 770347 FAX: (0732) 351746
MGR snowchains and snowgrips for car & commercial applications. 48 hourex-stock delivery.
RUD CHAINS LTD. 1-3 Belmont Road, Whitstable, Kent CT5 1QT (0227) 27661
Manufacturers of snow chains.
S.V.I. 5A Church Road, Tadley, Basingstoke, Hants RG26 TEL/FAX: (0734) 815495
Wide range of low price 4x4 accessories: Hi-Lift jacks/winches/tow ropes winches + ventilated discs, tyres
etc. Send SAE for catalogue.
SNOWCHAINS LTD. Wrotham Road, Borough Green, Kent TN15 8TG (0732) 884408
Most types and sizes of winter chains.
WEISENFELS SNOW CHAINS LTD. est Kingdom Trading Estate, Nr Sevenoaks, Kent TN15 6BR
(047) 485 3221
Manufacturers of snow chains.

LONDON

TRANSGLOBE INTERNATIONAL LTD. 143 Greenvale Road, London SE19 IP6
081-850 8884 FAX: 081-850 9100
The 'Widrod Carbar' eliminates rear end shunts when towing. Being a solid sectional bar utilising towing
eyes and/or 50mm ball, it can be used to tow inexperienced drivers - especially downhill or in heavy 'stop-
start' traffic - and even vehicles with poor brakes. Telephone for information and prices.

SURREY

DUCKBILL EARTH ANCHORS LTD. Unit 5E Vallance-by-Ways, Lowfield Heath Road,
Charlwood, Horley, Surrey RH6 0BT (0293) 862989
Duckbill Earth Anchors for self rescue by winch.

SUSSEX, EAST

MARLOW ROPES LTD. Diplocks Way, Hailsham, E Sussex BN27 3JS (0323) 847234
Rope manufacturer - Recovaline (KERR)/tow ropes in nylon, polypropoleyneand polyester/web strops.
Contact us for your local agent.

WEST MIDLANDS

GRIFF CHAINS LTD. Quarry Road, Dudley Wood, Dudley, W Midlands DY2 OED (0384) 69415/6/7
Manufacturers of snow chains.
TRUCKERS CARGO AID. Providence Street, Lye, Stourbridge, W Midlands DY9 8HS
(0384) 895700 FAX: (0384) 891994
Recovery equipment: Husky & Tifor winches, Hi-Lift jacks, snatch blocks,shackles, ground anchors, tow/
kinetic/winch ropes, webbing, lashing etc.

WORCESTERSHIRE
PATHFINDER SUPPLIES. 79 Easemore Road, Redditch, Worcs B98 8EY (0527) 67476
Made to measure winch cables, hydraulic hoses. Expanding range of chains, shackles and anchors.
Please send a S.A.E. for lists.

WALES

GWENT
GEMS CLEARWAY. Belmura House, Old Hill Crescent, Christchurch, Newport, Gwent NP6 1JN
(0633) 422706 FAX: (0633) 430117
Suppliers of towpoles/'A' frames/towing dollys/trailers, electric and hydraulic winchgear, chains/ropes/
shackles/pulley blocks/towropes etc.

SCOTLAND

TAYSIDE
RAMSEY LADDERS. 61 West High Street, Forfar, Angus, Tayside, Scotland (0307) 62255
Manufacturers of Sand Ladders.

DENMARK

D.G.A. Aadrovey no 18, 8870, Langaa, Jutland, Denmark.
TEL: 010 45 86 461655 or 461312 FAX: 010 45 86 462288
Manufacturers of Hi-Lift jacks under licence.

FRANCE

BARONG. 8 rue du Clos-Fiouri, 92370, Chaville, France TEL: (1) 47.50.05.12.
Manufacturers of the Barong articulated sand mat.
MANUTENTION AUTONOME. 77 rue Jules Guesde, Z.I. La Mouche, 69230 St Genis Laval, France
TEL: 78.50.76.39
Manufacturers of the Cric Gonflable "Sepi Air-Jack".

SOUTH AFRICA

GIFTS INTERNATIONAL LTD. P.O. Box 1640, 634 Grand Parade Centre, Adderley Street, Cape
Town, R.S.A. TEL: (021) 461 5969
Suppliers of Air Jacks.
MACLOED ENGINEERING. Johannesburg, R.S.A.
TEL: (011) 316-1613 FAX: (011) 316-161
"Trac-Mat" traction recovery aid for 4x4 and light vehicles for extracting vehicles from mud.

VIDEOS
ENGLAND

DEVON
> **FREE RANGE TELEVISION LTD.** Studio West, Barn Close, Langage, Plymouth PL7 5HQ
> (0752) 335597 FAX: (0752) 335598
> Producers & distributors of the annual *ARC National Rally* video. See our advertisement for details.

HAMPSHIRE
> **STEWART VISION VIDEO PRODUCTION.** 5a Church Road, Tadley, Basingstoke,
> Hants RG26 6AU (0734) 815495 FAX: (0734) 815495
> Fourwheel drive video production specialists, advertising, promotions etc. World coverage, rallies,
> expeditions, you name it we video it. Call us now!

ISLE OF MAN
> **DUKE MARKETING.** P.O. Box 46, Douglas, Isle of Man, British Isles
> (0624) 23634 FAX: (0624) 29745
> Major trade/retail supplier of pre-recorded videos including motorsport, accident compilations etc. List
> available on request.

LONDON
> **FOUR WHEEL FILMS.** Unit 12, 39 Tadema Road, London SW10 0PY
> 071-376 3056 MOBILE: (0836) 780128 FAX: 071-376 4510
> Producers & distributors of *The Land Rover Story* by James Taylor, *The 1993 Welsh Hillrally.*

NOTTINGHAMSHIRE
> **TOPPS VIDEOS.** 35 Kirkby Road, Sutton-in-Ashfield, Notts NG17 1GG (0623) 440337
> Experience the world's toughest off-road event in your own living room - *The Camel Trophy* from £10.99.
> Also Rallying, *Havoc* crash videos, etc.

WARWICKSHIRE
> **PP VIDEO PRODUCTIONS.** Bishops Itchington, Leamington Spa, Warwicks CV33 0BR
> The video *Off Road Survival Guide* includes Vehicle Design/Transmission Off Road Driving Techniques,
> The Best Tyre For Your Needs, Greenlaning, Vehicle Recovery/Winching, Trials/Comp. Safari/Quads/
> Pilot Racing.

YORKSHIRE, WEST
> **CLUB OFF ROAD.** 5 Quarryside Road, Mirfield, West Yorkshire WF14 9QG
> Distributors of the *Tartan Trail* video, following the fortunes of entrants in the 3-day Scottish Off Road
> Challenge - £13.50 incl. VAT/p&p

presents

THE 1993
ARC NATIONAL RALLY

Held in the glorious surroundings of Eastnor Deer Park, this 55 minute video will bring back fond memories of the two days of non-stop action known officially as 'The 1993 Association of Rover Clubs National Rally'.

Featuring Competition Safari, Winch Recovery, RTV Trials, Team Recovery, CCV Trials, the ever popular Gymkhana and a short compilation of action sequences from the previous two meetings, it is a must for any club enthusiast at home or abroad.

Don't just take our word for it - this is what Dave Barker had to say in Video Review
(Land Rover Owner Dec '93) :-

"Some excellent camera work, sound and a good commentary"

ORDER YOUR COPY NOW

ONLY £15 (+ £1.75 p&p)

- -

To: FREE RANGE TV LTD., Studio West,
Barn Close, Langage, Plymouth PL7 5HQ

NAME ....

ADDRESS ....

TELEPHONE NUMBER ....

I enclose £ .... for .... 1993 ARC Videos (£16.75 per tape inc p&p)
Please make cheques payable to Free Range Television Ltd.

WHEELS
CROSS REFERENCE: See also TYRES

ENGLAND

CHESHIRE
NATIONAL TYRES AND AUTOCARE. 80-82 Wellington Road North, Stockport, Cheshire SK4 1HR 061-480 7461 FREEPHONE: (0800) 626666 FOR NEAREST BRANCH
4x4 wheels and tyres, other tyres, exhausts, batteries & range of auto services. Check for service before travelling, 400 branches nationwide.

ESSEX
CYCLONE WHEELS (U.K.) LTD. 2D Bentalls Industrial Estate, Heybridge, Essex CM9 7NW (0621) 851128 (0621) 851138
CPS quality alloy wheels and Cyclone white & chrome steel wheels at the most competitive prices. Also BF Goodrich/General/Sport King tyres.

EASTERN LTD. 15 West Station Yard, Spital Road, Maldon, Essex CM9 6TW (0621) 858912 (4 lines) FAX: (0621) 857425
Large range of wheels and tyres including BF Goodrich, Yokohama, General and Marshall. Phone for your free copy of our full colour brochure now.

ELITE AUTOS & DESIGNS. Unit A, Suttons Business Park, 136/138 (A13) New Road, Rainham, Essex RM13 8DE (0708) 525577 FAX: (0708) 556684
A complete range of 4x4 wheels inc 8 spoke chrome & white, plus 4x4 tyres, Monroe shock absorbers, Cobra/Recaro seats, quality steering wheels.

HEREFORDSHIRE
PERFORMANCE INDUSTRIES UK LTD. 1 Hatton Garden Industrial Estate, Kington, Hereford HR5 3RB (0544) 231214 FAX: (0544) 230904
Europe's largest 4x4 wheel and accessory distributor for all makes of 4x4. Wheels/tyres/alloy bumper bars & roofracks/suspension and much more.

KENT
THE ORIGINAL HANDBUILT WHEEL CO. Unit 2C, Longfield Road, Noth Farm Bus.Estate, Tunbridge Wells, Kent TN2 3EY (0892) 30730 FAX: (0892) 515816
Manufacturer of the Weller range of wheels.

MIDDLESEX
AIM PRODUCTS. 149 High Street, Wealdstone, Harrow, Middx HA3 5DX 081-427 3907
Distributors of 'Wonder Wheels' alloy wheel cleaner - ideal for removing dirt & baked-on brake dust without staining coatings or harming lacquers.

STAFFORDSHIRE
REMALINE. 18 Bronte Court, Off Masefield Drive, Leyfields, Tamworth B79 8DN (0827) 64062 (0827) 50633
Suppliers of premium quality off-road 4x4 wheel rims, tyres and wheel arch extensions for Land Rover, Range Rover and Discovery.

SUFFOLK
B.J.L. FIELDEN LTD. Starhouse Farm, Onehouse, Stowmarket, Suffolk IP14 3EL
TEL: (0449) 675071 MOBILE: (0836) 619479 FAX: (0449) 678282
Sole 4x4 agent for Wolfrace wheels. Whites, chromes, steels & other alloys. Tyres, nuts, caps & lock nuts. Please phone for free brochure.

WINCHES

CROSS REFERENCE: See also VEHICLE RECOVERY

ENGLAND

DEVON

DAVID BOWYER'S OFF-ROAD CENTRE. East Foldhay, Zeal Monachorum, Crediton, Devon EX17 6DH (0363) 82666 FAX: (0363) 82782
New and secondhand electric winches at very reasonable prices. Also British Roo Bar fitting kits and recovery equipment.
SCITEC (UK) LTD. Ebsleigh House, Bridestow, Okehampton, Devon (083786) 225
Manufacturers of the Freewheeler emergency winch which attaches to a Land Rover wheel.
SUPERWINCH LTD. South Station Yard, Abbey Rise, Whitchurch Road, Tavistock, Devon PL19 9BS (0822) 614101
Manufacturer of mechanical & electric winches, freewheeling hubs and Fairey Overdrive units.
WESTERN WINCHES. 17 Chantry Court, Cothill, Plympton, Plymouth PL19 8DE (0752) 348691
Suppliers of electrical, mechanical & manual winches for vehicle, trailer mounting etc.

HAMPSHIRE

AQUA-MARINE MANUFACTURING (UK) LTD. 216 Fair Oak Road, Bishopstoke, Eastleigh, Hants SO5 6NJ (0703) 694949 FAX: (0703) 601381
Distributors of Rule electric vehicle winches and Dutton-Lainson manual and electric winches for your recovery, towing and other lifting applications.
SOUTHERN WINCH CENTRE. Unit 13 Monks Brook Industrial Park School Close, Chandlers Ford, Eastleigh, Hants SO5 3RA (0703) 270600 FAX: (0703) 271242
Agents for Superwinch, Warn & Tirfor Winches. Replacement bumpers, fitting kits and accessories. Also available on mobile telephone: (0860) 701496

HERTFORDSHIRE

BUSHEY HALL WINCHES & EQUIPMENT LTD. Unit 7, Lismirrane Industrial Park, Elstree Road, Elstree, Herts WD6 3EE 081-953 6050 FAX: 081-207 5308
The best in winch technology backed by a professional fitting and after- sales service. Send for details of winches & off-road accessories.

KENT

MAYWOOD WINCH COMPANY. 66 Marlowe Road, Larkfield, Aylesford, Kent ME20 6TW (0732) 843018 MOBILE: (0831) 225784 FAX: (0732) 871277
Superwinch stockists. New & s/hand winches available from stock, electric of hydraulic. All makes of winches serviced and repaired.

LANCASHIRE

WINCH & ENGINEERING LTD. 35 St Mary's Street, Preston, PR1 5LN (0772) 653737
Portable power winches - six models to fit your ball hitch (front or rear). Save expensive installation costs and gain added versatility.

MERSEYSIDE

RYDERS INTERNATIONAL. Knowsley Rd, Bootle, Liverpool L20 4NW
051-922 7585 FAX: 051-944 1424 TELEX: CHARCOM G Ryderauto 627110
Sole U.K. concessionaires for Warn battery/electric and hydraulic vehicle winches, accessories, spare parts, repairs and servicing. See our display advertisement on REAR COVER.

WORCESTERSHIRE

PATHFINDER SUPPLIES. 79 Easemore Road, Redditch, Worcs B98 8EY (0527) 67476
Made to measure winch cables, hydraulic hoses. Expanding range of chains, shackles and anchors. Please send a S.A.E. for lists.

YORKSHIRE, SOUTH

TIFOR LTD. Old Lane, Halfway, Sheffield S19 5G2 (0742) 482266 FAX: (0742) 475649
Manual/powered lifting and pulling equipment, load measuring devices. Essential equipment for all off-road users in emergency situations.

SCOTLAND

TAYSIDE, CENTRAL AND FIFE
OUTREACH PLC. Foundry Loan, Larbert, Stirlingshire FK5 4PH (0324) 563333 (0324) 563399
Powerwinch VR192 12 volt, remote control electric winch - fully portableto fit front/rear 50mm ball
instantly. £320.00 + VAT for complete kit. Rover wheel.

Alexander Associates
Imaging and Database Consultants
(Typesetters for MACK'S '94-95)

All your imaging needs from concept to finished products - be they: brochures,
logos, stationery, leaflets, company magazines, parts catalogues, technical
manuals, photography repro, computer graphics design, 3D views, typesetting,
illustration, corporate image creation, copywriting and DTP.

Creative Design

Our Bureaux have full capability to scan, clean up, enhance and manipulate your
original full colour or monochrome photographs or images for incorporation into
your brochure or adverts. 3D views can be created from plan and elevation
drawings.

London Bureau   Tel: 081 575 8485.   Fax: 081 813 0370
Southwest Bureau   Tel: 0726 832 900.   Fax: 0726 833 630

Trade and Private entires are listed under their FULL TITLE, thereafter entries consisting wholly or partly of intials have been determined by the second and subsequent letters.

Example 1: R.J. Harvey has been listed under 'R' and not 'H' (as Harvey, R.J.)
Example 2: Tom McGuigan has been listed under 'T' and not 'M' (as McGuigan, Tom)

Index

Please mention MACK'S when you phone or fax. 147

Please mention MACK'S when you phone or fax.   149

M

M & M LAND ROVER SERVICES LTD.   61
M & M. LAND ROVER SERVICES LTD.   74
M P P. 70
M. BURGINS & SON.36
M.C. MOTORS.   60
M.H. LEADER.   55
M.M.B. INTERNATIONAL.117
M.M.S. LAND ROVERS.   57
MACHINE MART LTD.   99
MACLOED ENGINEERING.140
MAD BARON ENTERPRISES.   30
MAGASIN GLOBE TROTTER.   116
MAIDENHEAD CB RADIO CENTRE.   28
MAINAIR SPORTS LTD.   124
MALCOLM DUNNING SADDLERY LTD. 19
MALPATECH LTD. 32
MANBY SHOWGROUND DRIVING CENTRE.   78
MANCHESTER LAND ROVER BREAKERS.   55, 130
MANSFIELD LAND ROVERS.   98
MANTEC SERVICES.108
MANUTENTION AUTONOME.   140
MAP HOMES.   118
MAP SHOP.   120
MAP-HOME. 115
MARGRET MOTORS.   14
MARJORIE KING PHOTOGRAPHICS.   132
MARK PEACOCK LANDROVERS. 59
MARK SMITH & CO.   43, 47
MARLOW INSURANCE BROKERS.   63
MARLOW ROPES LTD.   139
MARQUEZ MOTORS.   41
MARSH & JEFFREY LTD.   15
MARSLAND CHASSIS.   17
MASTA.   123
MASTER GLASS LTD.   10
MAYFIELD MOTORS.   31
MAYWOOD WINCH COMPANY. 145
McARDLE COACHBUILDERS LIMITED. 9
McARDLE FABRICATIONS.   103
McCARTNEYS.   70
McDONALD ENGINEERING SERVICES.   83
MEDIAID.   132
MEECHING COUNTRY WEAR.   20
MERCIA 4x4. 36
MERCURY TRAILER CENTRE.   5
MERLIN AUTOMOTIVE.   10
MERLIN MOTORSPORT.   91
MERSEYSIDE LAND ROVER SERVICES LTD.   83
MERV PLASTICS.   33
MGR UK.   139
MICHAEL FLETCHER LTD.61
MICHELDEVER TYRE SERVICES. 125
MICHELIN TYRE PLC.   126
MICHELIN TYRE PUBLIC LTD COMPANY.   120
MICKEY THOMPSON PERFORMANCE TYRES. 125
MID NORFOLK OFF ROAD CENTRE.   78
MID WALES FOUR WHEEL DRIVE CLUB.24
MIDDLEWOOD LANDROVERS.   60
MIDLAND LAND ROVER SERVICES.   93
MIDLAND ROVER OWNERS CLUB LTD. 23
MIDLAND TURBO. 88
MIKE AGER MOBILE.   70
MILITARY & CIVILIAN.   73
MILITARY SCENE.   73
MILL HILL SPARES. 130
MILNER CONVERSIONS.   34
MINUS 40.   116
MISSION SUPPLIES LTD.   114
MMB INTERNATIONAL.   9
MOBILE ADVENTURE CC. 116
MOBILE AIR PRODUCTS LTD.   70
MOBILE MAINTENANCE SERVICES.   57
MOBILE MECHANICAL REMEDIES.   70
MOBILITY ACCESSORIES. 7
MOCAL AEROQUIP.90
MOLD CB & RADIO.31
MONARCH GARAGE.   61
MOONRAKER (UK) LTD.   28
MOORLAND OFF-ROAD ADVENTURE SPORT. 79

MORROCH LETTINGS.   105
MOTIVAIR COMPRESSORS LIMITED.   99
MOTOR & DIESEL ENGINEERING.   34
MOTOR BOOKS.   14
MOTOR CLIMATE SERVICES.   72
MOTOR SAFARI.   79
MOTOR TRAVELLER.   4
MOTOR UPHOLSTERY SUPPLIES. 66
MOTORWAY REMOULDS LTD.   127
MUDDYTRAX - LAND ROVER SPARES. 84
MULTI-CLEAN SYSTEMS. 18
MUNSTER SIMMS ENGINEERING LTD. 115
MURVI.   117
MVS. 113

N

NAILSEA LAND ROVER CENTRE. 47
NATIONAL POWER STEERING.   97
NATIONAL TYRES . 9, 39, 97, 98, 125, 144
NATIONWIDE TRIM.   66, 93
NAVENBY 4x4 SALES.   135
NEATKENT LTD.   49
NENE VALLEY OFF ROAD. 57
NEO SYNTHETIC OIL CO. U.K.   68
NETWORK RADIO COMMUNICATIONS LTD.   30
NEW CONCEPT.   139
NEWARK LAND ROVER REPAIRS.58
NEWBURY 4WD CENTRE. 47
NEWCASTLE & NANTWICH ROVER OWNERS CLUB.   23
NEWTON HILL GARAGE. 61
NICK DIMBLEBY.   132
NICK KERNER ENGINEERING.   47
NICOLAS PAXTON. 58
NOMAD AFRICA.   108
NOMAD PHARMACY.   123
NOMAD.   113
NORFOLK LAND ROVER CENTRE.   33, 56
NORTECH RADIO COMMUNICATIONS. 29
NORTH EASTERN MOTORS LTD. 59
NORTH HANTS TYRES.   125
NORTH LAKES 4x4 CLUB. 23
NORTH RIDING AUTOMOTIVE. 60
NORTH STAFFS TYRE & BATTERY.   126
NORTH WALES LAND ROVER CENTRE. 86
NORTH WEST FOUR WHEEL DRIVE.   54
NORTH YORKSHIRE OFF ROAD CENTRE.   79, 96
NORTHERN IRELAND 4 WHEEL DRIVE CLUB.   24
NORTHERN PARAMEDICAL SERVICES. 134
NORWEGIAN LAND ROVER CLUB.   25

O

OAK TREE GARAGE.   53
OAKES BROS.   47
OAKFORD RESOURCES LTD.   68
OAKWOOD ENTERPRISES. 68
OASIS.81, 123
ODDESEY GUIDES. 110
OFF ROAD ADVENTURE. 78, 96
OFF ROAD EXPERIENCE. 78
OFF ROAD MOTIVATIONS.   77
OFF-ROAD EXPERIENCE/GLEN TANAR. 96
OKAPI AFRICA.   106
OLYMPIC TYRE CO.126
ON THE BALL LTD. 7
ONE STOP ELECTRONICS. 29
ONE STOP OVERLAND SHOP.   107
OPTRON.   122
OPTRONICS UK.   7
ORDNANCE SURVEY.   120
ORIGINAL HANDBUILT WHEEL CO.   144
OSELLI POWER & PERFORMANCE ENGINEERING.   88
OUTBACK TRADING COMPANY.20
OUTREACH PLC.   146
OVERFINCH LTD.   87
OVERLAND LATIN AMERICA.   105
OVERLAND LTD.   108
OVERLAND SAFARI.   105
OVERLAND VEHICLE SERVICES. 56
OVEX. 105

Please mention MACK'S when you phone or fax.

ADD YOUR OWN

(Can't find your local dealer or favourite supplier in *MACK'S*? So here's your chance!)
Don't forget if you would like to see these in *MACK'S* '95-96, please let me know - See Page2.

Name. ....
Address ....
Tele. No. .... Mobile .... Fax. ....
Description ....
....

Name. ....
Address ....
Tele. No. .... Mobile .... Fax. ....
Description ....
....

Name. ....
Address ....
Tele. No. .... Mobile .... Fax. ....
Description ....
....

Name. ....
Address ....
Tele. No. .... Mobile .... Fax. ....
Description ....
....

Name. ....
Address ....
Tele. No. .... Mobile .... Fax. ....
Description ....
....

Name. ....
Address ....
Tele. No. .... Mobile .... Fax. ....
Description ....
....

Name. ....
Address ....
Tele. No. .... Mobile .... Fax. ....
Description ....
....

Name. ....
Address ....
Tele. No. .... Mobile .... Fax. ....
Description ....
....

Name. ....
Address ....
Tele. No. .... Mobile .... Fax. ....
Description ....
....

Name. ....
Address ....
Tele. No. .... Mobile .... Fax. ....
Description ....
....

ADD YOUR OWN

(Can't find your local dealer or favourite supplier in *MACK'S*? So here's your chance!)
Don't forget if you would like to see these in *MACK'S* '95-96, please let me know - See Page 2.

Name. ....
Address ....
Tele. No. .... Mobile .... Fax. ....
Description ....
....

Name. ....
Address ....
Tele. No. .... Mobile .... Fax. ....
Description ....
....

Name. ....
Address ....
Tele. No. .... Mobile .... Fax. ....
Description ....
....

Name. ....
Address ....
Tele. No. .... Mobile .... Fax. ....
Description ....
....

Name. ....
Address ....
Tele. No. .... Mobile .... Fax. ....
Description ....
....

Name. ....
Address ....
Tele. No. .... Mobile .... Fax. ....
Description ....
....

Name. ....
Address ....
Tele. No. .... Mobile .... Fax. ....
Description ....
....

Name. ....
Address ....
Tele. No. .... Mobile .... Fax. ....
Description ....
....

Name. ....
Address ....
Tele. No. .... Mobile .... Fax. ....
Description ....
....

Name. ....
Address ....
Tele. No. .... Mobile .... Fax. ....
Description ....
....

Name. ....
Address ....
Tele. No. .... Mobile .... Fax. ....
Description ....
....

VEHICLE DATA

(For details of your 4x4 - very useful when ordering Mail Order parts etc.)

MAKE & TYPE:

VEHICLE MAKE .... MODEL .... WHEELBASE LENGTH ....

REGISTRATION No. .... YEAR OF MANUFACTURE ....

COLOUR .... BODY STYLE ....

....

....

ENGINE/GEARBOX/CHASSIS:

ENGINE SIZE (cc) .... FUEL TYPE ....

ENGINE No. .... SUFFIX ....

GEARBOX No. .... SUFFIX ....

CHASSIS No. ....

....

....

AXLE TYPE:

FRONT .... REAR ....

SERIAL NUMBER ....

RATIO ....

....

LUBRICANTS: (Make and/or type)

ENGINE OIL .... QUANTITY ....

GEARBOX OIL .... " ....

TRANSFER BOX OIL .... " ....

DIFFS/SWIVEL HOUSING OIL .... " ....

STEERING OIL .... " ....

.... " ....

.... " ....

FLUIDS:

ANTIFREEZE .... " ....

.... " ....

PARTS:

CONTACT BREAKER POINTS .... " ....

SPARK PLUGS .... " ....

AIR FILTER .... " ....

OIL FILTER (Internal) .... " ....

OIL FILTER (External) .... " ....

BRAKE PADS .... " ....

BRAKE SHOES .... " ....

.... " ....

.... " ....

.... " ....

.... " ....

.... " ....

DOCUMENTATION REMINDER

M.O.T. DUE .... INSURANCE DUE .... ROAD TAX DUE ....

Please mention MACK'S when you phone or fax.